THE RHETORIC OF JUDGING WELL

RHETORIC AND DEMOCRATIC DELIBERATION
VOLUME 29

Rhetoric and Democratic Deliberation focuses on the
interplay of public discourse, politics, and democratic action.
Engaging with diverse theoretical, cultural, and critical
perspectives, books published in this series offer fresh
perspectives on rhetoric as it relates to education, social
movements, and governments throughout the world.

A complete list of books in this series is located at the back
of this volume.

THE RHETORIC
OF JUDGING WELL

THE CONFLICTED LEGACY OF
JUSTICE ANTHONY M. KENNEDY

EDITED BY
DAVID A. FRANK AND FRANCIS J. MOOTZ III

The Pennsylvania State University Press | University Park, Pennsylvania

Library of Congress Cataloging-in-Publication Data

Names: Kennedy, Anthony M., 1936– | Frank, David
    A., editor. | Mootz, Francis J., III, editor.
Title: The rhetoric of judging well : the conflicted
    legacy of Justice Anthony M. Kennedy / edited by
    David A. Frank and Francis J. Mootz III.
Other titles: Rhetoric and democratic deliberation ; v. 29.
Description: University Park, Pennsylvania : The
    Pennsylvania State University Press, [2023] | Series:
    Rhetoric and democratic deliberation ; volume 29 |
    Includes bibliographical references and index.
Summary: "A collection of essays providing an
    interdisciplinary account of U.S. Supreme Court
    Justice Anthony M. Kennedy's judicial rhetoric"—
    Provided by publisher.
Identifiers: LCCN 2022046672 | ISBN 9780271094847
    (hardback)
Subjects: LCSH: Judicial process—United States. |
    Kennedy, Anthony M., 1936– | Law—United States—
    Decision making. | Judgments—United States. |
    Judges—United States. | United States. Supreme
    Court. | Law—United States—Interpretation and
    construction. | Rhetoric. | LCGFT: Essays.
Classification: LCC KF8775 .K437 2023 | DDC
    347.73/14—dc23/eng/20230105
LC record available at https://lccn.loc.gov/2022046672

This volume is published with the generous support
of the Center for Democratic Deliberation at The
Pennsylvania State University.

The Pennsylvania State University Press is a member
of the Association of University Presses.

It is the policy of The Pennsylvania State University
Press to use acid-free paper. Publications on uncoated
stock satisfy the minimum requirements of American
National Standard for Information Sciences—
Permanence of Paper for Printed Library Material,
ANSI Z39.48–1992.

For Michael and Justin: That you both are merciful and seek justice is a gift to your parents.
DAF

For Catherine and Daniel: You each inspire me in very different ways.
FJM III

CONTENTS

Part 6 Assessment

ACKNOWLEDGMENTS

No one writing in the cusp between law and rhetoric has a better explanation of "rhetorical knowledge" as a powerful touchstone for judgment and judging than Jay Mootz. His vision and body of scholarship inform our collaboration and his recent coedited book on Justice Scalia. I thank him for securing a splendid recording of Justice Kennedy, who spoke to us and the scholars who have joined us about his view of the law and civility. I also thank him for arranging a video symposium for our book and for working with me to assemble an outstanding cast of rhetoricians and legal academics. He is a real mensch.

David A. Frank
Eugene, OR
June 2021

I am deeply grateful to David Frank for a stimulating conversation over dinner at Mon Ami Gabi in Las Vegas that led directly to this book project. Fortunately, what happens in Vegas at a law and rhetoric conference doesn't stay in Vegas. David is one of the best scholars of Chaïm Perelman's New Rhetoric, and I was fortunate to have him as a partner for this project. I would also like to thank Jim Gardner, a trusted conversation partner for more than thirty years, for extremely helpful observations and suggestions on an early draft of my chapter. Finally, I appreciate the spirit with which all the contributors to the volume made my chapter, and all the chapters, better by participating in a working papers symposium to finalize the book. I have rarely experienced such a model of Gadamer's hermeneutical ideal of conversation. Finally, I am grateful that my colleague Leslie Jacobs, who holds the Anthony M. Kennedy Endowed Chair, generously sponsored the working papers symposium under the auspices of the chair.

Francis J. Mootz III
Sacramento, CA
June 2021

INTRODUCTION

Francis J. Mootz III and David A. Frank

Justice Anthony M. Kennedy is widely acknowledged to have been the single most important justice on the United States Supreme Court during the past three decades, primarily by serving in the often-cited role as the "swing justice." He famously disowned this moniker, insisting, "the cases swing, I don't" (Duehren 2015). His unease is understandable. A justice who "swings" between results generated by credible judicial philosophies would be regarded as a lightweight, a person easily moved by extraneous considerations that result in decisions that are erratic and unprincipled. A sympathetic commentator explains that "Justice Kennedy is often described as a 'rudderless and unpredictable' individual because of the perception that his rhetorical flourishes represent his inability to adopt consistent and predictable positions on issues."[1] Another friendly critic concludes that Justice Kennedy has only himself to blame for these negative accounts. "He has disclaimed any larger approach to constitutional interpretation, changed his votes on several high-profile issues, repudiated past votes without sufficient explanation, and attempted to court the media. Scholars fault his opinions as (at best) incompletely theorized, characterizing his approach to judicial decision-making as inconsistent, unprincipled, undefined or confused" (Colucci 2009, ix). Justice Kennedy is accused of a nonrigorous approach to judging that might be characterized as sophistic.

On the other hand, critics have long chided Justice Kennedy for his soaring prose and metaphysical musings that go far beyond the doctrinal elaboration of the relevant constitutional text. In some of his more notable opinions, Justice Kennedy invoked broad principles that seemed better suited for a class in moral philosophy. These critics do not regard Justice Kennedy as an opportunist acting without a judicial methodology. Instead, they regard him as guided by inappropriately malleable concepts, speaking in the "mystical aphorisms of the fortune cookie," as Justice Antonin Scalia acerbically made the point in his dissent in *Obergefell v. Hodges* (2015, 719n22). Many commentators were less caustic but equally bemused by his opinion recognizing constitutional protection of gay marriage in *Obergefell*, with one calling it a "Kennedy Special" because its "rhetoric is as gorgeous as its legal reasoning is gauzy," having been expressed in many "sweetly teary-eyed turns of phrase" (Stern 2015).

How can one approach such a complex and multilayered rhetorical legacy? Our answer was to organize this volume, which brings together a diverse group of scholars from a variety of theoretical and doctrinal perspectives to uncover and assess Justice Kennedy's rhetoric. From Michael Gagarin, the leading classics scholar on the legal systems of ancient Greece, to Beth Britt, a prominent rhetorical critic in an English department, to Ashutosh Bhagwat, a constitutional law scholar and former clerk for Justice Kennedy, the volume provides a rich source of insight into Justice Kennedy's judicial rhetoric. Given the diversity and range of approaches, it should not be surprising that a simple consensus does not emerge. If the contributors agree on one thing, though, it is the importance of exploring how Justice Kennedy defended his rulings with a complex and unique voice.

Although the contributors use distinct vocabularies expressing different disciplinary interests, they all speak against the backdrop of a deep historical relationship between the study of rhetoric and the practice of law. Aristotle (2002) describes rhetoric as the ability to see in any given situation the available means to persuade a particular audience. This definition certainly captures the agonistic arguments made by lawyers at trial before a jury, but it extends to the entire scope of the work of lawyers. Lawyers constantly engage in hermeneutical discernment and rhetorical persuasion in settings as diverse as an initial meeting with a client and a strategy session with a team of lawyers to prepare for an appellate oral argument. The study of rhetoric has flourished by exploring law as an exemplary type of persuasion. Unfortunately, law has attempted to speak in a univocal voice that compels assent rather than inviting agreement through persuasion. Gerry Wetlaufer aptly notes that the rhetorical conceit of contemporary legal theory is to deny the rhetorical nature of legal practice.[2] Despite the shared provenance of the two disciplines, then, they hardly speak the same language. In response, we briefly provide a shared baseline to permit a diverse readership to better situate the chapters that follow.

Classical rhetoric grew out of reflections on the practice of the sophists to assist Athenians to argue their cases in trials before an untrained jury, marking a deep connection with legal practice as it developed in Greece and Rome. The classical authors acknowledged three types of rhetoric: *forensic* (an inquiry into what happened), *deliberative* (a dialogue about what should be done), and *epideictic* (a celebration of community values). Legal rhetoric was classified as forensic in nature, but contemporary legal practice incorporates all three types of rhetoric, especially in constitutional argument. For example, a case challenging an affirmative action plan adopted by an employer will simultaneously address how and why the plan was developed, how to fashion a rule that best serves the antidiscrimination cause in this setting, and how the resolution of the case expresses and affirms our communal values of liberty and equality. Lawyers often lump these considerations together under the amorphous phrase "policy arguments," but rhetorical critique provides a much finer-grained vocabulary for addressing legal argumentation.

The forms of persuasion are also helpful categories to explore legal rhetoric. In the classical system, persuasion was a product of logos (the argument itself), ethos (the character of the rhetor), and pathos (the disposition of the audience as engendered by the rhetor). These elemental forms of persuasion track well in the legal setting. The argument is central, but securing the adherence of an audience is not simply a matter of logical deduction. The logos, or "word," rarely compels assent on its own. Rather, logos in law offers only verisimilitude (the appearance of truth). To persuade an audience, it is imperative to prepare it to hear your argument (pathos) and to present the argument as an extension of a trusted speaker's character (ethos). Commendations and critiques of Justice Kennedy's opinions are best analyzed in these terms. Justice Kennedy's famous opinions often suffer from a weak logos, to the extent that generally accepted constitutional doctrine does not support his result, but he provides powerful arguments drawing on his ethos and premised on creating the proper disposition of his audience.

The reader must remain mindful of Wetlaufer's lament that law has abandoned its rhetorical roots. This is seen in the reduction of rhetoric to mere stylistic flourish. In the case of Justice Kennedy, critics charge that he engages in "mere" rhetoric, which is seen as a frivolous and cognitively empty style. In contrast, the classical approach to rhetoric acknowledged the significance of style without capitulating to emotivism and irrationalism. The principal elements of a rhetorical argument track the divisions of the contemporary legal brief and argument: invention, arrangement, style, memorization, and delivery. It is difficult to disentangle these elements, which means that an overly stylized approach may undermine the argument at its core.

We are not suggesting that legal theory is rhetorically bankrupt. The great legal realist Karl Llewellyn sought to reinvigorate the ancient understanding of law as a rhetorical practice. In an introductory footnote to an essay on the broad social developments of law, Llewellyn expressed his hope that someday, "someone will help the second year [law] student orient himself. Nor does anyone bother to present to him the difference between logic and persuasion, nor what a man facing old courts is to do with a new vocabulary; in a word, the game, in framing an argument, of diagnosing the peculiar presuppositions of the hearers" (1934, 205). The aim of Llewellyn's liberal education in law is properly understood as rhetorical competence. He named the required approach "Spokesmanship," deriving it from theories first developed in ancient Greece as "rhetoric—in essence: the effective techniques of persuasion" (Llewellyn 1930, 185). He explains that this calls for more than ornamentation and that the ancient tradition illuminates a path between certainty and relativism (Mootz 2011, 143–46). In this volume, we draw on the rhetorical expertise of humanistic scholars and the legal expertise of law professors, with both seeking to understand and critique the legal analysis offered by Justice Kennedy.

We have divided the volume into five parts and a concluding assessment, but the intersections between the chapters could have resulted in any number of organizing principles. In this introduction, we briefly review the chapters that follow in an effort to provide only one of the plausible frames for reading the volume. We invite readers to draw their own comparisons and contrasts between the chapters.

Part 1 brings classical Greek conceptions of rhetoric to bear on Justice Kennedy's opinions. Michael Gagarin demonstrates that the classical approach to interpreting legal texts established hermeneutical strategies that persist in contemporary legal practice. Against the view that legal interpretation is simply assessing facts in light of a clear and stable rule, the ancients also understood that the rule is sometimes dynamic and complex, requiring sophisticated argumentation. Gagarin then compares these different interpretive arguments as they are used in Justice Kennedy's opinions in *Obergefell* and *Citizens United v. Federal Election Commission* (2010). Given the lack of attention to his interpretive choices in these cases, we might conclude that the ancients better understood their role in selecting interpretative approaches that generate different results. Gene Garver critiques Justice Kennedy's appeal to the "self-evident" horror of "partial birth abortion" for drawing on the ancient notion of moral pollution. Justice Kennedy could privatize the behavior of gays and lesbians and avoid seeing their marriage as an affront to the community, but in *Gonzales v. Carhart* (2007), he regarded the medical procedure as a deeply disturbing evil that tainted the society. Garver uses ancient concepts to clearly reveal the animating structure of Justice Kennedy's argument.

In part 2, the chapters assess Justice Kennedy through the Roman theory of stasis. Martin Camper begins by identifying the "interpretive stases" that are employed to argue about the meaning of texts and to provide relevant lines of argument. Contrary to some readings, he claims that the central interpretive challenge in *Obergefell* was to define the scope of liberty rather than to expand the definition of marriage. His analysis tracks how legal meaning is created through rhetorical argument rather than a hermeneutic of plain meaning. Susan E. Provenzano's contribution connects classical stasis theory to modern concepts of rational liberty to develop a normative baseline for assessing, rather than simply describing, the arguments made in support of a judgment. Justice Kennedy's opinion in a First Amendment case serves as the test of her evaluative theory, as she compares the more sophisticated uses of stases by Justice Kennedy to the simpler approach by Justice Scalia in dissent. This more robust use of stasis theory describes how Justice Kennedy was rhetorically successful. Finally, Sean O'Rourke contends that the current conservative majority on the Court is following Justice Kennedy more than Justice Scalia. Using the rhetorical doctrines of *controversia*, stasis, and topical argument, O'Rourke compares the opinions in *Romer v. Evans* (1996) by Justices Kennedy and Scalia to outline the rhetoric of judging well. Most significantly, and with potential connections with Provenzano's work, he observes that engaging in rhetorical exchanges by arguing both sides of a case cultivates a "habit of thought" that is normative rather than merely technical.

In part 3, the contributors look to contemporary rhetorical theorists to provide a ground for understanding Justice Kennedy's exercise of judgment. Applying Kenneth Burke's dramatistic theory, Clarke Rountree investigates the degree to which Justices Kennedy and Scalia provide a reasonable and artful reconstruction of the "acts" in question in *Lawrence v. Texas* (2003). Justice Kennedy describes the acts of the Court in *Bowers v. Hardwick* (1986) as mistaken at that time and the acknowledged scope of personal freedom as underdeveloped. An affinity to Burke's theory does not guarantee a laudable result, but Rountree argues that a dramatist opinion that accounts for the past, present, and future is more likely to represent good judging. Next, Francis J. Mootz III argues that Justice Kennedy employed a form of natural law argument that is best explained by Chaïm Perelman and Lucie Olbrechts-Tyteca's notion of an appeal to the "universal audience." In the positivist era, an "ontological gap" exists between the critique of current practices and laws, on one hand, and the disavowal of natural law foundations that gird decision-making with eternal norms, on the other. Justice Kennedy did not have the vocabulary to make a rhetorical appeal to the public to regard itself as a universal audience that moves beyond positivist accounts of law, but this in fact is the nature of his argument. Mootz emphasizes that natural law argumentation will not always be persuasive. As with all things rhetorical, the rhetor cannot avoid the obligation to argue responsibly simply by invoking the universal audience. Finally, Darien Shanske uses contemporary concepts of rhetorical knowledge to describe the failure of Justice Kennedy's sovereignty jurisprudence. Eschewing reliance on dialogically secured rhetorical knowledge as a thick source of guidance, Justice Kennedy fell back on rule-based reasoning with regard to the boundaries of sovereignty. In the post-Trump era, there is renewed concern about securing the federal system of sovereignty, but Justice Kennedy collapsed his decisions into a singular respect for ultimate federal power. Shanske bemoans his failure to generate a communal achievement of creating meaningful context-sensitive distinctions.

Justice Kennedy's ethos is the topic of the chapters in part 4. Ashutosh Bhagwat deftly demonstrates that in his First Amendment opinions, Justice Kennedy displayed optimism about the ability of citizens to assess the effects of speech in the public square and political settings. By extending First Amendment protections to speech that many people would regard as corrosive of democracy, especially in the infamous *Citizens United* case, he demonstrated a perhaps naive confidence in the citizenry. Bhagwat hypothesizes that Justice Kennedy was aspirational, creating a legal agora that he then called on citizens to inhabit with robust dialogue. In stark contrast, Jim Gardner characterizes Justice Kennedy as exhibiting neurotic tendencies in his efforts to defend his holdings in controversial cases. In *Vieth v. Jubelirer* (2004), an important redistricting case, Justice Kennedy could not bring himself to make a firm decision and appeared to be indecisive rather than reflective. Gardner concludes that Justice Kennedy's open struggle to resolve the question at hand served to undermine his ethos. Finally, Leslie Jacobs argues that, despite Justice Kennedy being known as the champion of liberty, his ethos was grounded more in equality at its core, with liberty rhetoric surrounding it. Even though liberty is at stake in many of these key opinions, Jacobs establishes that inequal treatment fueled the fervor of his rhetoric. The implications of this approach are seen in Justice Kennedy's abortion jurisprudence, in which he abandons the equality core and the liberty analysis, standing alone, fails to carry the day.

In part 5, the authors interrogate Justice Kennedy's misjudgments regarding women, racial minorities, and immigrants. Given his notoriety as the justice who single-handedly integrated gays and lesbians into the legal fabric of civil society, it might strike some people as strange that Justice Kennedy's rhetoric is wanting in his treatment of various underrepresented groups. Beth Britt argues that Kennedy utilizes a disembodied rhetoric of liberty when addressing reproductive rights, adopting a formal "view from nowhere." While the Court's attention is directed to the fetus, the woman is virtually invisible in his opinions. In the same vein, Britt argues, Justice Kennedy's opinions in the gay rights cases also embrace a sterile principle of liberty that ends with a celebration of a narrow view of marriage. In a related manner, Kathryn Stanchi distinguishes the personalization of the parties in the gay rights cases to the starkly depersonalized women in the abortion opinions. In a fascinating accounting, Stanchi demonstrates that the words "dignity," "autonomy," "liberty," and "freedom" are common in Justice Kennedy's opinions on gay rights but hardly used in the abortion cases. The disparity between the empathy shown to gay litigants and the lack of empathy for women seeking an abortion is palpable. Rebecca Zietlow argues that Justice Kennedy's blind spot extended to African Americans, to the extent that he rejected racial classifications but could not see his way to understanding the continuing effects of systemic racism. Nevertheless, his opinions did hold the conservative "color-blind" jurisprudence at bay, even if he could not advance the cause of equality beyond racial classifications. Finally, Leticia Saucedo contends that Justice Kennedy's rhetoric in cases involving immigrants tended to place the liberty, autonomy, and dignity of the federal government above concern for immigrants. However, in cases in which the immigrants were seeking to assimilate to American customs and values, Justice Kennedy tended to humanize and even celebrate them as deserving of autonomy and dignity. Perhaps the stinging effect of this jurisprudence is best seen in *Trump v. Hawaii* (2018), which was announced the day before Justice Kennedy retired.

In the concluding assessment, David Frank thematizes the volume under the provocation of two themes: What does it mean to judge well? Does Justice Kennedy judge well? He begins by articulating the baseline concept of "rhetorical knowledge" that conceptualizes the efforts to persuade in situations of uncertainty. Against this backdrop, he argues that the contributors develop several noteworthy themes that cut across the organization of the volume.

First, the contributors each demonstrate that classical and contemporary rhetorical theories and analytical practices can inform our understanding of contemporary legal discourse. Second, the concept of rhetorical knowledge, as developed in the rhetorical tradition, provides an appropriate baseline for assessing Justice Kennedy's opinions. Finally, the analysis is recursive insofar as the examination of Justice Kennedy's rhetoric provides more detailed explanation of what it means to judge well, effecting a nonvicious hermeneutical circle of understanding.

What does the impressive erudition in this volume accomplish? First, it reveals that the "superficial rhetoric" of some of Justice Kennedy's most prominent cases is a matter of stylistic flourish of some interest but that there are deep rhetorical lessons to be learned from his body of judicial opinions. Justice Kennedy's rhetoric is inextricably yoked to his articulation of legal doctrine. There is much more at work than elegiac phrases describing marriage or the exercise of free speech that order his thinking and expression. This volume makes substantial headway in uncovering these rhetorical themes. We invite you to enjoy the interdisciplinary investigations that follow.

We close with the suggestion that a unifying feature of Justice Kennedy's rhetoric may be its epideictic appeal to the citizenry to fulfill the promise of the American experiment of constitutional democracy. His former clerk Ashutosh Bhagwat makes this claim directly in his chapter, and it is echoed by another former clerk in Leah Litman's tribute to Justice Kennedy upon his retirement. As Litman summarizes,

> Instead of the pointed zingers that his colleagues directed at him (some of which should probably have never made their way into the U.S. Reports), the justice chose to write about the inherent goodness of America—not necessarily who America is, but who America should be, at least from the justice's perspective. [Several cases during Litman's term as a clerk contain] similar undercurrents of the justice's faith in the American constitutional project, and a desire to (re?)make America in that idealized image. . . . The justice's opinion in *Arizona v. United States* also adopted an instructive, almost admonishing, tone, this time about the importance of civility and rationality in politics. (2018)

Our sophisticated understanding of Justice Kennedy's judicial rhetoric should not obscure that a very human person penned those words with a

genuinely optimistic commitment to decency. As Gene Garver has emphasized in his pathbreaking book on Aristotle's *Rhetoric*, rhetoric primarily is
an art of character.

> Rhetorical argument differs from argument in general in that rhetori-
> cal argument is essentially ethical, and that rhetorical topics are the
> means of making argument ethical. . . . I would call the *Rhetoric*, in
> contrast to a hermeneutics of suspicion, a hermeneutics of trust. But
> even a hermeneutics of trust is not a hermeneutics of gullibility. . . . To
> rule on the basis of the law alone is a character flaw. Aristotle condemns
> the man who stands on his rights in demanding an ethically excessive
> sort of precision concerning justice in the distribution of goods. Simi-
> larly here. To argue on the basis of reason alone is a character flaw, a
> failure of ethos, and therefore a failure to persuade. Excessive precision
> is in both cases unethical because it takes something which should be
> within the range of praxis and judgment and makes it into a subject for
> more precise, scientific determination. (1994, 100–101, 161, 183)

This would seem to be an apt description of Justice Kennedy's struggle to
judge well by embracing an ethic of openness without being gullible. Pure in
heart is not sufficient, of course, even if it provides a strong foundation for
fostering rhetorical knowledge. But it is equally certain that no human, however dignified and respectful that person might be, could ever *fully* meet the
ethical demands of judging well. By exploring Justice Kennedy's struggles in
the rhetorical discernment and articulation of the law, though, we may hope
to gain insight into how to judge better.

Notes

1. Knowles 2019, 12, quoting Michael McConnell in Reuben 1992, 36. See also
Bartl 2014, 1–2.
2. Wetlaufer's incisive prose deserves an extended quotation:

> The irony is the fact that, on the one hand, law is the very profession of rheto-
> ric. We are the sons and daughters of Gorgias himself. But if law is, at its core,
> the practice of rhetoric, the *particular* rhetoric that law embraces is the rhetoric
> of foundations and logical deductions. And that particular rhetoric is one that
> relies, above all else, upon the denial that it is rhetoric that is being done. . . . If,
> as I suggest, law *is* rhetoric but the particular rhetoric embraced by the law oper-
> ates through the systematic *denial* that it is rhetoric, then it should come as no
> surprise that difficulties sometimes confront us. (1990, 1554–55)

References

Bartl, Anthony D. 2014. *The Constitutional Principles of Justice Kennedy: A Jurisprudence of Liberty and Equality.* El Paso: LFB Scholarly.

Bowers v. Hardwick. 1986. 478 U.S. 186.

Citizens United v. Federal Election Commission. 2010. 558 U.S. 310.

Colucci, Frank J. 2009. *Justice Kennedy's Jurisprudence: The Full and Necessary Meaning of Liberty.* Lawrence: University Press of Kansas.

Duehren, Andrew M. 2015. "At Law School, Justice Kennedy Reflects on Cases, Time as Student." *Harvard Crimson,* October 23, 2015. https://www.thecrimson.com /article/2015/10/23/justice-kennedy-harvard-law.

Garver, Eugene. 1994. *Aristotle's Rhetoric: An Art of Character.* Chicago: University of Chicago Press.

Gonzales v. Carhart. 2007. 550 U.S. 124.

Knowles, Helen J. 2019. *The Tie Goes to Freedom: Justice Anthony M. Kennedy on Liberty.* Updated ed. Lanham, MD: Rowman and Littlefield.

Lawrence v. Texas. 2003. 539 U.S. 558.

Litman, Leah. 2018. "Tribute: Justice Kennedy's Counter-Clerks." *SCOTUSblog,* June 29, 2018.   https://www.scotusblog.com/2018/06/tribute-justice-kennedys-counter -clerks.

Llewellyn, Karl N. 1930. *The Bramble Bush: On Our Law and Its Study.* Self-published.

———. 1934. "On Philosophy in American Law." *University of Pennsylvania Law Review* 82:205–12.

Mootz, Francis J., III. 2011. "Vico, Llewellyn, and the Task of Legal Education." *Loyola Law Review* 57:135–56.

Obergefell v. Hodges. 2015. 576 U.S. 644.

Reuben, Richard C. 1992. "Man in the Middle." *California Lawyer* 12 (October): 34–38.

Romer v. Evans. 1996. 517 U.S. 620.

Stern, Mark Joseph. 2015. "Decoding Anthony Kennedy's Gay Marriage Decision." *Slate,* June 26, 2015. https://slate.com/news-and-politics/2015/06/supreme-court-2015 -decoding-anthony-kennedys-gay-marriage-decision.html.

Trump v. Hawaii. 2018. 585 U.S. __, 138 S. Ct. 2392.

Vieth v. Jubelirer. 2004. 541 U.S. 267.

Wetlaufer, Gerald B. 1990. "Rhetoric and Its Denial in Legal Discourse." *Virginia Law Review* 76:1545–97.

PART I

JUDGMENT IN CLASSICAL RHETORIC

I

JUSTICE KENNEDY AND THE INTERPRETATION
OF LEGAL TEXTS: THE CLASSICAL BACKGROUND

Michael Gagarin

The interpretation of legal texts, whether explicit or implicit, is fundamental to the operation of any legal system. Litigants in Athenian courts during the classical period (ca. 420–320 BCE) were well aware of this, and although their legal system was very different from ours, they devised many different interpretative strategies that are also used today. Central to the arguments used by Justice Kennedy in *Obergefell v. Hodges* (2015), for example, is the interpretation of the Fourteenth Amendment, and his clear presentation of his own interpretative strategy, though mocked and criticized by dissenters in the case, has clear parallels in Athenian forensic pleadings.[1]

By contrast, Justice Kennedy's arguments in *Citizens United v. Federal Election Commission* (2010) seem designed to avoid explicit interpretation of the free speech clause of the First Amendment; instead, he assumes an interpretation that suits the needs of the case he seeks to build. Thus, in both cases, interpretation, explicit in the former case and implicit in the latter, is essential to the conclusions he reaches.

In this chapter, after a brief sketch of the Athenian legal system, I examine some Athenian arguments about interpreting laws and then discuss Justice Kennedy's arguments in these two cases. I should stress that I am a classicist, not a lawyer, and so I approach the interpretation of current legal texts as an amateur, just as those who interpreted legal texts in Greece did so as amateurs.

The Athenian Legal System

Athens in the fifth and fourth centuries BCE had a legal system unlike any other. Written laws were enacted beginning in the seventh century; however, these laws were never systematically organized into a code. Nor was there a written constitution, but the word *politeia*, often translated "constitution," designated the overall system of government, established partly by law but largely by tradition.[2]

Both the system of government and the legal system excluded women and slaves from participation but otherwise were fully democratic. An assembly, open to all adult male citizens, made important decisions by majority vote. A council of five hundred, selected by lot from citizens over thirty years old, prepared the agenda for assembly meetings. Most administrative offices were also assigned by lot and changed annually. Thus, leadership did not depend on holding office but on a person's ability to persuade a majority of the citizens in the Assembly to support his position. The legal system was similarly democratic, participatory, and rhetorical. Lawsuits were brought by ordinary citizens and were tried by juries consisting of two hundred or more members, who were selected by lot on the day of the trial from among those male citizens, thirty or older, who composed the jury pool for that year (who were also selected by lot). Trials consisted of a pleading by the plaintiff and then by the defendant, each of whom normally spoke for himself. A water-clock timed the pleadings to ensure equal time for both sides. In some cases, each side was allowed a second, shorter rebuttal speech. Sometimes one or more friends would deliver parts of a litigant's case. When the pleadings were finished, the jury voted without formal deliberation, dropping a token into one of two urns. The side with the majority won, and there was no appeal. No trial lasted more than one day.

Each side could call witnesses, who simply delivered a deposition. In the fourth century, this was read out to the court by the clerk and then affirmed by the witness. Litigants could also have the clerk read out the text of a law or other documentary evidence that they had provided. An official, selected by lot, kept order, together with a clerk and other assistants, but there was no judge in our sense, and each juror decided his vote on the basis of the pleadings. A litigant who could afford it could hire a logographer (speech writer) to compose his pleading, but the litigant had to deliver it himself. Logographers kept copies of the speeches they wrote, and some one hundred of these have survived; they are the main source for our knowledge of Athenian law.

The Interpretation of Laws in Athens

In such a system, a litigant's entire case depended on his pleading. The jury learned the facts of the case from the two litigants, parts of which would be confirmed by their witnesses, and when the two accounts differed, the relative persuasiveness of a litigant's account could be the crucial factor in winning the case. The jury also learned about the applicable law or laws from the litigants' speeches, together with the texts of any laws that were read out by the clerk, and each juror would decide for himself the meaning and applicability of any particular law. Guidance in making this decision came primarily from the pleadings of the two parties, and since the jury decided the entire case in a single vote, this one vote had to take into consideration both the facts and the law.

Since there was no written constitution, there was, strictly speaking, no such thing as judicial review as we know it, but there was a procedure that was quite similar (Lanni 2009; Sundahl 2009). After 403 BCE, the Athenians distinguished explicitly between a law (*nomos*) and a decree (*psēphisma*), the former being a general rule, whereas the latter concerned a specific individual or situation. Laws were prioritized, and one could challenge the validity of a decree by claiming that it conflicted with or violated one or more laws. The procedure for such a challenge was a *graphē paranomōn* ("indictment for illegal [decrees]"), and the indictment, which was written on a wax tablet, had to contain the text of the decree and next to it the text of the law or laws allegedly violated.

This was the procedure used in the most famous trial in classical Athens, the case "On the Crown" (ca. 330 BCE). Aeschines brought this case against Ctesiphon, a close colleague of Demosthenes, for proposing a decree to award a crown to Demosthenes in recognition of his public service. Aeschines claims that the decree is illegal because it violates two laws. He also argues that Demosthenes does not deserve the crown. In the course of his speech, he uses a striking metaphor to argue for a strict, objective understanding of the law: "For justice is not something undefined, but has been defined in your laws. As in carpentry, when we would like to know what is straight and what is not, we set a ruler next to it by which it can be judged, so too in indictments for illegal proposals we have at hand as a ruler of justice that wax tablet there with the decree and the laws written down next to it. [To Demosthenes] Just show that these agree with one another and then step down" (Aeschines 2000, 3.199–200). Demosthenes, not surprisingly, rejects this idea of a "ruler of justice," and, in fact, each side discusses the meaning of each of the laws written on the tablet.

Aeschines's metaphor has a striking modern parallel. In 1936, Supreme Court Justice Owen Roberts, in an opinion that declared unconstitutional one of Franklin Roosevelt's New Deal proposals, formulated a geometric image very similar to Aeschines's ruler of justice, the so-called T-square rule: "When an act of Congress is appropriately challenged in the courts as not conforming to the constitutional mandate, the judicial branch of the government has only one duty—to lay the article of the Constitution which is invoked beside the statute which is challenged to decide whether the latter squares with the former. All the court does, or can do, is to announce its considered judgment upon the question" (*Butler* 1936, 62).[3] To be sure, the T-square rule allows for the court's "considered judgment," which Aeschines's ruler of justice would seem to exclude, but the message conveyed by both is that the decision, whether one legal text is consistent with another, more fundamental legal text, is a relatively simple, objective decision, akin to a problem in plane geometry.

Although it is a comforting thought that the legality of a decree or the constitutionality of a law can be easily determined, in practice disputes about the meaning of a law or the constitution almost always arise. In "On the Crown," Aeschines and Demosthenes (not surprisingly) reach opposite conclusions about whether Ctesiphon's proposed decree conflicted with the two laws. For example, there was a law prohibiting the award of a crown to any official who had not passed the audit required of all officials at the end of their term. Demosthenes held a minor position that year as Keeper of the Walls and had not yet been audited for this, so Aeschines argues that he is ineligible to receive a crown (Aeschines 2000, 3.9–31). Demosthenes counters that the law meant that someone could not receive a crown for his service in a specific office before passing the audit for that office and that his crown was to be awarded for his years of public service and had nothing to do with the office he currently held. He then cites several precedents of officials who had been honored before passing their audits (Demosthenes 2005, 18.111–19).[4]

"On the Crown" is one of the rare cases in which the speeches for both sides have survived. Most often, only one side survives, but these single speeches offer an array of different kinds of interpretation of laws. The plaintiff in Lysias 10, for example, argues for applying the spirit rather than the letter of the law. He has brought a libel suit against a man who accused him of killing his father. He anticipates that the accused will argue that the law on libel only prohibits the use of certain specific words, including "patricide" (*patrophonos*), and that the accused did not use that word but instead said that the plaintiff killed his father. The speaker argues that being a patricide and killing one's father are the same thing, and surely the legislator who enacted the law would have wanted to prohibit anyone from calling a person the latter as well as the former: "It would be a large task for the legislator to write down all the words that have the same meaning, so by mentioning one he made clear that he was speaking about all of them" (Lysias 2000, 10.7).

This argument exemplifies a common strategy in Athenian litigants' interpretations of the laws, the appeal to the legislator and his intent in enacting the law in question. Today the same sort of appeal is commonly made to the intentions of the authors of the US Constitution (or one of its amendments). In both cases, these appeals are problematic. In Athens, even if the author of a law was known (which was rarely the case),[5] no information was available concerning his intentions other than the text of the law itself, so that any discussion of his intent was mere speculation. For the authors of the Constitution, we have documents such as *The Federalist Papers*, but even when these convey clearly the view of James Madison or Alexander Hamilton on a particular point, it is very unlikely that all the signers of the final document had exactly the same intention. Today, as in Athens, the only true guide to the meaning of a legal text is the actual text of the law or constitution in question. From this, one may try to infer the intent of its author(s), but this is simply one strategy for interpreting the law in a way that will support one's case. Another example of interpretation is Hyperides, *Against Athenogenes* 3.13: "[He] will at once tell you that the law declares that agreements made between two parties are binding. Yes, agreements that are just. But for unjust agreements the law says the exact opposite; they are not binding." In fact, the law in question said nothing about unjust agreements. There is also Demosthenes 22.8: "[My opponent will say that] the law does not allow the Council to request an award [from the Assembly], . . . but nowhere does it prevent the Assembly from granting one."

Another interpretive strategy is to ask the jurors to be legislators; for example, the speaker in Lysias 14.4 argues, "Since you are deciding a case of this type for the first time since we made peace [i.e., since the end of civil war in 403 BCE], it is appropriate that you should be not simply jurors but legislators. You are fully aware that in the future the city will treat such matters in whatever way you decide today. The task of a responsible citizen and just-minded juror is to interpret the laws in the way that will benefit the city in the future." But in another speech, a different speaker on the same side in this case argues differently: "If anyone thinks that the penalty is substantial and the law too severe, you need to remember that you have not come here to be legislators but to vote according to the established laws" (Lysias 2000, 15.9). Applying the view of the first speaker today would mean that when the Constitution does not address a particular situation, the Supreme Court should act as legislator. Most justices today would strongly agree with the second speaker that the Court should not act as legislator, even though it appears to most outside observers that this is exactly what the Court often does.

Justice Kennedy and the Greeks on Interpretation

Some of the arguments of Justice Kennedy and his dissenters in *Obergefell* and *Citizens United* closely resemble Athenian arguments just outlined. In both cases, Justice Kennedy interprets amendments to the constitution (the Fourteenth and the First Amendments, respectively) as they may apply to matters that surely were not imagined by the authors of those amendments.[6] In both cases, Justice Kennedy's concern is freedom, but not necessarily all freedoms.

Obergefell v. Hodges *(2015)*

In *Obergefell*, Justice Kennedy begins his opinion with the Due Process Clause of the Fourteenth Amendment, under which no state shall "deprive any person of life, liberty, or property, without due process of law." Previous courts have established that "the fundamental liberties protected by this Clause include most of the rights enumerated in the Bill of Rights. . . . In addition these liberties extend to certain personal choices central to individual dignity and autonomy, including intimate choices that define personal identity and beliefs" (*Obergefell* 2015, 663). The range of possible protections within this description is large indeed.

Justice Kennedy then proceeds to lay out the methodological principles that will guide his opinion:

> The identification and protection of fundamental rights is an enduring part of *the judicial duty to interpret the Constitution.* That responsibility, however, has not been reduced to any formula. . . . Rather, it *requires courts to exercise reasoned judgment* in identifying interests of the person so fundamental that the State must accord them its respect. . . . *History and tradition guide and discipline this inquiry but do not set its outer boundaries.* . . . *That method respects our history and learns from it without allowing the past alone to rule the present.* . . . The generations that wrote and ratified the Bill of Rights and the Fourteenth Amendment did not presume to know the extent of *freedom in all of its dimensions,* and so they entrusted to future generations a charter protecting the right of all persons to enjoy liberty *as we learn its meaning.* When *new insight*

reveals discord between the Constitution's central protections and a received legal stricture, a claim to liberty must be addressed. (*Obergefell* 2015, 663–64; emphasis added)

The view described here envisions a much more complex process of judicial deliberation than does an appeal to the intent of the authors of the Constitution, because according to Justice Kennedy, these authors "did not presume to know" the full meaning of what they were writing or what their words would mean for future generations, and even when their intent is known, it is only one factor that may "guide and discipline" our current understanding but does not control it. In this way, Justice Kennedy effectively gives the Court a similarly broad latitude to interpret the Constitution as Athenian litigants (and the jurors who heard them) had when they cited the legislator's intent as guiding their understanding of a law, since they could present almost any plausible interpretation of a law as the legislator's intent.

The flexibility that Justice Kennedy envisions here for judicial deliberation is arguably necessary in a case like *Obergefell* because the Constitution nowhere envisions the possibility of same-sex marriage and certainly does not explicitly protect it. In fact, it would probably have been difficult, if not impossible, for our Founding Fathers to comprehend either the meaning of same-sex marriage or the nature of the social world of the twenty-first-century United States in which a case like this could arise.

Justice Kennedy then introduces four principles and traditions that "demonstrate that the reasons marriage is fundamental under the Constitution apply with equal force to same-sex couples" (*Obergefell* 2015, 644–48). These include that

- the right to personal choice regarding marriage is inherent in the concept of individual autonomy;
- the right to marry is fundamental because it supports a two-person union unlike any other in its importance to the committed individuals;
- the right to marry . . . safeguards children and families and thus draws meaning from related rights of childrearing, procreation, and education; and
- marriage is a keystone of our social order.

Not all of these principles and traditions are self-evident. The right to personal choice in marriage would be accepted by most people in the Western world, but other traditions support arranged marriages, and neither system has been proven better or more successful. The other three principles are even more questionable, especially in the twenty-first century. Two-person unions that are of great importance to the committed individuals can now regularly be found outside of marriage. The nuclear family envisaged by the third principle constitutes an ever smaller percentage of arrangements that we now consider to be families with or without children. And although marriage could perhaps in the past have been considered a keystone of our social order, in today's world, it does not have the same importance.

Even if we accept that these principles and traditions have the force Justice Kennedy assumes, it is not easy to see how they demonstrate that same-sex couples should be allowed to marry. Perhaps the most relevant is the right to personal choice, but even here, there are legitimate restrictions on that right. We disallow child marriages, for example, as well as incestuous and polygamous marriages, though the last of these prohibitions would seem to be open to the same objections that Justice Kennedy directs at the prohibition on same-sex marriage.[7]

Justice Kennedy ignores such concerns and instead turns to the question of how to understand the nature of the rights protected by the Bill of Rights and the Fourteenth Amendment and, more specifically, the right to marry. He begins with a condensed summary of the methodological principles already established: "The right to marry is fundamental as a matter of history and tradition, but rights come not from ancient sources alone. They rise, too, from *a better informed understanding* of how constitutional imperatives define a liberty that remains urgent in our own era" (*Obergefell* 2015, 671–72). Then, in order to reach this better informed understanding, he turns to the Equal Protection Clause of the Fourteenth Amendment, which states that no state shall "deny to any person within its jurisdiction the equal protection of the laws," and he proceeds to defend same-sex marriage on the basis of equality: "In interpreting the Equal Protection Clause, the Court has recognized that *new insights and societal understandings* can reveal unjustified inequality within our most fundamental institutions that once passed unnoticed and unchallenged" (673).[8] From here, Justice Kennedy concludes that, according to the Court's new understanding, same-sex marriages are a right, protected by the Constitution, and must be recognized by all states.

Justice Kennedy is saying, in essence, that as our world changes, our understanding of the fundamental rights protected by the Constitution may change along with it, so that a right established many years ago may now mean something quite different. This view is generally accepted with regard to literature; our understanding of Shakespeare is not what it was a century or two ago, and few people would seriously maintain that it should be the same. But many would argue that a legal text is different. If its meaning is continually changing, then no one knows what it really means, and the law loses its authority. Thus, some argue that legislation, regular but not frequent, is the only proper means for keeping the law up-to-date. For others, the flexibility that law requires may be provided by new legislation, but when legislation lags, change can and should be implemented by reinterpretation. These conflicting views derive from the tension in any legal text, including our Constitution, which requires permanence in order to have authority but flexibility in order to remain relevant to a changing world.

Justice Kennedy's majority opinion is followed by four separate dissenting opinions, each joined by one or two other dissenters. I focus on that of Chief Justice John Roberts, which is the most comprehensive of the four.[9]

Chief Justice Roberts begins with a clear stand against judicial legislation: "This Court is not a legislature. Whether same-sex marriage is a good idea should be of no concern to us. Under the Constitution judges have power to say what the law is, not what it should be. The people who ratified the Constitution authorized courts to exercise 'neither force nor will but merely judgment'" (*Obergefell* 2015, 686).[10] Chief Justice Roberts's position, however, is not without ambiguity. On the one hand, the Court must say "what the law is"; the Constitution has a specific meaning that the Court must merely declare (the originalist view). On the other hand, the Court must "exercise . . . judgment" in deciding what the Constitution means (essentially Justice Kennedy's position).

Chief Justice Roberts continues along the same lines; for example, "The real question in these cases is what constitutes 'marriage,' or—more precisely—*who decides* what constitutes 'marriage'?" (*Obergefell* 2015, 688). He then argues (702–3) that no precedent supports Justice Kennedy's broad understanding of freedom but that Justice Kennedy's claim (703–4) that "the right to personal choice regarding marriage is inherent in the concept of individual autonomy" echoes the widely condemned decision in *Lochner v. New York* (1905).

Chief Justice Roberts then adds (with notable sarcasm),

> To be fair, the majority does not suggest that its individual autonomy right is entirely unconstrained. The constraints it sets are precisely those that accord with its own "reasoned judgment," informed by its "new insight" into the "nature of injustice," which was invisible to all who came before but has become clear "as we learn [the] meaning"

of liberty. . . . The truth is that today's decision rests on nothing more than the majority's own conviction that same-sex couples should be allowed to marry because they want to, and that "it would disparage their choices and diminish their personhood to deny them this right." (*Obergefell* 2015, 703, Roberts, J., dissenting)

Near the end, Chief Justice Roberts returns to his main criticism that despite the Constitution's limiting the Court's role to judgment, the Court is acting as a legislature: "Those who founded our country would not recognize the majority's conception of the judicial role. They after all risked their lives and fortunes for the precious right to govern themselves. They would never have imagined yielding that right on a question of social policy to unaccountable and unelected judges" (709).

The decision in *Obergefell* depends primarily on the question of the judicial role in interpreting the Constitution. Justice Kennedy and Chief Justice Roberts both agree that the Court should only exercise its judgment and should not legislate, but they disagree widely on just what it means to exercise judgment.

Citizens United v. Federal Election Commission *(2010)*

In Justice Kennedy's opinion in *Citizens United*, he does not directly address any of the broad questions about judicial interpretation that he raises in *Obergefell*. The central issue in this case is whether a federal statute prohibiting independent corporate expenditures for electioneering communications is constitutional. Courts had previously ruled that Congress could prohibit corporate advertisement in elections because of its potential corrupting influence on the political process. Justice Kennedy frames the case as whether this prohibition is legitimate regulation of speech or suppression of speech. He concludes that it is suppression and that the law in question is therefore unconstitutional.

The basis of Justice Kennedy's opinion is the free speech clause of the First Amendment: "Congress shall make no law . . . abridging the freedom of speech." The meaning of "freedom of speech" had been an issue in countless prior court cases, resulting in many precedents. Justice Kennedy cites twenty-one of these prior cases in which "the Court has recognized that First Amendment protection extends to corporations" (*Citizens United* 2010, 558 U.S. at 342). Thus, Justice Kennedy never asks the basic questions that a layperson might ask, such as how a corporation can "speak" or whether there is any difference between corporate "speech" and the speech of individuals.

Rather, his arguments are mostly focused on the complex details of these previous cases. Thus, although the arguments in *Citizens United* are more complex than in *Obergefell* and Justice Kennedy's entire opinion is about 40 percent longer than in *Obergefell* (twenty-one versus fifteen pages), there is much less discussion of the nature of judicial deliberation and the interpretation of legal texts. Apparently in his mind, the meaning of "freedom of speech" as applied to corporate "speech" has already been decided.

Although the language of the free speech clause, as Justice Kennedy understands it, might seem to exclude the possibility of any regulation of speech, Justice Kennedy does acknowledge that "the Government may regulate corporate political speech through disclaimer and disclosure requirements, but it may not suppress that speech altogether" (*Citizens United* 2010, 558 U.S. at 319). The main question then becomes whether certain regulations enacted by Congress and permitted by two recent Supreme Court decisions—*Austin v. Michigan Chamber of Commerce* (1990) and *McConnell v. Federal Election Commission* (2003)—amount to legitimate regulation of speech or suppression of speech. Since the airing of the film in question would clearly violate these congressional regulations, Justice Kennedy turns to his main task, finding grounds for overturning these two cases. He argues that they were wrongly decided and that because both cases are fairly recent, any precedent that they set is not long-standing.

Because these prior cases upheld laws that regulated the political speech of corporations differently from that of individuals, Justice Kennedy devotes much of his argument to establishing the essential sameness of corporate and individual speech: "The right of citizens to inquire, to hear, to speak, and to use information to reach consensus is a precondition to enlightened self-government and a necessary means to protect it. . . . For these reasons, political speech must prevail against laws that would suppress it, whether by design or inadvertence. . . . Prohibited, too, are restrictions distinguishing among different speakers, allowing speech by some but not others" (*Citizens United* 2010, 558 U.S. at 340). By treating both corporations and individuals as "subjects" or "speakers," Justice Kennedy implies that there is no relevant difference between the two, so that the former cannot be regulated in ways that the latter are not. He does not explicitly argue for their sameness but rather assumes it, repeatedly using language that implies it: "it identifies certain preferred speakers"; "taking the right to speak from some and giving it to others"; "restrictions that operate to the disadvantage of certain persons"; "the exclusion of a class of speakers from the general public dialogue"; "restrictions on certain disfavored speakers" (341); "Corporations and other associations, like individuals, contribute to the 'discussion, debate, and the dissemination of information and ideas' that the First Amendment seeks to foster"; "The Court has thus rejected the argument that political speech of corporations or other associations should be treated differently under the First Amendment simply because such associations are not 'natural persons'" (343); "simply because the speaker is an association that has taken on the corporate form" (349). All these expressions imply that for the purpose of this case, a corporation is essentially a person engaging in political speech. Once this is established, little is left to be done in order to conclude that any regulation imposed on corporations but not individuals amounts to suppression of speech.

This reasoning evidently made sense to a majority of the justices, but to ordinary people, not trained in the intricacies of constitutional interpretation, it is rather bewildering to speak of corporations as "certain persons" or "a class of speakers." A corporation might be said to "speak" when it advertises, but advertisements have long been regulated in various ways (e.g., cigarettes, liquor, drugs, etc.). Corporate political "speech" may be speech in some sense, but in the eyes of most people, it clearly differs from the speech of an actual person.

Be that as it may, Justice Kennedy takes up one objection he foresees, that "the Framers may not have anticipated modern business and media corporations," and responds by pointing to "television networks and major newspapers owned by media corporations," which the framers surely would have protected from restrictions on publishing (*Citizens United* 2010, 558 U.S. at 353). But freedom of the press is addressed separately in the First Amendment, indicating that the framers distinguished between the press and other forms of speech and therefore would probably also have distinguished between individuals and media corporations as speakers. Justice Kennedy, however, ignores the "freedom of the press" clause in his single-minded focus on the protection of all corporations as speakers.

Justice Kennedy's final argument switches the focus from the right of corporations to engage in political speech to the right of individuals to obtain information from whatever sources they wish: "When Government seeks to use its full power, including the criminal law, to command where a person may get his or her information or what distrusted source he or she may not hear, it uses censorship to control thought. This is unlawful. The First Amendment confirms the freedom to think for ourselves" (*Citizens United* 2010, 558 U.S. at 356). As further support for this line of reasoning he later adds, "On certain topics corporations may possess valuable expertise, leaving them the best equipped to point out errors or fallacies in speech of all sorts, including the speech of candidates and elected officials" (364). This claim may be true in theory, and may pass muster in judicial argument, but if an ordinary person examines the history of corporate speech, one would be more likely to find corporate expertise being used to promote false information than otherwise.[11]

Justice Kennedy's conclusion is aptly summarized in the syllabus of the court reporter:

1. government may not, under the First Amendment, suppress political speech on the basis of the speaker's corporate identity. . . .
2. federal statute barring independent corporate expenditures for electioneering communications violated First Amendment. . . .
3. disclaimer and disclosure provisions of Bipartisan Campaign Reform Act of 2002 did not violate First Amendment, as applied to nonprofit corporation's film and three advertisements for the film. (*Citizens United* 2010, 130 S. Ct. at 876–77)

This last conclusion might seem to suggest that there are, in fact, significant differences between natural persons and corporations or associations, so that it is legitimate to regulate the latter in ways that do not apply to the former, but Justice Kennedy devotes very little of his argument to this third point and never examines its potential implications.

Conclusion

In sum, Justice Kennedy's opinions in these two cases and the arguments by which he justifies them seem to this nonspecialist to exemplify the lesson we learn from classical Athenian litigation that those who are skilled in judicial argument can justify different interpretations of a basic legal text and different methods of interpretation and that, therefore, the final decision that a person reaches about the meaning of a legal text is essentially the one that best supports the outcome of the case that the person desires. In one case, Justice Kennedy finds it helpful to discuss his view of judicial interpretation at some length, whereas in the other, almost nothing is said on this subject, implying that the meaning of the text is clear and needs no discussion. In one case, he builds his argument on the history of the subject, whereas in the other, he argues against the recent history of the subject and overturns precedents. The Athenians, aside from Aeschines's isolated "ruler of justice," had no difficulty acknowledging the rhetorical nature of judicial decision-making. We, on the other hand, generally decry the role of rhetoric in judicial decision-making while engaging in it nonetheless. These two decisions of Justice Kennedy's stand as a fine illustration of this.

Notes

1. Justice Kennedy was quite familiar with the rhetorical literature of classical Greece, from his general education at Stanford and elsewhere.

2. The *Athēnaiōn Politeia*, or *Constitution of the Athenians*, a work attributed to Aristotle but probably written by his pupils, describes the Athenian government and legal system in the late fourth century BCE.

3. Ironically, one year later, in *West Coast Hotel Co. v. Parrish*, 300 U.S. 379 (1937), Justice Roberts provided the swing vote in the first case in which the Court switched from opposing government measures to regulate the economy to supporting them, measures that included a few months later the National Labor Relations Act and the Social Security Act.

4. Regardless of the relative strengths of the arguments about the meaning of the law, this issue was almost certainly not the deciding factor in the case, since both sides devoted only a small fraction of their pleading to it (Gwatkin 1957; Harris 2000).

5. Athenians commonly attributed their laws to Solon, even when the law in question was certainly enacted after his time.

6. I am aware that the comparison of modern judicial opinions to ancient forensic pleadings may be inexact, but both kinds of texts contain arguments about the interpretation of an authoritative legal text (statute or constitution), and these arguments can legitimately be compared.

7. In fact, there is more support in our tradition for marriage being an arrangement between more than two people than there is for same-sex marriage. Cf. Chief Justice John Roberts's dissent in *Obergefell*: "It is striking how much of the majority's reasoning would apply with equal force to the claim of a fundamental right to plural marriage" (*Obergefell* 2015, 704).

8. Justice Kennedy cites, for example, the gradual elimination by the Court of gender-based inequalities in marriage laws.

9. Chief Justice Roberts's dissent (*Obergefell* 2015, 686–713) is nearly as long as Justice Kennedy's majority opinion (651–81).

10. The quoted words are from Hamilton 1961.

11. Cigarette companies, for example, long denied the health risks of smoking, and oil companies denied climate change, despite their knowledge to the contrary in both cases.

References

Aeschines. 2000. *Aeschines*. Translated by Christopher Carey. Austin: University of Texas Press.

Aristotle. 2002. *The Athenian Constitution*. Translated and edited by P. J. Rhodes. London: Penguin Classic Books.

Austin v. Michigan Chamber of Commerce. 1990. 494 U.S. 652.

Citizens United v. Federal Election Commission. 2010. 558 U.S. 310.

Demosthenes. 2005. *Speeches 18–19.* Translated by Harvey Yunis. Austin: University of Texas Press.

Gwatkin, William E., Jr. 1957. "The Legal Arguments in Aischines' *Against Ctesiphon* and Demosthenes' *On the Crown.*" *Hesperia* 26:129–41.

Hamilton, Alexander. 1961. "Federalist No. 78." In *The Federalist,* edited by Clinton Rossiter. New York: New American Library.

Harris, Edward M. 2000. "Open Texture in Athenian Law." *Dike* 3:27–79.

Hyperides. 2001. *Against Athenogenes.* In *Dinarchus, Hyperides, Lycurgus.* Translated by Craig R. Cooper. Austin: University of Texas Press.

Lanni, Adrianne. 2009. "Judicial Review and the Athenian 'Constitution.'" In *Démocratie athénienne—démocratie moderne: Tradition et influences,* edited by M. H. Hansen, 235–76. Geneva: Hardt Foundation.

Lochner v. New York. 1905. 198 U.S. 45.

Lysias. 2000. *Lysias.* Translated by Stephen Todd. Austin: University of Texas Press.

McConnell v. Federal Election Commission. 2003. 540 U.S. 93.

Obergefell v. Hodges. 2015. 576 U.S. 644.

Sundahl, Mark. 2009. "The Living Constitution of Ancient Athens: A Comparative Perspective on the Originalism Debate." *John Marshall Law Review* 42:463–504.

United States v. Butler. 1936. 297 U.S. 1.

West Coast Hotel Co. v. Parrish. 1937. 300 U.S. 379.

2

SEX AND MORAL POLLUTION IN THE RHETORIC OF JUSTICE KENNEDY

Eugene Garver

Excess is always a comfort, and sometimes a career. Moderation, on the other hand, is nothing but pure tension.

—Albert Camus, *The Rebel*

Appearance Versus Reality and the Normative Versus the Actual

Justice Kennedy's opinion in *Gonzales v. Carhart* contains the following two sentences: "While we find *no reliable data* to measure the phenomenon, *it seems unexceptionable* to conclude some women come to regret their choice to abort the infant life they once created and sustained. . . . It is *self-evident* that a mother who comes to regret her choice to abort must struggle with grief more anguished and sorrow more profound when she learns, only after the event, what she once did not know: that she allowed a doctor to pierce the skull and vacuum the fast-developing brain of her unborn child, a child assuming the human form" (2006, 159–60; emphasis added). I would be embarrassed to write these lines. They are easy to dismiss as a judge making an argument for a result he's already decided on, rationalizing rather than reasoning; maybe that is true. One common rhetorical strategy is to convince an audience that what the speaker says is actually what the speaker believes. The tactics for doing so can be stylistic: "It seems unexceptionable to conclude . . ." "It is self-evident . . ." I do not want to look at the stylistic side of Justice Kennedy's rhetoric but at a more substantive aspect.

We hold some truths to be self-evident. But is "A mother who comes to regret her choice to abort must struggle with grief more anguished and sorrow more profound when she learns, only after the event, what she once did not know" one of those self-evident truths? When we hold a truth to be self-evident, that does not mean that everyone agrees with it, and it does not mean that there is not evidence to the contrary that has to be disposed of one way or another. That evidence that points in the other direction is merely apparent, measured against the truths the community holds as self-evident.

To ask for or try to supply evidence means that you do not trust the judgment of the community for whom Justice Kennedy claims to be speaking. If there are women who do not feel remorse, that would not make Justice Kennedy's claims false. It would mean there was something wrong, something unnatural, about those women. Real women do not have abortions without regret; real women do not have partial birth abortions without horror. To argue against a self-evident truth takes a different form of argument from simply showing that Justice Kennedy relied on a questionable amicus brief and should look at a wider range of evidence.

In *Gonzales v. Carhart*, where the issue was whether to uphold a law banning what the law's opponents called "partial birth abortion," deciding the issue turned on whether to endorse popular opinion, "community standards," what the community supposedly takes to be self-evident, or instead to look for credible reasons, from science, from history, from judgments of some more reputable group than the majority.

The persuasive public speaker generally draws their premises from well-regarded and accepted premises asserted by well-regarded and reliable people. Justice Kennedy does just that. But we are not doomed to affirming everything a community generally holds to be true. We can, as Justice Kennedy himself does in the line of sexual orientation cases from *Romer v. Evans* (1996) through *Obergefell v. Hodges* (2015), instead discount common opinions as private judgments, even if held by most of the right-thinking members of a community. According to that argumentative strategy, people's opinions about homosexuality are private opinions because homosexuality itself has become a private affair, just as birth control did in *Griswold v. Connecticut* (1965) and abortion in *Roe v. Wade* (1973). Privatization is the most effective way of undermining a self-evident truth; only universal and public truths can be self-evident.

The difference between Justice Kennedy's argument in *Gonzales* and in *Romer* et al. is which side of the issue one should take on, when to endorse popular opinion and when to privatize it. The issue is stated succinctly in

Justice Henry Brown's not usually praised opinion in *Plessy v. Ferguson*: "We consider the underlying fallacy of the plaintiff's argument to consist in the assumption that the enforced separation of the two races stamps the colored race with a badge of inferiority. If this be so, it is not by reason of anything found in the act, but solely because the colored race chooses to put that construction upon it" (1896, 551).[1]

Whose opinions are authoritative is the crux in how to appeal to what everybody knows, *endoxa*, to settle questions of law.

Appearance and Reality in Common Opinion

Socrates asks Euthyphro, in the Platonic dialogue that has the latter's name, "Consider this: Is the pious loved by the gods because it is pious, or is it pious because it is loved by the gods?" (Plato 1975, 14). Euthyphro does not understand the question—most of us would not—because most of the time we do not have to face it; unless someone or some situation forces the question on us, we lead our lives perfectly comfortably without ever having to distinguish *endoxa*, reputable opinions of the community, from truth. Almost all the time, we live perfectly well without answering the question of whether something is true because most people take it to be true—what better measure of truth could we have than consensus?—or that most people's opinions converge on the truth, so that being true is the usual reason for us to hold the opinions we do.

Rhetorical argument often consists in either driving truth and consensus apart, as with Justice Kennedy in *Lawrence v. Texas* (2003) and Justice Brown in *Plessy*, or in making the two coincide, as Justice Kennedy does in *Gonzales*. There are two options here. It can be that there is no difference between thinking that something is true because decent people think it so and thinking that decent people take it to be true because it is true. Or, we offer an argument to deny that identity, and then we discount what most people think is true as only apparently true, apparent to those people. We have to get beyond common opinion to see the truth.

Ethical deliberation has to confront these different possibilities for the relation of appearance and reality because of the nature of the problems the judge faces. Practical thinking gets started when someone feels a discrepancy between the way things are and the way they ought to be and wants to close that gap. Ethical reasoning consists in exploring the different ways of reconciling the actual and the normative, and the conflicting strategies of identifying what is true with the way things appear to the community and driving those two apart are a principal resource in reintegrating what is and what ought to be.

The identity between what reputable people think and what is true is a principle that lies behind the common thought that because something is good, it will happen, that if something is good to believe, it must be true. And so the arguments go: racial segregation is wrong, and so the evidence will show that it harms Black children; abortion is wrong, and so evidence will show that it harms women. We see things a certain way because of the kind of people we are. Our characters and ideals determine how we see the world—therefore the self-evidence that Justice Kennedy finds in *Gonzales*.

Euthyphro is not very bright and never gets the point of Socrates's question. But Justice Kennedy has to. The distance between the actual and the normative forces him to argue about the relation between appearance and reality, between opinions that are only what someone thinks and opinions that are held because they are true and track reality.

In *Gonzales*, the fact that partial birth abortion looks barbaric to the community for which Justice Kennedy speaks means that it *is* barbaric and should be prohibited. And the stylistic side of Justice Kennedy's rhetoric shows that he speaks for the community: "It seems unexceptionable to conclude . . ." "It is self-evident . . ." By contrast, In *Lawrence* and *Obergefell*, the fact that the community thinks homosexual behavior is disgusting is no longer reason to ban it but instead reason to reform how the community thinks or to report that that reform has already taken place. This is the difference in rhetorical argument between the premise "This is disgusting" and the premise "People think that this is disgusting."

Sex and Moral Pollution

I have claimed that the reason Justice Kennedy can vote to uphold laws forbidding "partial birth abortion" but find unconstitutional laws abridging rights involving sexual orientation is that he comes down first on one side and then the other of the dilemma that Socrates poses to Euthyphro. That the American people are revolted by partial birth abortion is arguably reason for banning it because they *should* be disgusted: this practice displeases the gods because it is impious. They might be equally revolted by gay people in our midst, but those opinions are not grounded in reality, not according to the decisions Justice Kennedy wrote about those issues. The American people are wrong to think that the behavior is impious because they are disgusted.

Of course, you will not find words like "piety" or "holiness"—or "the gods" or "God"—in Justice Kennedy's opinions. But I want to claim that partial birth abortion and sexual orientation cases are both about moral pollution, a most acute form of the gap between the way things are and the way they ought to be: there is something critically wrong with our community, and it has to be purged and cleansed. That Justice Kennedy is thinking in terms of pollution is most clear in *Gonzales*. Reva Siegal interprets *Gonzales* as saying that "guilt and abortion have virtually become synonymous. It is superfluous to ask whether patients experience guilt; it is axiomatic that they will" (2008, 1658, quoting the congressional testimony of the antiabortion activist Vincent Rue). The "guilt" she mentions is not being guilty of a crime but of a shameful act of pollution. And she sees how the decision does not need evidence.

Justice Kennedy faces a common rhetorical problem. He wants to talk about something for which he lacks the language. The law, with the language of rights and justice and law, cannot talk about the evil that Justice Kennedy wants to ban. Existing law and prior Supreme Court decisions will not allow him to claim that partial birth abortion is criminal and certainly not that the woman choosing one—or, as he prefers, "the mother"—is guilty of a crime. He cannot use the language of rights without begging questions about the legal status of a fetus. He lacks the language for saying why partial birth abortion is "worse" than abortions in general.

If Justice Kennedy's rhetoric is the language of moral pollution, then partial birth abortion does not just putatively harm an individual fetus; its ugliness infects the entire community, and the fact that it is legal makes the pollution all the worse. We do not have to be active participants, as a woman and a doctor are, to be tainted or disgraced by the practice. You do not have to *do* anything to be polluted. Innocence does not insulate you against being polluted.

Whether Euthyphro's father was guilty of negligent homicide is irrelevant to whether his action sullied his family and is in need of purgation (*catharsis*) rather than punishment. Oedipus's ignorance did not stop his actions from polluting Thebes. We do not have to impute criminal intent to women, doctors, or homosexuals to see their activities as polluting our community. If many people feel that the entire community is polluted by someone's having a partial birth abortion or a gay marriage, that doesn't mean at all that such a society thinks it bears collective guilt. I might have no responsibility for failing to prevent these abhorrent actions; moral pollution has nothing to do with what the rest of the community did or did not do. I began by saying that the purpose of ethical reasoning is to bring "is" and "ought" back into harmony and noted that we commonly short-circuit the hard business of acting to bring them together by seeing the world as it ought to be. Here examples could be seeing homosexuality as leading to God's punishment in the form of AIDS. Moral pollution does not have to be physical pollution to be real.

It is worth focusing a little more closely on the *Euthyphro*. Euthyphro runs into Socrates when both are on their way to court, Socrates to defend himself against charges of blasphemy and Euthyphro to prosecute his father for polluting his family through his negligently killing one of his slaves.[2] It takes a while for their conversation to get to the point where Socrates asks whether something is pious because the gods like it or the gods like it because it is holy.

In between is an examination of Euthyphro's stance about piety. He claims to be an authority on piety. He is so much wiser than the rest of Athens that he claims to have an obligation to do something that he knows most people think is impious but that he claims is pious: prosecuting his father for polluting his family. There is a paradox here: How can somebody be an authority on what the community takes to be true? Could a community be wrong about what it takes as its basic values? Euthyphro's putative expertise is as much a violation of community norms as is Socrates's profession of ignorance. Justice Brown's opinion in *Plessy* again cuts to the heart of the matter: Who gets to make the authoritative interpretation of the meaning of the community's basic ethical principles?

In *Gonzales*, Justice Kennedy's answer is easy. The voice of the community is decisive. *Vox populi, vox deo*. That is what self-evidence means. In *Romer* through *Obergefell*, that answer is not good enough. Because the community believes something, even holds it self-evident, does not make it true. Things are pious if they please the gods, not the other way around. Neither Euthyphro nor Socrates has much success arguing against Athenian common opinion. What rhetorical strategy could Justice Kennedy use to discount American common opinion in the sexual orientation cases?

Pollution and Epideictic Rhetoric

Moral pollution calls for a specific kind of rhetoric. Aristotle divides rhetoric into three kinds. In deliberative rhetoric, there is something that we want, an end, and we do not have it. We then calculate what we can do to achieve the end. Things are then as we think they ought to be. People are hungry, and we should deliberate about how to reduce poverty. Next, in judicial rhetoric, we argue whether someone committed a crime; if so, punishment will erase the gains they acquired through the crime, restoring the identity of how things are and how they ought to be. When performing an abortion becomes a crime, the people involved can be punished: the immoral act is isolated and does not contaminate the community. One reason doctors are targeted, by murderers or by law, is to preserve the innocence of the pregnant woman.

But epideictic rhetoric displays the values of the community, and in Justice Kennedy's opinions that I have focused on, the values exhibited are cases of moral pollution that threatens the community. The meaning of my marriage changes when gay marriage exists too. We insist on the values of the community especially when they are under threat by an action that is ignoble or disorderly. The community has to figure out how to cleanse itself from pollution so that things are once again as they ought to be. If a practice threatens the values of a community expressed as disgusting and unnatural, the Court either has to condemn it—people are against it because it is wrong in *Gonzales*—or, although many people think the practice degrades the community, the Court argues that it does not sully the community, as in *Romer* to *Obergefell*.[3]

Justice Kennedy captures the nature of epideictic rhetoric perfectly when he cites *Planned Parenthood v. Casey* (1992) in *Gonzales*. The issue, as he frames it, is not about whether a woman's rights are violated or whether the state has the power to prevent wrongs, but "the government may use its voice and its regulatory authority to show its profound respect for the life within the woman" (*Casey* 1992, 873; *Gonzales* 2007, 128). A law banning partial birth abortion is legitimate because it is a legitimate government function to show "profound respect." Epideictic rhetoric is puzzling because it seems to be speech without practical effect. People can well not be troubled by homosexual activity, but when the government declares that it is protected activity, they can worry that the community they thought they were a part of is not the one they live in now.[4]

In epideictic reasoning, we make norms and nature coincide by an act of declaration, rather than discourse that leads to some further action. *Bowers v. Hardwick* (1986) and *Lawrence* were challenges to laws that were never enforced; *Gonzales* outlawed a rarely performed surgical procedure. The practical effects of the laws involved are not important; it is the fact of their being said in the name of the community that matters. Punishing the woman having an abortion is an issue avoided in the politics of abortion, and punishing doctors performing the procedure is not at issue in this particular case.

What matters is not who caused the abomination but how to purify society from its occurrence, and the solution is to declare the procedure illegal.

Justice Ruth Bader Ginsburg, in her dissent in *Gonzales*, rightly says that "the law saves not a single fetus from destruction, for it targets only a *method* of performing abortion" (Gonzales 2007, 181). But her observation misses the point of Kennedy's opinion as a piece of epideictic rhetoric, where the presumption is that the issue will be about justice and injustice, not the noble and the base. Her dissent is parallel to arguing against outlawing biological weapons on the grounds that soldiers would be just as dead from artillery fire. The issue is not harm but something so revolting that it must be unnatural and for that reason has to be prohibited. Just as Oedipus can be innocent but still pollute Thebes, the motives of the woman asking for an abortion are beside the point; this is a stain, not a crime. The method of abortion is then all-important because this is a matter of pollution, not injustice.

Pollution is precisely a practice where harm is not the grounds of its prohibition. The identity of the community is at stake in the gay marriage and abortion cases. So, again, Justice Ginsburg may be right when she said that "the law saves not a single fetus from destruction" (*Gonzales* 2007, 181), but Justice Kennedy wants us to think that the identity and nature of all women is threatened if partial birth abortion is left approved of by law. I may be innocent of abortion, but I am defiled by its presence in the community.

But in *Lawrence*, Justice Kennedy makes the opposite response to the pollution of homosexuality. "The fact that the governing majority of a State traditionally viewed a particular practice as immoral is not a sufficient reason for upholding a law prohibiting the practice" (*Lawrence* 2003, 577).[5] In this case, according to Justice Kennedy, the fact that people find homosexuality a stain is not sufficient reason for prohibiting it. People are just as likely to think that the marriages of all of us are threatened by gay marriage as that the sexual and reproductive behavior of all of us are threatened by those rare instances of partial birth abortion. But those opinions do not count in deciding whether laws prohibiting homosexual conduct or gay marriage are constitutional.

Public Versus Private in Epideictic Rhetoric

Justice Kennedy's claim that "while we find *no reliable data* to measure the phenomenon, *it seems unexceptionable* to conclude some women come to regret their choice to abort the infant life they once created and sustained" seems easy to rebut (*Gonzales* 2007, 159). All we have to do is find reliable data to the contrary.

But such refutations do not come so easy in practical reasoning, which has to be resistant to giving up the well-regarded opinions of the community. Someone who disagrees is not a well-regarded member of the community. Any evidence contrary to Justice Kennedy's claim that no woman who does not regret her choice deviates from the community's normative standards of how women should behave. Real women do not enjoy abortions. As Siegel puts it, "Choosing against motherhood and subverting the physiology of pregnancy will make women ill—and in all events cannot represent what women really want, because any *real* woman wants what is best for her child. Women who seek abortions must have been confused, misled, or coerced into the decision to abort a pregnancy—because the choice to abort a pregnancy cannot reflect a normal woman's true desires or interests. Using law to restrict abortion protects women from such pressures and confusions—and frees women to be true women" (2007, 145).

In *Gonzales*, Justice Kennedy chooses as evidence anecdotes supplied in the amicus briefs filed by Operation Outcry over the scientific evidence presented by briefs on behalf of physicians and medical associations. Scientific evidence cannot counter community norms, as Chief Justice Earl Warren discovered when his presentation of purported scientific evidence backfired: the psychological findings made what should be self-evident, that state-imposed racially segregated schools violate principles of equality, open to evidence and so debate. Scientists, like Euthyphro when he presents himself as an expert on piety, are not part of the community, and so we are right to disregard what they say.

If a self-evident assertion cannot be rebutted by citing contrary evidence, how can it be countered? The majority of Colorado citizens voted for the constitutional amendment prohibiting cities and other jurisdictions from prohibiting discrimination on the grounds of sexual orientation. How could a court claim that this majority opinion is not the normative judgment of the community? The only way is by making those voters' opinions private beliefs rather than contributions to the authoritative opinion of the community (Rousseau's will of all versus the general will, if that helps).

As Barbara Flagg puts it, "One problem of moral community: whether and how the state may express moral disapproval of 'victimless' private conduct. . . . *Hardwick* held that a moral purpose provided adequate justification for a state's criminalization of one form of adult, private, consensual sexual activity. However, *Romer* discounted an analogous moral justification, identifying (impermissible) 'animus,' rather than (arguably permissible) moral disapproval, as the motivating force behind Amendment 2" (1997, 833–34).

What look like norms of the community can be rebutted by making them private and so of no legal standing. Apparent pollution is privatized; privatization is a way that appearances become mere appearances. *Lawrence* made homosexuality doubly private and therefore harmless. First, homosexual conduct was no longer public but a subject of private choice. It did not pollute. Second, people's disgust at homosexuality was now private too; it did not count as a reason for prohibition. It was an opinion that was no longer an *endoxon*. One common device for privatizing something is to put it inside the gates of a family; something that was within the zone of privacy can become public just because people think it pollutes all of us. Euthyphro wants to make public the actions of his father, who had jurisdiction within the household and was there beyond criticism. Euthyphro can only make them public by persuading the jury that his father's action is not private after all but pollutes the whole community.[6] The doubling of pollution in Euthyphro's case is paradigmatic: partial birth abortion is a stain on the community, but so is its legality.

As I just said, what look like norms of the community can be rebutted by making them private and so of no legal standing. But in another sense, making them beyond legal criticism transforms the public and its authoritative opinions. The community has to change the way things look to accord with a new vision of reality. Gay marriage is now one way of forming a family, while having a partial birth abortion is no way to be a woman, and so the maximally intimate relations between woman and fetus become exposed to public judgment.[7]

I noted that it is a peculiarity of epideictic rhetoric that displaying and defending the values of a community is practical reasoning without apparent practical effect. Disputes about whether an opinion is public or private are naturally bitter and unresolvable. Once again, *Euthyphro* is on point:

> What things is the disagreement about, which causes enmity and anger? Let us look at it this way. If you and I were to disagree about number, for instance, which of two numbers were the greater, would the disagreements about these matters make us enemies and make us angry with each other, or would we not quickly settle it by resorting to arithmetic? Is it not about right and wrong, and noble and disgraceful, and good and bad? Are not these the questions about which you and I and other people become enemies, because we differ about them and cannot reach any satisfactory conclusion? (Plato 1914, 25)

Disputes are especially bitter when one side takes its opinions as veridical and the other as merely opinions, when one side sees the issue as public and the other as private and so outside debate. In the contemporary United States, disputes about sex are paradigmatically bitter, and Justice Kennedy's rhetoric aimed at displaying and taking a side in those disputes.

Epideictic rhetoric is most at home with the strategy of making appearances and reality coincide by changing appearances rather than acting to make things be as they ought. That is why, compared to deliberative and judicial rhetoric, it looks impractical. We can remove the stain of partial birth abortion by banning the practice or, more exactly, by making an official declaration of the community that the practice is a danger to us all. But we can remove the stain of homosexuality by changing the way people think about what is noble—romantic love—and what is shameful. Homosexuality does not count as unnatural anymore, and opinions to the contrary become private, without political weight.[8]

Rhetorical Argument as Practical Reasoning

Sexual discrimination cases, from *Romer* through *Obergefell*, extend legal protection and recognition to homosexual acts and people by removing them from public judgment and transferring them to the private realm. *Gonzales* does the opposite. It refuses to count partial birth abortion as a private act but sees it instead as open to judgment by the public. But I need to add a couple of final complications. First, placing something in the private realm of the family is not necessarily progress; any rhetorical argument can be used for welcome and disturbing purposes.[9] Alternatively, progress can come in the other direction. Spousal abuse used to be invisible to the law because it took place beyond the wall of privacy; it has become common reputable opinion that it should be publicly cognized as a crime and as much an act of moral pollution as homosexuality once was. Second, the domain of the private shifts over time. If today it is family, it once was a business that was private and so none of the law's business. *Lochner* should give pause to the idea that the more things are taken out of the public realm, the better.[10]

In moral pollution, one person's acts besmirch all of us; their legal imprimatur is a stain on the community. The community is transformed, to the horror of some and the satisfaction of others. My act of childbirth is not the same as it was before the existence of partial birth abortion. My marriage is not the same once homosexual marriage has legal sanction. The obvious response is to remove these threats to the identity of the community and its sacred institutions. Justice Kennedy's language in *Gonzales* shows him doing just that. His arguments in the sexual orientation cases are more ambitious.

Consider for a final time Justice Ginsburg's dissent in *Gonzales*, which meets head-on Justice Kennedy's presupposition about pollution: "As *Casey* comprehended, at stake in cases challenging abortion restrictions is a woman's 'control over her [own] destiny.' 'There was a time, not so long ago,' when women were 'regarded as the center of home and family life, with attendant special responsibilities that precluded full and independent legal status under the Constitution.' Those views, the Court made clear in *Casey*, 'are no longer consistent with our understanding of the family, the individual, or the Constitution.' Women, it is now acknowledged, have the talent, capacity, and right 'to participate equally in the economic and social life of the Nation'" (*Gonzales* 2007, 171; internal citations omitted). The nature of childbirth changes when it is one alternative response among others to pregnancy, as the meaning of my marriage changes when same-sex couples can marry as well. The community changes when new options become possible or old ones impossible, and the community can be polluted by the presence of an option, even if no one, or almost no one, chooses it. The Court in *Casey* spoke as though there was a single "understanding of the family, the individual, or the Constitution." If we think instead that we share a range of available meanings, the boundaries of which can be contested, and therefore a range of judgments and decisions, then individual acts of childbirth and marriage, and their corresponding institutions, change their meaning as they are held up against new norms.

It is hard to find examples of radical conversion, someone who quickly changes from taking homosexuality to be an abomination to thinking of it as a practice deserving toleration and respect. Moral and political change occur more often as some practice enters or exits from the range of legitimate choices. Entry and exit often take place, we have seen, by a practice's becoming public or private. But now the narrative has three stages instead of two, and this picture accords with how people are actually persuaded to change their evaluative judgments. First something is impossible, then it is possible, and only then is it desirable or respectable. Homosexuality is first, in *Bowers*, something that has to be condemned publicly, since its existence threatens the community. Then, in *Lawrence*, it is a private matter, affecting only the people engaging in the activity, and finally it can become public again, as homosexual couples become fully recognized as members of the community through publicly sanctioned marriage. Battles over abortion and homosexuality, and over moral pollution in general, are fights over the admission and exclusion of public possibilities. A community's identity consists in the truths it holds to be self-evident. Justice Kennedy's rhetoric of moral pollution exhibits how moral progress can, and sometimes cannot, occur.[11]

Notes

1. To give a little more context: "A statute which implies merely a legal distinction between the white and colored races—a distinction which is founded in the color of the two races and which must always exist so long as white men are distinguished from the other race by color—has no tendency to destroy the legal equality of the two races, or reestablish a state of involuntary servitude. Indeed, we do not understand that the Thirteenth Amendment is strenuously relied upon by the plaintiff in error in this connection" (Plessy 1896, 543).

2. I ignore several questions and details in presenting this summary. I take them up in Garver 2014. The standard work on Greek ideas of moral pollution is Parker's Miasma: Pollution and Purification in Early Greek Religion (1996).

3. The closest contemporary jurisprudence comes to pollution is the idea of stigma, which Justice Kennedy employed in other cases, especially the homosexuality cases, but not in matters of abortion. And if the appropriate response to miasma is catharsis, it is assertions of dignity that counter stigmata.

4. See the assertion in Casey that laws can have a persuasive as well as a prohibitive force: "Regulations which do no more than create a structural mechanism by which the State, or the parent or guardian of a minor, may express profound respect for the life of the unborn are permitted, if they are not a substantial obstacle to the woman's exercise of the right to choose. . . . Unless it has that effect on her right of choice, a state measure designed to persuade her to choose childbirth over abortion will be upheld if reasonably related to that goal" (Casey 1992, 877–78).

5. Casey 1992, 850: "Some of us as individuals find abortion offensive to our most basic principles of morality, but that cannot control our decision. Our obligation is to define the liberty of all, not to mandate our own moral code." Lawrence 2003, 558: though "for many persons [objections to homosexual conduct] are not trivial concerns but profound and deep convictions accepted as ethical and moral principles," the power of the state may not be used "to enforce these views on the whole society through operation of the criminal law" (citing Casey 1992, 850).

6. As I show, Euthyphro's argument is especially far-fetched and therefore significant, because his father's actions took place in another place and time, in Naxos years before the prosecution (Garver 2014).

7. As Geoffrey Stone writes, "Over the next several decades, the AMA [American Medical Association] launched an aggressive campaign to rid the nation of abortion. The success of this campaign was facilitated by the late nineteenth-century 'social purity' movement, which sought to impose conservative religious and normal 'values on the whole society,' and to give the state 'greater power over areas of life once considered private'" (2017, 219).

8. The truthful person (ho alêtheutikos) "is someone who is truthful both in what he says and how he lives when nothing about justice is at stake, simply because that is his state of character. Someone with this character seems to be a decent person [ho epieikês]. For the lover of truth [ho philalêthês] who is truthful when nothing is at stake will be still keener to tell the truth when something is at stake" (Aristotle 2019, 75; Greek added to Irwin translation).

9. See the analysis of arguments that display self-confidence and those that exhibit the complications of a practical situation in Gardner, chapter 10 in this volume.

10. For the change in the primary sense of the private for constitutional law, see Kahn 2005.

11. For an analogous analysis of death, see Kahn 2020. As Kahn observes, "No set of observations can tell us whether to register a death as a sacrifice, a tragedy, or a cost" (2020, 205).

References

Aristotle. 2019. *Nicomachean Ethics.* Translated by Terence Irwin. 3rd ed. Indianapolis: Hackett.

Bowers v. Hardwick. 1986. 478 U.S. 186.

Camus, Albert. 1991. *The Rebel: An Essay on Man in Revolt.* New York: Vintage Books.

Flagg, Barbara J. 1997. "Animus and Moral Disapproval: A Comment on *Romer v. Evans.*" *Minnesota Law Review* 82:833–54.

Garver, Eugene. 2014. "Euthyphro Prosecutes a Human Rights Violation." *Philosophy and Literature* 38 (2): 510–27.

Gonzales v. Carhart. 2007. 550 U.S. 124.

Griswold v. Connecticut. 1965. 381 U.S. 479.

Kahn, Paul W. 2005. *Putting Liberalism in Its Place.* Princeton: Princeton University Press.

———. 2020. "Democracy and the Obligations of Care." In *Democracy in Times of Pandemic: Different Futures Imagined,* edited by Miguel Poiares Maduro and Paul W. Kahn, 196–208. Cambridge: Cambridge University Press.

Lawrence v. Texas. 2003. 539 U.S. 558.

Lochner v. New York. 1905. 198 U.S. 45.

Obergefell v. Hodges. 2015. 576 U.S. 644.

Parker, Robert. 1996. *Miasma: Pollution and Purification in Early Greek Religion.* Oxford, UK: Clarendon.

Planned Parenthood of Southeastern Pennsylvania v. Casey. 1992. 505 U.S. 833.

Plato. 1914. *Euthyphro; Apology; Crito; Phaedo; Phaedrus.* Translated by W. R. M. Lamb. Loeb Classical Library. London: W. Heinemann.

———. 1975. "Euthyphro." In *The Trial and Death of Socrates,* edited by G. M. A. Grube. Indianapolis: Hackett.

Plessy v. Ferguson. 1896. 163 U.S. 537.

Roe v. Wade. 1973. 410 U.S. 113.

Romer v. Evans. 1996. 517 U.S. 620.

Siegel, Reva B. 2007. "Dignity and the Politics of Protection: Abortion Restrictions Under Casey/Carhart." *Yale Law Journal* 117:1694–796.

———. 2008. "The Right's Reasons: Constitutional Conflict and the Spread of Woman-Protective Anti-abortion Argument." *Duke Law Journal* 57:1641–92.

Stone, Geoffrey R. 2017. *Sex and the Constitution: Sex, Religion, and Law from America's Origins to the Twenty-First Century.* New York: Liveright.

PART 2

JUDGMENT IN STASIS THEORY

3

JUSTICE KENNEDY'S DEFINITIONAL CONSTRUCTION OF GAY RIGHTS IN *LAWRENCE* AND *OBERGEFELL*: LEGAL RHETORICAL ANALYSIS WITH THE INTERPRETIVE STASES

Martin Camper

Definition played a key rhetorical role in the public debate over same-sex marriage in the United States. Critics of same-sex marriage charged proponents with changing marriage's traditional definition as a bond between two people of opposite sex. Meanwhile, same-sex marriage advocates argued that marriage's core definition, love of and commitment to another person, is not dependent on the gender of the people involved. Pro-traditional-marriage slogans such as "marriage = 1 man + 1 woman" and the pro-same-sex-marriage symbol of a pink equals sign illustrate that, for much of the public, the answer to the question of whether same-sex marriage should be legal hinged on one's view of the institution's essential definition.

But a close reading of the text that made same-sex marriage a constitutional reality reveals that the definition of another term was actually the crux of the decision. In his opinion for the majority in *Obergefell v. Hodges* (2015), Supreme Court Justice Anthony Kennedy expends most of his rhetorical energy defining the word *liberty* in the Fourteenth Amendment: "nor shall any state deprive any person of life, liberty, or property, without due process of law" (U.S. Const. amend. XIV, §1). Known as the Due Process Clause, this passage is at the center of a decades-long dispute over substantive due process: whether this clause protects rights that are not mentioned anywhere in the Constitution from state infringement. Justice Kennedy's argument for legally recognizing a right to same-sex marriage rests on the definition of *liberty* in this clause.

Much of the legal scholarship on this case focuses on how Justice Kennedy develops substantive due process doctrine. In contrast, this chapter shines light on how Justice Kennedy rhetorically constructs—or employs the argumentative affordances of language to persuasively formulate—a definition of Fourteenth Amendment *liberty* that supports a constitutional right to same-sex marriage in *Obergefell* and to same-sex sex in *Lawrence v. Texas* (2003), as the former case builds on the discursive strategies of the latter. The creation and application of law is a thoroughly rhetorical process, and analyzing the discursive architecture of these decisions contributes to our knowledge of how constitutional rights are argued into existence. To carry out this investigation, this chapter employs an ancient theory of rhetoric that was birthed in the courtroom and thus is well suited for this analysis: *stasis theory*.

Analyzing Arguments over Legal Texts: The Interpretive Stases

Stasis theory was developed by ancient Greek and Roman teachers of rhetoric as a tool for inventing courtroom arguments. It outlines a comprehensive and sequential set of general issues, or *stases* (singular: *stasis*), that recur in virtually all legal cases. The theory pairs each stasis with a set of supporting lines of argument, or *topoi* (singular: *topos*), that advocates can use to support or attack claims concerning each issue type. The stases, with their associated topoi, provided ancient legal rhetors with a road map of the possible turns a court case could take, which they could prepare for in advance with stock arguments. Ancient rhetoricians realized that stasis theory described how disagreement can proceed in all genres of discourse, but their discussions of the theory, as found in Cicero's *De inventione*, the anonymous *Rhetorica ad Herennium*, and Quintilian's *The Orator's Education*, generally assume a legal context.[1]

Despite the origins of stasis theory in courtroom discourse, it remains an underutilized tool for analyzing modern legal rhetoric. Only a few scholars have argued that stasis theory offers a comprehensive, systematic method for analyzing legal arguments (Dicks 1976; Hohmann 1989; Könczöl 2009; Provenzano and Larson 2020; Provenzano and O'Rourke, chaps. 4 and 5 in this volume). These scholars primarily focus on one branch of the theory, the set of stases that assess the defendant's allegedly criminal actions: *conjecture*, whether the defendant committed the act; *definition*, how to classify the committed act in legal terms; *quality*, how to evaluate the defendant's act; plus *jurisdiction*, whether the proper legal procedures have been followed (Cicero 1976a, 1.8.10; Quintilian 2001, 3.6.66.).

While this set of *situational stases* covers large swaths of legal argumentation, employing only these stases neglects one critical area: interpretation
of the law. Virtually all of the treatments of stasis theory in ancient to early
modern Western rhetorical manuals detail a second set of stases that identify general, recurring issues concerning the interpretation of legal texts: the
interpretive stases. Five interpretive stases can be identified in ancient rhetorical handbooks: *ambiguity*, when a word or phrase in a text elicits two or more
divergent readings; *definition*, when the semantic scope or limits of a word
in a text are uncertain; *letter versus spirit*, when the exact words of a text seem
to clash with the author's intent; *conflicting passages*, when two or more parts
of a text seem to be discordant; and *assimilation*, when an unwritten meaning is inferred from a written text (Cicero 1976a, 1.12.17–13.17; [Cicero] 1981,
1.11.19; Quintilian 2001, 3.6.66). As with the situational stases, there can be
procedural questions in the stasis of *jurisdiction* concerning the appropriate
means of arriving at an interpretation (Camper 2018, 139–62). Each interpretive stasis comes with a set of topoi, some of the most common being
historical context, authorial intention, and co-text, or the language surrounding the word, phrase, clause, or passage in question. In general, the extant
ancient Greco-Roman rhetorical handbooks take a descriptive approach to
explaining the interpretive stases. Some handbooks offer prescriptive advice
for employing the topoi in a given stasis, while other handbooks offer more
of an inventory of available strategies. Regardless, the aim is to equip students with the knowledge to compose effective arguments.

From this body of observation and advice arises a descriptive vocabulary for analyzing interpretive disputes in terms of points of disagreement
and the lines of argument that can support competing positions in those
disagreements. In contrast to modern argument theories, the interpretive
stases and their topoi are tailored to the particulars of hermeneutical argumentation, which stem from the complex act of making meaning from language that is disconnected from or has an unclear relationship to its original
context. Stasis theory makes critical distinctions between different hermeneutical issues, distinctions key to understanding what divides competing
interpretations and to evaluating the persuasive potential of an interpretive
argument. Because stasis theory's organizing principle is disagreement, it
is an appropriate analytical fit for the adversarial nature of judicial rhetoric.

As this chapter demonstrates through its examination of *Lawrence* and
Obergefell, the interpretive stases and their topoi constitute a critical tool for
rhetorical analysis of legal argumentation given the central role of written
law in modern jurisprudence. By identifying a legal argument's interpretive

stasis, a critic can characterize how a case with respect to a legal text is rhetorically framed, a key piece of analysis since the outcome of any case is
dependent on its framing (Mootz 2006, 109). The topoi associated with the
identified stasis then give the critic language to name and analyze the lines
of reasoning that the rhetor employs to justify a claim within that frame. The
next two sections apply this two-step sequence of analysis to Justice Kennedy's
arguments in *Lawrence* and *Obergefell*, followed by a section that applies this
same sequence of analysis to these cases' dissents.

Justice Kennedy's Definitional Construction of *Liberty*
to Include Gay Rights

In both *Lawrence* and *Obergefell*, Justice Kennedy's argument primarily operates in the interpretive stasis of definition, "a case in which a document
contains some word the meaning of which is questioned" (Cicero 1976a,
2.51.153). More precisely, the interpretive stasis of definition involves disputes
where there is agreement about the basic sense of a word in a text but there is
disagreement about the scope or limits of that sense. The word is not ambigu-
ous, with two or more possible discrete readings, but vague (Camper 2018,
45–46). All of the justices would agree that *liberty* in its most basic sense
means *freedom*, but they do not all agree about *what one has the freedom to do*
as guaranteed by the Fourteenth Amendment. Arguments in this stasis are
concerned with fine semantic distinctions as well as the criteria for including
or excluding something from the category indicated by the term (Camper
2018, 45, 49). In appellate contexts, nailing down these definitional criteria is
critical since lower courts will need a guide to applying the disputed term as
novel cases arise. In legal contexts more broadly, words in written laws often
have technical definitions; therefore, appealing to general usage of a word can
be unpersuasive. However, a shared understanding of the word's basic sense
offers some argumentative leverage. Within this chosen frame, Justice Kennedy advances his claim that same-sex sex and marriage are constitutionally
protected rights. Striking a balance between legal innovation and continuity,
Justice Kennedy rhetorically constructs a definition of *liberty* that is at once
already established and a warrant for declaring these two new rights.

 Both Cicero and the *Rhetorica ad Herennium*'s author advise that legal
advocates should, as a matter of framing, begin arguments in the definitional stasis with a concise and lucid explanation of the key term (Cicero
1976a, 2.17.53; [Cicero] 1981, 2.12.17). Justice Kennedy opens both opinions

with definitions of *liberty*: "Liberty protects the person from unwarranted government intrusions into a dwelling or other private places" (*Lawrence* 2003, 562); "The Constitution promises liberty to all within its reach, a liberty that includes certain specific rights that allow persons, within a lawful realm, to define and express their identity" (*Obergefell* 2015, 651–52). By beginning his opinions this way, Justice Kennedy frames the essential questions in these two cases as a matter of Fourteenth Amendment *liberty*. Justice Kennedy could have argued that the definition of *liberty* in this clause should be expanded to cover rights to same-sex sex and marriage. Instead, he argues that these rights fall within the definitional scope of *liberty* and, therefore, are not newly created rights but heretofore unrecognized ones. Intuiting Quintilian's insight that "there is usually more difficulty in establishing a definition than in applying it to a thing" (2001, 7.3.19), Justice Kennedy spends significant rhetorical energy constructing this inclusive definitional scope as already established.

Toward this end, in *Lawrence*, Justice Kennedy traces the definition of due process *liberty* in modern Supreme Court jurisprudence, following the *Rhetorica ad Herennium*'s advice of appealing to "previous judgment" to invalidate "the principle underlying the contrary definition" ([Cicero] 1981, 2.12.17, 2.13.19). He begins with 1965's *Griswold v. Connecticut*, which established that "a right to privacy" definitionally included "the marriage relation and the protected space of the marital bedroom" (*Lawrence* 2003, 564–65). Next, he points to 1972's *Eisenstadt v. Baird*, which definitionally expanded the right to privacy to "the right to make certain decisions regarding sexual conduct [that] extends beyond the marital relationship." Justice Kennedy further notes that the Court defined the right to privacy as "fundamental," a necessary qualification according to some jurists and legal scholars for a right to be definitionally covered by *liberty* (565).

Then, Justice Kennedy observes that in 1973, *Roe v. Wade* "recognized the right of a woman to make certain fundamental decisions affecting her destiny and confirmed once more that the protection of liberty under the Due Process Clause has a substantive dimension of fundamental significance in defining the rights of the person" (*Lawrence* 2003, 565). *Roe* is critical to Justice Kennedy's history because it definitionally expands the right to privacy, particularly in sexual matters, to *fundamental destiny-shaping choices*, and it definitionally links this right to *liberty* in the Fourteenth Amendment, a connection neither *Griswold* nor *Eisenstadt* makes. As legal commentators have noted, Justice Kennedy definitionally subsumes a right to privacy under *liberty* (Knowles 2019, 166). Finally, in this section of the opinion, Justice

Kennedy contends that *Carey v. Population Services International* in 1977 further solidified that the right to privacy in relational and sexual matters is not definitionally limited "to the protection of rights of married adults" (*Lawrence* 2003, 566). Later in the opinion, Justice Kennedy cites *Planned Parenthood v. Casey* as further precedent that in 1992 cemented "the substantive force of liberty protected by the Due Process Clause" (573) and "that our laws and tradition afford constitutional protection to personal decisions relating to marriage, procreation, contraception, family relationships, child rearing, and education" (574).

By outlining these definitional precedents, Justice Kennedy can proclaim that *Bowers v. Hardwick*, which in 1986 ruled that antisodomy laws were constitutional and which *Lawrence* overturned, "was not correct when it was decided," defending *Lawrence* from charges of constitutional revisionism inspired by changing social mores rather than law. *Griswold, Eisenstadt, Roe*, and *Carey* were all decided prior to *Bowers*, and therefore, as Justice Kennedy argues, a definition of *liberty* that would cover same-sex sex as a private matter had already been affirmed by the Court by 1986. Justice Kennedy bolsters this argument by quoting from Justice John Paul Stevens's *Bowers* dissent: "Individual decisions by married persons, concerning the intimacies of their physical relationship, even when not intended to produce offspring, are a form of 'liberty' protected by the Due Process Clause of the Fourteenth Amendment. Moreover, this protection extends to intimate choices by unmarried as well as married persons" (*Lawrence* 2003, 578).

Maintaining that this precedent-established reading of the Fourteenth Amendment has persisted to the present day, Justice Kennedy locates *Bowers*'s flaw not in an incorrect definition of *liberty* but in an incorrect definition of the right to "sodomy." As Cicero explains, "it will be necessary to show the connexion between the act . . . and [the preferred] definition" (Cicero 1976a, 2.17.53). In order for the precedent-established definition of *liberty* to be applied to same-sex sex, this activity must be described such that it fits within the term's scope. One method of defining an object, according to Cicero, involves enumerating its parts: "definitions are made partly . . . by enumeration, when the thing which has been set up for definition is divided into its members," "for example a body has head, shoulders, hands, sides, legs, feet and so forth" (Cicero 1976b, 5.28, 6.30). Justice Kennedy critiques *Bowers* for reducing (i.e., underenumerating) the petitioners' claim to "simply the right to engage in certain sexual conduct." He contends that *Bowers* failed to see how antisodomy laws regulate "the most private human conduct, sexual behavior, and in the most private of places, the home," and "seek to control a personal relationship that . . . is within the liberty of persons to choose without being punished as criminals" (*Lawrence* 2003, 567). Justice Kennedy maintains that *Lawrence* does not change *liberty*'s definition but rectifies *Bowers*'s misanalysis of the right to same-sex sex by enumerating the other aspects of freedom involved.

In *Obergefell*, Justice Kennedy replicates his approach in *Lawrence*, outlining a history of the Court's definition of *liberty* to show that it already encapsulates a right to same-sex marriage. He begins with *Eisenstadt* and *Griswold*, asserting that they define liberty to include "certain personal choices central to individual dignity and autonomy, including intimate choices that define personal identity and beliefs" (*Obergefell* 2015, 663). A little later, Justice Kennedy cites precedent establishing that "the right to marry is protected by the Constitution": *Loving v. Virginia* (1967), *Zablocki v. Redhail* (1978), and *Turner v. Safley* (1987). He specifically quotes from *Loving*, which in 1967 stated that the right to marry "is one of the vital personal rights essential to the orderly pursuit of happiness by free men" (664). Justice Kennedy then cites a string of cases demonstrating that the Court has consistently discussed the right to marry as definitionally covered by due process *liberty*, including *M.L.B. v. S.L.J.* (1996), *Cleveland Board of Education v. LaFleur* (1974), *Griswold*, *Skinner v. Oklahoma ex rel. Williamson* (1942), and *Meyer v. Nebraska* (1923) (*Obergefell* 2015, 664–65).

Justice Kennedy concedes that all of these cases assume a right to marry in the context of opposite-sex unions (*Obergefell* 2015, 665); therefore, he must show that the Court's reasons for definitionally covering the right to opposite-sex marriage under *liberty* equally apply to the right to same-sex marriage. One way to accomplish this task is to establish a genus of *marriage* whose defining qualities characterize both *opposite-sex* and *same-sex unions* as its species. As Cicero writes, "species is a concept whose special characteristic can be referred to a head and source, as it were in the genus" (Cicero 1976b, 7.31). Justice Kennedy thus contends, "In defining the right to marry these cases have identified essential attributes of that right based in history, tradition, and other constitutional liberties inherent in this intimate bond" (*Obergefell* 2015, 665). On the basis of Court precedents, including *Loving*, *Zablocki*, *Lawrence*, *United States v. Windsor* (2013), *Griswold*, *Turner*, *Pierce v. Society of Sisters* (1925), *Meyer*, and *Maynard v. Hill* (1888), Justice Kennedy offers four reasons for protecting marriage as a due process *liberty*: respecting individual autonomy, recognizing marriage's unique significance, protecting children, and maintaining a stable society (665–70). Since "these reasons apply with equal force to same-sex couples," Justice Kennedy concludes, "same-sex couples may exercise the right to marry" (665). Again, Justice Kennedy rhetorically leaves the definition of *liberty* unmodified and instead provides a definition of same-sex marriage that necessarily qualifies it for protection under the Fourteenth Amendment.

Justice Kennedy's Justifications for Applying *Liberty* So Defined to Gay Rights

Even though Justice Kennedy constructs an expansive definition of *liberty* that existed prior to *Lawrence* and *Obergefell*, there remains the problem that these rights have never been declared before. Justice Kennedy must justify applying this term, so defined, to these rights for the first time. His main defense is that *liberty* in the Fourteenth Amendment is intentionally broad, in effect following advice in the *Rhetorica ad Herennium*: "We shall ascertain the writer's intention and present the reason why he had in mind what he wrote, and show that that text is clear, concise, apt, complete, and planned with precision" ([Cicero] 1981, 2.9.13). Justice Kennedy employs the authorial intention topos in *Lawrence*: "Had those who drew and ratified the Due Process Clauses of the Fifth Amendment or the Fourteenth Amendment known the components of liberty in its manifold possibilities, they might have been more specific. They did not presume to have this insight. They knew times could blind us to certain truths and later generations can see that laws once thought necessary and proper in fact serve only to oppress" (*Lawrence* 2003, 578–79); and in *Obergefell*: "The generations that wrote and ratified the Bill of Rights and the Fourteenth Amendment did not presume to know the extent of freedom in all of its dimensions, and so they entrusted to future generations a charter protecting the right of all persons to enjoy liberty as we learn its meaning" (*Obergefell* 2015, 664). Thus, Justice Kennedy ties the Court's declaration of same-sex intimacy and marriage rights to the Constitution's intended meaning.

If the framers intentionally employed broad language to cover rights that would be recognized in the future, then, as Justice Kennedy argues, judges are responsible for determining what rights count as protected liberties (*Obergefell* 2015, 663). However, he resists reducing that determination to a single method, contending that this definitional process "requires courts to exercise reasoned judgment in identifying interests of the person so fundamental that the State must accord them its respect" (663–64). He says that such a process is similar to the "analysis of other constitutional provisions that set forth broad principles rather than specific requirements." Knowing how his conservative colleagues limit *liberty*'s definition, Justice Kennedy writes, "History and tradition guide and discipline this inquiry but do not set its outer boundaries. . . . That method respects our history and learns from it without allowing the past alone to rule the present" (664). He later cautions, "If rights were defined by who exercised them in the past, then received practices could serve as their own continued justification and new groups could not invoke rights once denied" (671). Justice Kennedy thus faults the conservatives' definition of *liberty* for being incomplete, one of the grounds of definitional refutation noted by Quintilian (2001, 7.3.23). He then cites *Loving* and *Lawrence* as examples where the Court has rejected a history-only definition (*Obergefell* 2015, 671). The definitional process that Justice Kennedy defends allows for a "better informed understanding of how constitutional imperatives define a liberty" (671–72). For Justice Kennedy, the definitional bounds of *liberty* are expandable but constrained (see Knowles 2019, 48).

In *Obergefell*, Justice Kennedy supports a definition of *liberty* that includes a right to same-sex marriage by making a connection between the Fourteenth Amendment's Due Process and Equal Protection Clauses. This appeal to cotext follows Cicero's advice that "it must be shown that from what precedes or follows in the document the doubtful point becomes plain" (Cicero 1976a, 2.40.117).[2] Justice Kennedy writes, "In any particular case one Clause may be thought to capture the essence of the right in a more accurate and comprehensive way, even as the two Clauses may converge in the identification and definition of the right" (*Obergefell* 2015, 672). Citing precedent in which equal protection is invoked to abolish legally sanctioned sex discrimination in marital contexts, Justice Kennedy writes, "the Equal Protection Clause can help to identify and correct inequalities in the institution of marriage, vindicating precepts of liberty and equality under the Constitution" (674). As he explains, state laws prohibiting same-sex marriage "are in essence unequal: Same-sex couples are denied all the benefits afforded to opposite-sex couples and are barred from exercising a fundamental right." He concludes, "the Equal Protection Clause, like the Due Process Clause, prohibits this unjustified infringement of the fundamental right to marry" (675). By asserting that these two clauses have mutually defining power to identify rights, Justice Kennedy lends further textual support to the right to same-sex marriage.

Cicero notes that "the definition of the opponents may also be attacked if we show that to approve it is dishonourable and inexpedient, and point out what disadvantages will follow if their definition is accepted" (Cicero 1976a, 2.17.54). Justice Kennedy in effect follows this advice by showing the negative consequences of defining *liberty* to the exclusion of same-sex sex and marriage rights. In *Obergefell*, Justice Kennedy writes that defining *liberty* to exclude the right to same-sex marriage "would disparage [same-sex couples'] choices and diminish their personhood" (*Obergefell* 2015, 672). There are fewer appeals to consequences in *Lawrence*, yet there Justice Kennedy writes that *Bowers*'s "continuance as precedent demeans the lives of homosexual persons" (*Lawrence* 2003, 575).

Conservative Objections to Justice Kennedy's Definition of *Liberty*

In the conservatives' dissents in *Lawrence* and *Obergefell*, they reject Justice Kennedy's definitional framing, insisting that Justice Kennedy is creating new, textually unmoored rights. They thus attempt to shift the stasis from definition to assimilation, the latter of which, as Cicero explains, "arises . . . when from a statement written somewhere one arrives at a principle which is written nowhere" (Cicero 1976a, 2.50.148). This slippage between the stases of definition and assimilation is common enough that centuries ago Quintilian wrote, "There is some link between [assimilation] and Definition, because if a Definition is weak it often slips into [assimilation]" (2001, 7.8.1). If a key term in a legal text cannot be persuasively defined to support a legal rhetor's argument, the rhetor may resort to some kind of inference, or assimilation, that bridges the gap between the term and the argument. Because inferential, or assimilative, interpretive arguments go beyond the explicit terms of the text, they are more easily rebutted. This shift in stasis can be accomplished rhetorically by attacking the opposing side's definition of a key term.

Predictably, all of the dissents in *Lawrence* and *Obergefell* explicitly reject Justice Kennedy's definition of *liberty* in the Fourteenth Amendment as broadly covering a right to privacy and autonomy. Citing *Washington v. Glucksberg* (1997), Justices Antonin Scalia, Samuel Alito, and John Roberts each limit the term *liberty* to fundamental rights that are grounded in the country's history and tradition (*Lawrence* 2003, 588, 593; *Obergefell* 2015, 697–98, 737). Justice Clarence Thomas narrowly defines *liberty* as "freedom from physical restraint"; however, he also entertains a definition in line with the broader "American legal tradition" as "individual freedom *from* governmental action" but "not as a right *to* a particular governmental entitlement" (*Obergefell* 2015, 725, 726). None of these definitions encompass a right to same-sex sex or marriage for the dissenting justices in *Lawrence* or *Obergefell*, respectively.

On the basis of this putative failure of definition, the conservatives conclude that the majority's rulings in both cases infer, or assimilate, constitutional rights without a firm textual basis, a violation of originalist hermeneutics. The conservatives then employ several topoi, a number of which are identified in ancient rhetorical discussions of assimilation, to rhetorically unmoor these rights from the text further. These topoi flow from a hermeneutic that stipulates that constitutional interpretations should be limited to the text's original intended or public meaning. Chief Justice Roberts's dissent in *Obergefell*, the lengthiest of the four dissents, and Justice Scalia's dissent in *Lawrence*, the lengthier of the two dissents, exhibit the main topoi found across the conservatives' responses.

One topos, identified by Cicero, is the insistence of strictly adhering to the text: "He will deny that anything should be considered except the letter of the law" (Cicero 1976a, 2.50.152). Chief Justice Roberts charges the majority with disregarding the text: "The right it announces has no basis in the Constitution," and "If you are among the many Americans . . . who favor expanding same-sex marriage, by all means celebrate today's decision. . . . But do not celebrate the Constitution. It had nothing to do with it" (*Obergefell* 2015, 687, 713). In addition to rejecting Justice Kennedy's due process argument, Chief Justice Roberts rejects Justice Kennedy's argument from co-text that a right to same-sex marriage can also be found in the Equal Protection Clause, criticizing "the majority [for] fail[ing] to provide even a single sentence explaining how the Equal Protection Clause supplies independent weight for its position" (707). Chief Justice Roberts further derides Justice Kennedy's reasoning by asserting that the majority's ruling was "based not on neutral principles of constitutional law, but on its own 'understanding of what freedom is and must become'" (688). Chief Justice Roberts's derision closely follows Cicero's advice to attack any assimilation by declaring, "inference is no better than divination" (Cicero 1976a, 2.50.153).

Another way to attack an assimilative argument is to associate it with prior assimilations of the same text that the audience views negatively (see Camper 2018, 123–24). Chief Justice Roberts disparages the majority's ruling even further by linking Justice Kennedy's interpretation of *liberty* to prior decisions now overturned and widely scorned: *Dred Scott v. Sandford* (1856) and *Lochner v. New York* (1905). Chief Justice Roberts contends that in *Dred Scott* "the Court relied on its own conception of liberty and property" (*Obergefell* 2015, 695), stripping all African Americans of citizenship and upholding the rights of white Americans to own Black people anywhere in the Union.[3] Likewise, Chief Justice Roberts argues that *Lochner*, which struck down a

New York law limiting the number of hours bakers could work, "empower[ed] judges to elevate their own policy judgments to the status of constitutionally protected 'liberty'" (697).

Just as rhetors can link present assimilations to past assimilations, they can project from present assimilations to future assimilations. The negative form of this topos is the *slippery-slope* objection: the present inference will lead to an undesirable inference in the future (Camper 2018, 132–33). In *Obergefell*, Chief Justice Roberts writes, "It is striking how much of the majority's reasoning would apply with equal force to the claim of a fundamental right to plural marriage," a widely stigmatized arrangement (*Obergefell* 2015, 704). Chief Justice Roberts's words serve as a warning that Justice Kennedy's justification of same-sex marriage will ultimately undo the two-person requirement for marriage. In *Lawrence*, Justice Scalia issues a similar slippery-slope warning: "State laws against bigamy, same-sex marriage, adult incest, prostitution, masturbation, adultery, fornication, bestiality, and obscenity" are "called into question by today's decision" (*Lawrence* 2003, 590). Indeed, Justice Scalia correctly predicts the next logical step for the Court: "what justification could there possibly be for denying the benefits of marriage to homosexual couples exercising '[t]he liberty protected by the Constitution'?" (605).

Reinforcing the shift from the stasis of definition to assimilation, Justice Scalia contends that there are significant gaps in the definitional links Justice Kennedy traces through precedent as the foundation of the *Lawrence* ruling. First, Justice Scalia observes that *Griswold* and *Eisenstadt* do not ground a right to privacy in the Fourteenth Amendment's Due Process Clause (*Lawrence* 2003, 594–95). He then attacks *Roe*, which does ground a right to privacy in this clause, for violating the conservative definitional requirement that an unenumerated liberty be within the country's history and tradition. Instead, Justice Scalia argues, the Court based its interpretation on "its own normative judgment that antiabortion laws are undesirable." Further, he says that *Casey* undermined *Roe*'s claim that abortion is a fundamental right because it decided that restrictions did not need to be "narrowly tailored to serve a compelling state interest," the standard, according to Justice Scalia, for fundamental rights (595). Given the key role *Roe* plays in Justice Kennedy's definitional construction of *liberty*, Justice Scalia's counters are a sharp rhetorical blow.

One final significant assimilative topos that undermines Justice Kennedy's reasoning can be found in Justice Scalia's *Obergefell* dissent, where Justice Scalia counters Justice Kennedy's argument from intent. Justice Scalia contends that even though the Due Process Clause is vague, "it is unquestionable that the People who ratified that provision did not understand it to prohibit a practice [limiting marriage to opposite-sex couples] that remained both universal and uncontroversial in the years after ratification" (*Obergefell* 2015, 715–16). Justice Scalia also argues that Justice Kennedy's premise—that the authors and ratifiers of the Constitution's Due Process Clauses "did not presume to know the extent of freedom in all of its dimensions"—could lead to another conclusion, that "they left the creation of additional liberties, such as the freedom to marry someone of the same sex, to the People, through the never-ending process of legislation" (716). Justice Scalia's argument echoes the *Rhetorica ad Herennium*'s advice to claim that "the absence of a text concerning the matter here involved was intentional, because the framer was unwilling to make any provision" ([Cicero] 1981, 2.12.18).

Rhetorical Lessons from Justice Kennedy's Definitional Construction of Gay Rights

The interpretive stases and topoi provide a precise analytical tool for parsing how legal rhetors construct the meaning of a law through argument. When coupled with knowledge about a particular audience, the stases and topoi can support assessments about the likely efficacy of particular interpretive arguments. Thus, this chapter concludes by drawing rhetorical lessons from Justice Kennedy's arguments in *Lawrence* and *Obergefell* for legal rhetors arguing for new rights, especially before conservative audiences, given the Court's strong rightward tilt and the wide dominance of originalist hermeneutics. The following lessons are based on how well Justice Kennedy's arguments constructed these two rights as emanating from the text, a requirement for originalist jurisprudence, and on his conservative colleagues' responses.

Legal rhetors arguing for new rights should follow Justice Kennedy's example of tying the argued rights as directly to the text as possible. Justice Kennedy did well to argue in the definitional stasis, anchoring same-sex sex and marriage rights in Fourteenth Amendment *liberty*; likewise, he did well to avoid arguing in the assimilative stasis by not grounding these rights in a nonconstitutional term like *privacy* (see Barnett 2002–3; Colucci 2009, 21–22, 28; Knowles 2019, 170). One way to solidify a text-based argument is to appeal to authorial intention, as Justice Kennedy did; but, if possible, this topos should be supported by citations of the framers' or ratifiers' words. Appealing to co-text can be another effective topos for tying a right to the text, but it can also, if not supported well, raise more questions than it answers.

Again, finding evidence to support original intent or public meaning can aid an argument from co-text; Justice Kennedy's invocation of the Equal Protection Clause would have been stronger if he had noted that the original draft of the Fourteenth Amendment joined equal protection and liberty in one clause (Lash 2014, 85–89). Slippery-slope objections to expanding the meaning of a passage could be answered by articulating a principle that draws a clear line between the proposed right and future undesirable rights.

Rights rhetors will naturally employ the topos of previous judgments, but they should follow Justice Kennedy's *Obergefell* opinion, which, in contrast to *Lawrence*, cites more precedents that can link the disputed right to the text in question. Like Justice Kennedy, advocates should use precedent to argue that they are not offering a new reading of the text but a new application of it. In an unenumerated-rights case, one can answer the charge that a putative right was not recognized in the country's history or tradition by showing that the country has continually expanded the bounds of freedom by recognizing new rights (see *Bowers* 1986, 217; Carpenter 2012, 224). One could also critique the belief that limiting interpretations of legal texts to historical understandings is hermeneutically neutral, since history too is subject to interpretation (see *Michael H.* 1989, 137). As for a topos to rebut arguments for maintaining a static or limited view of a term or clause in a text, one could point to past cases where conservatives have defined a constitutional or statutory term in different ways depending on the case (Camper 2018, 123; see also Langford 2017, 58–59). Rights rhetors should then be sure that they themselves are hermeneutically consistent.

There is no guarantee that these strategies will persuade a conservative-majority Court to recognize new or expanded rights, but the audience for these arguments is not just jurists but also lawyers, journalists, law professors, politicians, and the public. The more these text-based arguments are circulated widely throughout society, the more likely they will gain adherence among a broad range of rhetors, increasing the chances that there will be enough people in places of influence to make the conclusions of these arguments law. Justice Kennedy's rhetoric may not have persuaded his conservative colleagues, but he laid the constitutional foundation for future expansion of relational and sexual rights (Campbell 2012; Kinnear 2019). The interpretive stases and topoi, which constitute a critical tool for analyzing arguments about legal texts, elucidate how Justice Kennedy strategically constructed that foundation through argument. Justice Kennedy's rhetoric, thus elucidated, can serve as a model for legal rhetors who, with the help of the interpretive stases and topoi as an enduring and flexible guide, can follow, adapt, and improve on this model as part of the perennial struggle to make our society ever more just and free.

Notes

1. For centuries, it was believed that Cicero was the author of the *Rhetorica ad Herennium*. Modern scholars, however, reject this attribution. Although the author is unknown, the text's association with Cicero has led the editors of the Loeb edition of this work to identify the author as "[Cicero]," meaning pseudo-Cicero.

2. Although Cicero is specifically speaking about ambiguities, his advice applies equally to vague or broad terms.

3. The *Dred Scott* ruling was based on the Fifth Amendment's Due Process Clause, which is identical to the Fourteenth Amendment's Due Process Clause, with the former amendment applying to the federal government and the latter applying to states.

References

Barnett, Randy E. 2002–3. "Justice Kennedy's Libertarian Revolution: *Lawrence v. Texas.*" *Cato Supreme Court Review* 2002–3:21–42.

Bowers v. Hardwick. 1986. 478 U.S. 186.

Campbell, Peter Odell. 2012. "The Procedural Queer: Substantive Due Process, *Lawrence v. Texas*, and Queer Rhetorical Futures." *Quarterly Journal of Speech* 98 (2): 203–29.

Camper, Martin. 2018. *Arguing over Texts: The Rhetoric of Interpretation.* New York: Oxford University Press.

Carey v. Population Services International. 1977. 431 U.S. 678.

Carpenter, Dale. 2012. *Flagrant Conduct: The Story of* Lawrence v. Texas. New York: Norton.

Cicero. 1976a. *De inventione.* Translated by H. M. Hubbell. Cambridge: Harvard University Press.

———. 1976b. *Topica.* Translated by H. M. Hubbell. Cambridge: Harvard University Press.

[Cicero]. 1981. *Rhetorica ad Herennium.* Translated by Harry Caplan. Cambridge: Harvard University Press.

Cleveland Board of Education v. LaFleur. 1974. 414 U.S. 632.

Colucci, Frank J. 2009. *Justice Kennedy's Jurisprudence: The Full and Necessary Meaning of Liberty.* Lawrence: University Press of Kansas.

Dicks, Vivian I. 1976. "Courtroom Controversy: A Stasis/Stock Issues Analysis of the Angela Davis Trial." *Journal of the American Forensic Association* 13 (2): 77–83.

Dred Scott v. Sandford. 1856. 60 U.S. 393.

Eisenstadt v. Baird. 1972. 405 U.S. 438.

Griswold v. Connecticut. 1965. 381 U.S. 479.

Hohmann, Hanns. 1989. "The Dynamics of Stasis: Classical Rhetorical Theory and Modern Legal Argumentation." *American Journal of Jurisprudence* 34 (1): 171–97.

Kinnear, Olivia. 2019. "Legal Relationships, Illegal Marriage: Explaining Plural Marriage and a Legal Inconsistency." *Tulane Journal of Law and Sexuality* 28:59–76.

Knowles, Helen J. 2019. *The Tie Goes to Freedom: Justice Anthony M. Kennedy on Liberty.* Updated ed. Lanham, MD: Rowman and Littlefield.

Könczöl, Miklós. 2009. "What There Is Left and How It Works: Ancient Rhetoric and the Semiotics of Law." *International Journal for the Semiotics of Law* 22 (4): 399–410.

Langford, Catherine L. 2017. *Scalia v. Scalia: Opportunistic Textualism in Constitutional Interpretation.* Tuscaloosa: University of Alabama Press.

Lash, Kurt T. 2014. *The Fourteenth Amendment and the Privileges and Immunities of American Citizenship.* New York: Cambridge University Press.

Lawrence v. Texas. 2003. 539 U.S. 558.

Lochner v. New York. 1905. 198 U.S. 45.

Loving et ux. v. Virginia. 1967. 388 U.S. 1.

Maynard v. Hill. 1888. 125 U.S. 190.

Meyer v. Nebraska. 1923. 262 U.S. 390.

Michael H. v. Gerald D. 1989. 491 U.S. 110.

M.L.B. v. S.L.J. 1996. 519 U.S. 102.

Mootz, Francis J., III. 2006. *Rhetorical Knowledge in Legal Practice and Critical Legal Theory.* Tuscaloosa: University of Alabama Press.

Obergefell v. Hodges. 2015. 576 U.S. 644.

Pierce v. Society of Sisters. 1925. 268 U.S. 510.

Planned Parenthood of Southeastern Pennsylvania v. Casey. 1992. 505 U.S. 833.

Provenzano, Susan E., and Brian N. Larson. 2020. "Civil Procedure as a Critical Discussion." *Nevada Law Review* 20 (3): 967–1035.

Quintilian. 2001. *The Orator's Education.* 5 vols. Edited and translated by Donald A. Russell. Cambridge: Harvard University Press.

Roe v. Wade. 1973. 410 U.S. 113.

Skinner v. Oklahoma ex rel. Williamson. 1942. 316 U.S. 535.

Turner v. Safley. 1987. 482 U.S. 78.

United States v. Windsor. 2013. 570 U.S. 744.

U.S. Const. amend. XIV, §1.

Washington v. Glucksberg. 1997. 521 U.S. 702.

Zablocki v. Redhail. 1978. 434 U.S. 374.

4

JUSTICE KENNEDY, NATURAL LIBERTY, AND CLASSICAL STASIS THEORY: ADVANCING FREE SPEECH WITH RHETORICAL KNOWLEDGE AND INTERPRETIVE ARGUMENTATION

Susan E. Provenzano

This chapter examines Justice Kennedy's use of rhetorical knowledge and interpretive argumentation to advance free speech rights. As Ashutosh Bhagwat observes in this volume and elsewhere, Justice Kennedy's Supreme Court tenure marked him as "the foremost defender of free-speech principles on the modern Court" (Bhagwat and Struhar 2013, 167) and almost "certainly the most free-speech-protective justice of his era" (Bhagwat, chap. 9 in this volume). This reputation finds support in quantitative and qualitative measures, with Justice Kennedy "more willing to find a First Amendment violation" and to take "substantially more speech-protective" positions to get there than the Court generally (Bhagwat and Struhar 2013, 168, 175). Against potential claims of partiality stands the "sheer variety" of protected speech and speakers in Justice Kennedy's opinions (Bhagwat and Struhar 2013, 179). This much is true of Justice Kennedy's free speech jurisprudence, but the question remains how well Justice Kennedy judged along the way.

I conclude that Justice Kennedy judged *relatively* well, landing on the positive side of the judging-well continuum, using his 2001 majority opinion in *Legal Services Corporation v. Velazquez* as an exemplar.[1] Judging well does not mean reaching the "best" result in free speech cases—what is "best" is often a debatable proposition. And it does not mean holding up Justice Kennedy's free speech rhetoric as a judging ideal or downplaying its faults. Nor is it to defend Justice Kennedy's rhetorical sincerity. As others in this volume have shown and I will echo here, Justice Kennedy's rhetoric is short on empathy—particularly for women (Stanchi, chap. 13 in this volume), communities of color (Zietlow, chap. 14 in this volume), and nonassimilative immigrants (Saucedo, chap. 15 in this volume)—and long on removed abstraction. His rhetoric can be disembodied and detached from individual knowers' experience (Britt, chap. 12 in this volume). Mindful of these rhetorical weaknesses, my claim is more modest: Justice Kennedy judged *relatively* well in *Velazquez* by developing rhetorical knowledge with an argumentative expansiveness that advanced natural liberty and speech rights.

My argument proceeds as follows. In part 1, I demonstrate the philosophical compatibility of judging well with a natural law Enlightenment view of liberty—which I call "natural liberty" for short—and these two philosophies' commitment to rhetorical knowledge in constituting law. I conclude that together, these philosophies set a normative benchmark for assessing Justice Kennedy's judging on the rhetorical knowledge axis. In part 2, I discuss how a descriptive rhetorical theory called "critical discussion-stasis theory" supplements this normative benchmark by pinning down more precise argumentative qualities of judging well. In part 3, I evaluate Justice Kennedy's judging in *Velazquez*. I offer Justice Antonin Scalia's dissenting opinion as a contrasting rhetorical example.

Judging Well and Natural Liberty: A Joint Commitment to Rhetorical Knowledge

I begin with Jay Mootz's definition of judging well, whose touchstone is rhetorical knowledge, that is, knowledge cultivated "through interpretive experiences that provide dynamic resources to exercise judgment in changing circumstances" (2018, 20). As Mootz has explained, judging well using rhetorical knowledge is not a methodology, and it is not a strategy; it is instead a profound philosophical commitment to the rule of law. This philosophy constitutes law by treating legal text as a responsive "fusion of horizons" marked by a "rich history of human thought, action, and understanding" (2018, 19). Those who judge well use that imprinted text to formulate reasonable, if not definitive, answers to legal questions that defy historical parallel (Mootz, chap. 7 in this volume).

Philosophically, judging well is compatible with the constitutional theory of natural liberty, which scholars have argued characterizes Justice Kennedy's jurisprudence (Kelso and Kelso 2011).[2] Vitally, both philosophies make rhetorical knowledge an interpretive cornerstone. Using rhetorical knowledge means "surveying accepted topics, norms, and opinions as resources for confronting the demands of the case at hand," joining them "in unique ways that serve to re-create the argumentative resources," and consequently, "develop[ing] a public discussion *along new lines of argumentation* that motivate justified action" (Mootz, chap. 7 in this volume; emphasis added). In the constitutional realm, natural liberty similarly views law as the product of "reasoned elaboration" applied to "current social realities." Natural liberty's interpretive approach builds on incremental interactions between the constitutional text and many forms of human deliberation, such as historical evidence, precedent, governmental practice, and social practice (Kelso and Kelso 2011, 31, 38–42). Although constitutional principles remain constant, through this interpretive process of reasoned elaboration, their contours are reshaped and adapted over time to confront issues that were unforeseeable at the country's founding (Kelso and Kelso 2011, 38).

Judging well and natural liberty eschew the false notion of "correct" textual readings that yield the flat pitch of pronouncing meaning from the omniscient vantage point of "reason." Instead, these philosophies encourage judges to reflect and to rely on textual interpretation's full vocal range. To these ends, the judging well and natural liberty philosophies encourage judges to seek answers not from a static past but from "unfolding values and experience"; they favor diverse interpretive methods and modes of argumentation; they are concerned with the real-world consequences of legal interpretation; and they honor institutional roles while acknowledging the difficult choices inherent in judging. Together, judging well and natural liberty offer a normative benchmark for assessing the use of rhetorical knowledge in constitutional interpretation—including Justice Kennedy's free speech rhetoric.

The Legal Topoi: A Fine-Grained Measure of Argumentative Quality

Setting a normative benchmark for evaluating Justice Kennedy's free speech rhetoric is just the starting point, however. That benchmark does not go so far as to identify the precise *argumentative qualities* of judging well. To pin down those argumentative qualities, I turn to a descriptive component of an adapted rhetorical theory: the critical discussion-stasis model for evaluating legal argumentation developed in my earlier work with Brian Larson.[3] This model's theory of legal topoi offers a finer-grained measure of argument quality under the normative benchmark of judging well.

Stasis Theory and the Legal Topoi

The critical discussion-stasis model combines two rhetorical theories: the contemporary normative theory of pragma-dialectics and descriptive classical stasis theory.[4] Classical stasis theory is a method of rhetorical invention and evaluation developed by the ancients—among them, Hermogenes from the Greek tradition and the Romans Cicero and Quintilian—to identify stock issues and arguments in legal cases (Camper 2018, 4–7; Nadeau 1964, 373–81). In ancient legal disputes, the stases set ordered predictable "stopping points" at which parties presented opposing standpoints for court resolution (Provenzano and Larson 2020, 986–87). As Martin Camper observes, the stopping points vary along stasis theory's two branches: (1) the "forensic" stases, which characterize legal argument broadly, and (2) the interpretive stases, which concern the interpretation of legal documents (Camper, chap. 3 in this volume). Both the forensic and interpretive stases carry rich potential for dissecting and evaluating how contemporary rhetors construct legal issues and deploy dialogic arguments supporting them.

Our model relies on the forensic stases, which theorists divide into three stock issues (Nadeau 1964, 373–81). First, parties reach a stasis of "conjecture" if they dispute questions of fact (Did the plaintiff's and defendant's cars collide?). Second, they reach a "definitional" stasis if they dispute the legal significance of agreed-on facts (Did defendant drive negligently?). Third, parties reach a stasis of "quality" if, after resolving factual and definitional questions, they haggle over mitigating or aggravating circumstances bearing on legal responsibility (Did the plaintiff compound the harm with his own negligent driving?). Each stasis, in turn, has supporting lines of commonplace arguments.[5] Some lines of argument pertain only to a particular stasis, while others can be used to support multiple stases.

Synthesizing these lines of argument, Larson and I constructed a high-level taxonomy of three legal topoi that can be used to argue any forensic stasis: (1) empirical, (2) conventional, and (3) value-based. The empirical topos consists of arguments grounded in observations about the world, the who, what, when, and where of factual events and legal texts. The conventional topos encompasses arguments that employ legal standards to categorize or interpret facts or legal texts, including interpretive canons and modes of legal reasoning. The value-based topos supports textual interpretation with appeals to underlying legal norms and real-world consequences (Provenzano and Larson 2020, 1025–29). This topos must stay "within the constraints that our legal system imposes on policy-oriented and emotionally appealing arguments" (Provenzano and Larson 2020, 1025). Such arguments make the "complex assertion that some consequence is good and that some rule or practice is justified" because the proposed interpretation of that text would actually "[bring] about that consequence" (Larson 2021, 169). The legal topoi, refined by rhetorical knowledge over centuries, represent an argumentative expanse that judges can use, in varying combinations and proportions, to reach reasonable resolutions of debatable legal questions.

The Legal Topoi as a Measure of Interpretive Argument Quality

As a taxonomy of legal argumentation, the legal topoi offer a measure of the argumentative quality of a judge's constitutional interpretation. The legal topoi also give judges diverse and adaptable lines of argument to meet the interpretive needs of each case, made possible because each topos varies in its expenditure of interpretive resources. The empirical topos draws on the fewest, the conventional topos employs more, and the value-based topos uses the most. This interpretive resource variation reflects the degree to which each topos must account for "alternative hypotheses" about a text's meaning (Larson 2021, 192–93). Accounting for competing textual meanings is a "problem-solving" inquiry into the text's "fusion of horizons"—an important quality of judging well (Mootz 2018, 4, 12).

For example, in constitutional cases, the empirical topos may generate arguments about the "plain meaning" of words in a statute facing constitutional challenge. If these arguments are resolved on this direct observational line, it often obviates resort to alternative meanings and sources.[6] In contrast, the conventional topos relies more heavily on inferential reasoning, requiring judges to use their own faculties to justify one meaning as more reasonable than another. Though constitutional interpretive tools such as verbal maxims, historical evidence, precedent, and governmental practice all have an empirical starting point—the maxims, evidence, precedent, and practice do exist—conventional arguments ultimately succeed or fail on the quality of the judge's reasoning about how those tools shape textual meaning and inform the current case's result.[7]

Analogical reasoning and precedent synthesis—forms of eductive and inductive reasoning, respectively[8]—are high-interpretive-resource conventional arguments. Take a free speech case where the judge draws an analogy between two facially distinct phenomena: (1) government-imposed limits on public radio editorializing (precedent) and (2) congressional constraints on attorneys' advocacy for welfare benefits (the case being judged). Analogizing the two requires cognition on at least three interpretive levels. First, the judge must discern from these phenomena comparable elements between the speech limits, the speech, the actors, the context, and the governing legal principles. Second, the judge must choose and defend the level of abstraction at which to pitch these comparisons. And third, the judge must explain why comparing other elements or using other levels of abstraction yields distinctions without an interpretive difference.[9]

Deductive reasoning by enthymeme likewise falls under the conventional topos, though it commands fewer interpretive resources than analogy or synthesis because it requires fewer moves. Deduction draws on an empirically observable principle that, when applied to the case at hand, yields an immediate conclusion—a conclusion that stands without reference to other interpretive aids (see Larson 2021, 146). For example, if constitutional principles hold that the First Amendment does not apply to government funding decisions that impact speech, then a case challenging a government subsidy withdrawal on the basis that it chills speech will fail outright on First Amendment grounds.

The value-based topos "moves even deeper into interpretive territory" than the conventional topos. For these arguments, the judge must choose from an array of sources that reveal the spirit or intent of the text and its legal and normative aims (Larson 2021, 193).[10] The judge must also link interpretation of these sources to probable external consequences—in essence making a predictive contention about real-world causation. And the judge must reason through how those envisioned consequences tie back to the text's legal and normative aims. Consider a judge who strikes down a state law criminalizing flag-burning using a value-based argument that the law would silence a wide range of peaceful dissenting symbolic protests. The judge must marshal sources supporting the First Amendment's commitment to peaceful protest and dissenting views and its extension of protection to symbols, proving up the First Amendment's imprimatur on these behaviors. The judge must also show how imprisoning citizens who burn the flag in peaceful protest would, in fact, deter these constitutionally sanctioned behaviors. And the judge must explain how ongoing or new behaviors incentivized by this First Amendment interpretation would, in the main, further those same constitutional commitments.

At the Supreme Court level, when the obvious interpretive avenues have failed to resolve the case, high-interpretive-resource conventional and value-based topoi should, more often than not, carry the day. It is these topoi that engage a judge's "refined cognitive processes," which "build on

[the] deep-seated capacity to judge" and to reach reasonable, reflective resolutions of intractable constitutional questions (Mootz, chap. 7 in this volume). To be sure, the simplicity of empirical arguments and the seeming inevitability of low-resource conventional deductive arguments hold great persuasive appeal. But it is the eductively and inductively reasoned conventional and value-based topoi that command attention to alternative hypotheses of textual meaning and that demand the use of rhetorical knowledge to resolve interpretive disputes. A judge who takes full advantage of the legal topoi but leans most heavily on those with the greatest interpretive currency, then, has used interpretive argumentation to judge well in difficult constitutional cases.

Using the Topoi in Free Speech Argumentation

By the normative benchmark of rhetorical knowledge and the legal topoi's measure of interpretive argument, Justice Kennedy judged relatively well in *Velazquez*.[11] *Velazquez* challenged an amendment to the federal Legal Services Corporation (LSC) Act, a statute funding nonprofit organizations whose lawyers represent indigent clients in welfare-benefits cases. The amendment's "suits for benefits proviso" barred LSC-funded lawyers from challenging the legality of state welfare laws on pain of losing their organizations' funding (*Velazquez* 2001, 540). Striking down the proviso on First Amendment grounds, Justice Kennedy reasoned that it was viewpoint discrimination to limit LSC-funded lawyers and clients to legal status quo positions. He conceived of welfare advocacy as a private speech space analogous to a limited public forum—a space whose functioning the government could not manipulate or distort by defunding a disfavored viewpoint.

The road to rejecting the LSC proviso was not empirically or deductively straight but was interpretively curved along two paths. On the first, *Velazquez* laid to rest the maxim that government funding is not speech regulation—a narrow view that had held sway for a decade, courtesy of *Rust v. Sullivan* (1991). To put this notion to bed, Justice Kennedy relied on rhetorical knowledge and high-interpretive-resource argumentation blending conventional and value-based topoi. The second path engaged in a reasoned elaboration of the public forum doctrine and extended Justice Kennedy's commitment to the distortion model of speech protection, which checks government manipulation of speech spaces, suppression of disfavored voices, and deprivation of listeners' information.[12]

Judging Well by Recasting and Constraining Rust v. Sullivan

In deeming the LSC proviso to be impermissible viewpoint discrimination, Justice Kennedy's first interpretive step was to maneuver around *Rust*, a 1991 decision that Justice Kennedy himself had joined. *Rust* had rejected health-care providers' First Amendment challenges to Title X of the Public Health Service Act. The act established grants to run Title X projects, whose mission was to offer government-funded "preconceptual" family-planning services. Section 1008 of the act forbade program doctors from counseling patients about abortion or referring them to abortion providers. The consequence for discussing abortion with patients was a loss of program funding. Writing for the majority, Justice William Rehnquist pronounced, "There is no question but that the statutory prohibition contained in §1008 is constitutional" (*Rust* 1991, 192). Despite the law's explicit speech restriction, the Court saw the issue not as speech regulation but as program definition. In this frame, Title X reflected a "value judgment favoring childbirth over abortion" in a speech space of the government's creation, where it was free to "fund one activity to the exclusion of another" (192–93). The Court emphasized that doctors still maintained a separate speech space to counsel patients on abortion. They just had to keep that work separate from their Title X projects. On this basis, *Rust* drew the binary distinction between spending programs and speech regulations.

Despite having joined *Rust*, Justice Kennedy did not read this distinction into the opinion. Instead, he retrospectively harmonized *Rust* with cases decided since then, re-creating these rhetorical resources to develop a new line of argumentation—one that limited *Rust*'s reach to government speakers. Justice Kennedy acknowledged *Rust*'s reasoning that Title X's ban on abortion counseling was not viewpoint discrimination but a program limit barring "counseling that was outside the scope of the federally funded program" (*Rust* 1991, 197). He then used the conventional topos of inductive reasoning from precedent to neutralize this programmatic rationale. Precedent following *Rust*, said Justice Kennedy, permits "viewpoint-based funding decisions" only when the "government is *itself* the speaker" or when the government "*use[s] private speakers* to transmit information pertaining to its own program."[13] The precedent did not countenance viewpoint-discriminatory funding in programs "designed to *facilitate private speech*" (*Velazquez* 2001, 541; emphasis added). Justice Kennedy thus used rhetorical knowledge to replace the funding-versus-regulation distinction with a government-versus-private-speaker distinction. And he was transparent about the interpretive process, acknowledging that *Rust* did not *explicitly say* that Title X's funding proviso was government speech but claiming rather that "later cases" have "explained *Rust* based on this understanding" (541).

This high-interpretive-resource inductive reasoning paved the way to deeming the LSC proviso viewpoint discrimination. Along these recast lines, Justice Kennedy reasoned eductively to differentiate *Rust*'s speakers and speech restrictions from *Velazquez*'s. He accepted *Rust*'s framing of Title X as a government-program speech space with a preset agenda, where doctors accepted Title X funding as a condition of doing the government's family-planning bidding. Using this frame allowed Justice Kennedy to distinguish the LSC program as one "designed to facilitate [the] private speech" of indigent clients' lawyers, "not to promote a governmental message" (*Velazquez* 2001, 542). The government's message was instead transmitted by government lawyers defending welfare-benefits programs: "Congress funded LSC grantees to provide attorneys to represent the interests of indigent clients. In the specific context of §504(a)(16) suits for benefits, an LSC-funded attorney speaks on the behalf of the client in a claim against the government for welfare benefits. The lawyer is not the government's speaker. The attorney defending the decision to deny benefits will deliver the government's message in the litigation. The LSC lawyer, however, speaks on the behalf of his or her private, indigent, client" (542). With this reasoning, Justice Kennedy mined another interpretive level to support the private-speaker rationale, this one grounded in the adversary system's structure.

Justice Kennedy's constraint on *Rust* concluded with value-based topoi concerning the abuse of government power and indigent access to legal representation. In contrast to the Title X program, Justice Kennedy argued, the LSC proviso left no alternative speech space for LSC lawyers to challenge the status quo. The moment that any question of legal validity arose in a case, the LSC attorney had to withdraw. For clients, too, "there often will be no alternative source" to "receive vital information respecting constitutional and statutory rights bearing upon claimed benefits" (*Velazquez* 2001, 546). Of equal concern was the anticonstitutional nature of a proviso aimed "at the suppression of ideas thought inimical to the Government's own interest" (549). Under these value-based topoi, the LSC proviso not only distorted the advocacy process but also shut down the lines of argument that were most threatening to the government entirely.

Justice Kennedy's reasoning was not without interpretive fault. In the first place, by joining the *Rust* majority, Justice Kennedy signed onto an opinion that did not judge well. With its unquestioning adherence to government prerogatives and its sense that the Title X program challenge presented an easy case, *Rust* lacks a strong rhetorical knowledge base, argumentative heft, and interpretive depth. Moreover, in *Velazquez*, Justice Kennedy arguably compounded *Rust*'s interpretive weaknesses in two ways. First, he accepted the opinion's dubious account of doctors as government mouthpieces for a nonabortion family-planning agenda. That characterization "founders on the reality" that Title X project doctors had "a professional obligation to serve the interests of their patients" as well as the fact that these doctors were unlikely to have viewed their confidential patient interactions as government communications (*Velazquez* 2001, 554, Scalia, J., dissenting). Second, Justice Kennedy may have misstepped by doubling down on *Rust*'s programmatic rationale. If a government program that sets speech restrictions at the out-set transforms participants into government speakers, "it is hard to imagine what subsidized speech would not be government speech" (554). Justice Kennedy tried tamping this down by warning that government funding condi-tions could not be "recast" as "a mere definition of its program in every case, lest the First Amendment be reduced to a simple semantic exercise" (547). It remains to be seen whether he succeeded.

Justice Kennedy's reasoning is also vulnerable to charges of nonempa-thetic, disembodied rhetoric. While *Velazquez* was attentive to the plight of indigent clients who are unable to challenge unlawful welfare-benefit schemes, in *Rust*, he showed no such concern for women who are unable to afford private abortion counseling—a reality that persists even if doctors can afford to run separate non–Title X abortion-counseling practices. A chari-table reading of this differential view between indigent clients in *Velazquez* and indigent women in *Rust* might view it as a product of Justice Kennedy's concern for structural integrity, an effort to maintain a sphere of legislative and executive autonomy: "When the government disburses public funds to private entities to convey a governmental message, it may take legitimate and appropriate steps to ensure that its message is neither garbled nor dis-torted by the grantee" (*Velazquez* 2001, 541). But a defensible contrasting reading is that Justice Kennedy values the legal process—a relatable concept for him—over the health and choices of women with unwanted pregnancies, a situation that he would never face.[14]

Despite these shortcomings, Justice Kennedy judged relatively better than Justice Scalia's dissenting opinion in *Velazquez*. Standing beside Justice Scalia's barbs at Justice Kennedy's government/private-speaker distinction, Justice Scalia wholeheartedly embraced *Rust*'s hard line between subsidy funding and speech regulation. For him, that was the end of the story: "Reg-ulations directly restrict speech; subsidies do not" (*Velazquez* 2001, 552).

Justice Scalia's argumentation relied primarily on the empirical topos, premised on the LSC Act's most readily observable feature—it is a government "spending program" (552). This empirical argument obviated the need for a considered response to Justice Kennedy's conventional topos synthesizing *Rust* with later cases.

From a doctrinal standpoint, Justice Scalia's framing of the LSC proviso as a spending program thrust the analysis into deferential First Amendment territory, which gave rise to low-resource deductive reasoning. Subsidies, Justice Scalia observed, can be said to regulate speech only when "the funding scheme is 'manipulated' to have a 'coercive effect' on those who do not hold the subsidized position." Subsidy schemes have a coercive effect only when they are "aimed at the suppression of dangerous ideas," but simply denying a subsidy under the LSC funding scheme's restrictions "does not coerce belief" (*Velazquez* 2001, 552). Ergo, the LSC funding scheme does not regulate speech and cannot be viewpoint discrimination.

Judging Well with a Reasoned Elaboration on the Public Forum Doctrine

Justice Kennedy's second interpretive path in *Velazquez* travels a more classic doctrinal route but is no less reliant on rhetorical knowledge or diverse interpretive legal topoi. On this path, Justice Kennedy engaged in a reasoned elaboration of the public forum doctrine and connected *Velazquez* to cases reflecting Justice Kennedy's commitment to the free speech distortion model, aimed at protecting the marketplace of ideas for speakers and listeners alike.

Justice Kennedy marked this path with rhetorical knowledge about the public forum doctrine. The key precedent was 1995's *Rosenberger v. Rector and Visitors of the University of Virginia*. In Justice Kennedy's majority opinion, *Rosenberger* struck down the university's refusal to fund printing costs for student newspapers expressing religious editorial viewpoints. Printing costs were backed by a Student Activities Fund (SAF) capitalized by student fees that the university paid to printing contractors on student newspapers' behalf. Because it was expending funds to "encourage a diversity of views from private speakers," the SAF established a "limited public forum," albeit a "metaphysical" one, distributing funds rather than physical access (*Rosenberger* 1995, 830–31). In contrast to traditional public forums such as streets and sidewalks, limited public forums permit government content discrimination but not viewpoint discrimination. *Rosenberger* concluded that refusing printing reimbursements to student newspapers espousing religious editorial views was impermissible viewpoint discrimination.

In *Velazquez*, Justice Kennedy engaged in a reasoned elaboration of *Rosenberger* and the public forum doctrine to buttress his viewpoint-discrimination reasoning, blending conventional and value-based topoi in the process. Justice Kennedy rejected Justice Scalia's dissenting empirical and deductive argumentation, which rested on a surface-level distinction between a government subsidy program and a limited public forum. According to Justice Scalia, limited public forums are designated speech spaces; subsidies are spending programs, not speech spaces; therefore, the LSC proviso is a permissible funding choice rather than government viewpoint discrimination. In contrast, Justice Kennedy used educative analogical reasoning to equate the SAF funding restriction with the LSC proviso on a higher plane of abstraction: they both facilitated preexisting private speech systems. In *Rosenberger*, student newspapers constituted an informational marketplace, which the SAF facilitated by reimbursing printing costs. In *Velazquez*, welfare-benefit advocacy existed by virtue of the state substantive law and legal systems; that advocacy was then facilitated by the LSC Act's funding. Although *Rosenberger's* limited public forum holding was not "controlling in a strict sense," both the SAF's limited public forum and the LSC subsidy program expressed a government view that a sphere of preexisting private speech is "necessary" and worth encouraging (*Velazquez* 2001, 544). So deemed, neither the university nor Congress could then step in and control that sphere of speech "in ways which distort its usual functioning" (555).[15] The SAF funding restriction and the LSC proviso violated the First Amendment by distorting an existing college publication structure and an advocacy system, respectively, withdrawing funding for expression that would normally flow freely in those systems. The LSC proviso's advocacy distortion was especially severe: in "restricting LSC attorneys in advising their clients and in presenting arguments and analyses," the proviso "alter[ed] the traditional role of the attorneys" (544).

Building on this value-based topos, Justice Kennedy linked the distortion conception to an even broader free speech value: maintaining a robust marketplace of ideas for listeners' benefit.[16] Under the LSC proviso, the impacted listener population was the judiciary. The proviso forced attorneys to "truncate" their arguments to judges, limiting the "speech and expression upon which courts must depend for the proper exercise of the judicial power." This "distorts the legal system . . . and the functioning of the judiciary" to "act within the sphere of its authority to resolve a case or controversy" (*Velazquez* 2001, 544). The LSC proviso not only threatened an independent, informed judiciary but also amounted to a congressional effort to "wrest the law from the Constitution which is its source." This, said Justice Kennedy, made for an even greater danger: a law fundamentally "inconsistent with accepted separation of powers principles" (546).

Conclusion

Velazquez presented critical interpretive needs concerning the complex relationship between government funding, the speaker rights of welfare-benefit lawyers and litigants, and the listener rights of judges—as well as the meaning of viewpoint discrimination and the public forum doctrine. Justice Kennedy's majority opinion managed those needs relatively well. From the standpoint of rhetorical knowledge, he treated the First Amendment and its precedent as interconnected text imprinted by human deliberation, knowledge, and experience over time. He did not take the easy argumentative path but instead blended conventional and value-based topoi to harmonize muddled precedent, blunted the effect of a wayward decision, and continued to shape the First Amendment's contours in the modern world. From a liberty perspective, Justice Kennedy engaged in a reasoned elaboration of the public forum doctrine and the speech-protective distortion model with interpretive vibrancy and dynamic argumentation, important hallmarks of judging well.

Notes

I am deeply grateful to my research assistant, Robert Weiss, for his thorough research and deep engagement with this work. My profound thanks go to editors Jay Mootz and David Frank for their vision, their generous counsel, and their astute editing. I am thankful as well to my fellow authors, whose constructive feedback improved the chapter. And I am indebted to Randy Kelso, Brian Larson, and Jason DeSanto, who took the time to comment very thoughtfully on my drafts.

　　1. Because judging well is a human endeavor subject to human judgment, it is best evaluated on a continuum rather than in binary terms.

　　2. As Mootz explains (chap. 7 in this volume), the Enlightenment take on natural law embraces "nontheistic, indeterminate" arguments, a secularized notion reflected in many constitutional rights provisions. In this respect, natural law principles are mediated through the Constitution's positive text.

　　3. Larson and I developed the model in our work concluding that the Federal Rules of Civil Procedure governing US civil cases operate as a system for argumentation designed to persuade rational judges to reach reasonable resolutions (Provenzano and Larson 2020).

　　4. Larson and I used the pragma-dialectics (PD) aspect of our model to evaluate whether the Federal Rules of Civil Procedure's phased sequencing is designed to

convince a *reasonable* critic to make *rational* decisions, the ultimate objective of a PD "critical discussion" (van Eemeren and Grootendorst 2004, 1), including a dialogic argument phase. We concluded that the Federal Rules capture this phase as PD envisions it, but neither PD nor the Federal Rules identify the argumentative topoi that arise at each stasis. That gap is filled by classical stasis theory (Provenzano and Larson 2020, 984–86).

5. These topoi, originally identified by Cicero (1976, 2001) and Quintilian (2001) and the author of the *Rhetorica ad Herennium* ([Cicero] 1981), are exhaustively catalogued for the interpretive stases by Camper (2018) and for the forensic stases by Hanns Hohmann (1989) and in my work with Larson (2020). Note that *Rhetorica ad Herennium* was originally attributed to Cicero, but in more recent history, scholars attribute the text to an unknown author.

6. In the interpretive stasis of definition, resolving the word's or phrase's basic apparent meaning ends the stasis and moves rhetors to other points of disagreement (Camper 2018, 165).

7. The conventional topos parallels the interpretive stasis of "assimilation," "when from a statement written somewhere one arrives at a principle which is written nowhere" (Camper 2018, 115, quoting Cicero 1976).

8. The conventional topos employs the same types of inferential reasoning that Camper recognizes for assimilation: deduction, induction, and eduction. In rhetoric, deduction appears as the probabilistic enthymeme (versus the logical syllogism), inductive reasoning generalizes inferentially from similar cases, and eduction reasons from one particular case to another, such as by analogy (Camper 2018, 119–23).

9. As Larson explains of argument by analogy, the contender has "the option to draw the category of assimilation at various levels of abstraction, all of which the precedent case may equally strongly implicate. Alternative hypotheses about the meaning of the text are considerably more numerous, and the need to choose imposes higher interpretive costs on the author" (2021, 192–93).

10. In the interpretive stasis branch, Camper refers to this topos as "sensibility," which employs a "range of values" to "determine how sensible an interpretation is" (2018, 30).

11. Indeed, *Velazquez* has been recognized among "the most important free speech majority opinions authored by Justice Kennedy" (Bhagwat and Struhar 2013, 179; see also Kelso and Kelso 2011, 46–47).

12. The speech-protective distortion model is a negative-rights view of the First Amendment premised on curbing government regulation that warps public debate (Bevier 1992, 102–3).

13. The precedent was *Board of Regents of the University of Wisconsin System v. Southworth* (2000), which upheld university-imposed student fees used to fund students' political and ideological speech on a viewpoint-neutral basis, and *Rosenberger v. Rector and Visitors of the University of Virginia* (1995), which struck down a university printfunding restriction for student newspapers that manifested beliefs about a deity or ultimate reality.

14. In *Hill v. Colorado* (2000), which upheld state provisions against counseling within eight feet of a person approaching a health-care facility, Justice Kennedy's dissent contained an exegesis on the moral rights of abortion protesters to "engage in peaceful face-to-face communication with individuals the petitioners believe are about to commit a profound moral wrong" (768).

15. Among those cases was *Federal Communications Commission v. League of Women Voters of California* (1984), which held that the government could not hamper the normal functioning of a broadcast system by banning public radio editorializing.

16. The distortion model of speech protection and listener protection topoi are value-based threads running throughout Justice Kennedy's free speech opinions. *Citizens United v. Federal Election Commission* (2010) struck down a ban on independent corporate expenditures for electioneering communications because it distorted the political marketplace and deprived voters of the ability to "obtain information from diverse sources in order to determine how to cast their votes" (899). Justice Kennedy's well-known concurrence in *International Society for Krishna Consciousness v. Lee* (1991) identified the primary evil of speech suppression as "allow[ing] the government to tilt the dialog heard by the public to exclude many, more marginal, voices" (702). And in 2017, Justice Kennedy in *Packingham v. North Carolina* invalidated a law banning registered sex offenders from using certain internet sites, grounded on the First Amendment's "fundamental principle" that "all persons have access to places where they can speak and listen, and then, after reflection, speak and listen once more" (1735).

References

Bevier, Lillian R. 1992. "Rehabilitating Public Forum Doctrine: In Defense of Categories." *Supreme Court Review* 1992:79–122.

Bhagwat, Ashutosh. 2019. "More Speech Everywhere: Justice Kennedy and the Public Forum." *Hastings Law Journal* 70:1185–92.

Bhagwat, Ashutosh, and Matthew Struhar. "Justice Kennedy's Free Speech Jurisprudence: A Quantitative and Qualitative Analysis." *McGeorge Law Review* 44:167–99.

Board of Regents of University of Wisconsin System v. Southworth. 2000. 529 U.S. 217.

Camper, Martin. 2018. *Arguing over Texts: The Rhetoric of Interpretation*. New York: Oxford University Press.

Cicero. 1976. *De inventione*. Translated by H. M. Hubbell. Cambridge: Harvard University Press.

———. 2001. *On the Ideal Orator (De oratore)*. Translated by James M. May and Jakob Wisse. New York: Oxford University Press.

[Cicero]. 1981. *Rhetorica ad Herennium*. Translated by Harry Caplan. Cambridge: Harvard University Press.

Citizens United v. Federal Election Commission. 2010. 558 U.S. 310.

Federal Communications Commission v. League of Women Voters of California. 1984. 468 U.S. 364.

Hill v. Colorado. 2000. 530 U.S. 703.

Hohmann, Hanns. 1989. "The Dynamics of Stasis: Classical Rhetorical Theory and Modern Legal Argumentation." *American Journal of Jurisprudence* 34 (1): 171–97.

International Society for Krishna Consciousness v. Lee. 1991. 505 U.S. 672.

Kelso, Charles D. and Randall Kelso. 2011. "The Constitutional Jurisprudence of Justice Kennedy on Liberty." *Dartmouth Law Review* 9:29–77.

Larson, Brian. 2021. "Precedent as Rational Persuasion." *Legal Writing: The Journal of the Legal Writing Institute* 25:135–212.

Legal Services Corporation v. Velazquez. 2001. 531 U.S. 533.

Mootz, Francis J., III. 2018. "Judging Well." *Washington University Jurisprudence Review* 11 (1): 1–37.

Nadeau, Ray. 1964. "Hermogenes on Stases: A Translation with an Introduction and Notes." *Speech Monographs* 31 (4): 361–424.

Packingham v. North Carolina. 2017. 582 U.S. __, 137 S. Ct. 1730.

Provenzano, Susan, and Brian Larson. 2020. "Civil Procedure as a Critical Discussion." *Nevada Law Journal* 20:967–1035.

Quintilian. 2001. *The Orator's Education*. Translated by Donald A. Russell. Cambridge: Harvard University Press.

Rosenberger v. Rector and Visitors of University of Virginia. 1995. 515 U.S. 819.

Rust v. Sullivan. 1991. 500 U.S. 173.

van Eemeren, Frans H., and Rob Grootendorst. 2004. *A Systematic Theory of Argumentation: The Pragma-Dialectical Approach*. Cambridge: Cambridge University Press.

5

ROMER V. EVANS: JUSTICE KENNEDY, JUSTICE SCALIA, AND THE RHETORIC OF JUDGING WELL

Sean Patrick O'Rourke

Recent rulings by the most deeply conservative Supreme Court since the New Deal have revealed tensions between and among the conservative working principles of judicial restraint, originalism, and textualism. As Noah Feldman has noted, Chief Justice John Roberts's decision in *June Medical Services v. Russo* (2020) and Justice Neil Gorsuch's opinions in *Bostock v. Clayton County* (2020) and *McGirt v. Oklahoma* (2020) expose growing philosophical divisions among the conservative justices and therefore raise questions about not only what constitutes "good" conservative judgment but also whose jurisprudence best represents a conservative judicial ideal (Feldman 2020, 67–69). At the center of this crisis is the judicial philosophy and legacy of Justice Antonin Scalia, which was celebrated by conservatives even before his death in 2016 and to which each of the three newest justices claimed adherence during their nomination hearings (Slocum and Mootz 2019). In practice, however, some of the six conservatives now on the Court seem in some ways more closely aligned with a less celebrated but perhaps underappreciated former member of the Court: Justice Anthony M. Kennedy.

Despite a consistent record of conservative voting in his thirty years on the Court, Justice Kennedy was roundly condemned by conservative politicians and pundits for siding with the liberal members of the Court in important rulings on closely contested questions about abortion, affirmative action, and especially LGBTQ+ rights. He was also condemned by those in the middle and on the left, who saw his "melodramatic" relishing of his role as the swing vote after Justice Sandra Day O'Connor's retirement as "self-dramatizing utopianism" that barely masked his judicial "arrogance" (Rosen 2007). The criticism had its effect: in the latter part of his career,

Justice Kennedy occasionally mentioned the "loneliness" of his position, a statement no doubt true if we compare Justice Kennedy's public reception with the enthusiastic followings of Justice Scalia and Justice Ruth Bader Ginsburg, two of his contemporaries on the Court. He was, after all, never the "Notorious AMK."

But perhaps lurking behind these public images is a jurisprudence—or at least an approach to judging—that might offer an alternative to the Scalian. To consider this possibility, in this chapter, I compare Justice Kennedy's majority opinion in *Romer v. Evans* (1996), arguably the first in a series of Supreme Court decisions leading to marriage equality and equal protection of the law for nonheterosexuals, with Justice Scalia's dissent in the same case.[1]

The case serves the purpose well because Justice Kennedy's opinion was loudly condemned by conservatives. The columnist James J. Kilpatrick nominated Justice Kennedy's effort the year's "worst opinion from the Supreme Court" (1996, C11). Lon Mabon, leader of the Oregon Citizens Alliance, declared the decision "an attack on the moral foundation of American culture" (Bates 1996, A1). And Gary Bauer, president of the Family Research Council, called May 20, 1996, "a very dark day for the liberty rights of the American people" (Asseo 1996, A1). The majority opinion was also forcefully challenged by Justice Scalia, who wrote a strongly worded dissent that accused Justice Kennedy of not judging well.

But what is "judging well"? Jay Mootz, in his provocative essay of the same name, argues that good judging is opposed to judges "imposing their will" but that judging well cannot be assessed, as it traditionally has, with reference to the rules of deductive logic or empirical analysis (2018, 36). To the contrary, he suggests, judging well is an art rooted in "hermeneutical and rhetorical capacities" that "[create] (rhetorical) knowledge and [reject] a subjective imposition of meaning." He adds, "An account of judging well that is grounded in an account of interpretation, persuasion, and judgment is sufficient to sustain the rule of law" (37). Mootz offers an approach rooted in Hans-Georg Gadamer's hermeneutics and Chaïm Perelman's new rhetoric.

Building on earlier descriptive work on the case (O'Rourke and Dellinger 1997), I seek here to pursue Mootz's suggestion by considering both *Romer* opinions through a different critical lens: the rhetorical doctrine of *controversia*. The practice of *controversia* can be traced as far back as the fragments of Protagoras (Mendelson 2002) but received its fullest ancient treatment in Cicero.[2] Cicero refined the Protagorean notion of debating both (or all) sides of a question into *a way of thinking* about complex issues at the heart of larger controversies. In his hands, controversial thinking became a habit of thought, a rhetorical method of invention well suited to law and legal practice: the ability to argue *in utramque partem*. As I have noted elsewhere, controversial thinking is a way of approaching the world, a rhetorical stance, predicated on the assumption that doubt begets possibilities for argument.[3] It serves as an inventional activity by cultivating fitting responses to the factual, legal, and equitable demands of a case and is evident in the text that the rhetor produces. At its heart is the *quaestio*, the question. Judicial rhetoric involves both general questions as to the nature of the human condition, justice, or even the law and the particular questions raised by the case, and a judge must be prepared to move nimbly among them. By so doing, the judge begins to create the realm of germane discourse and to define the circumstances and standards for good judgment. In this process, judges also provide readers entrée into their thought process—their starting principles, their sense of what is relevant and what is not, the different weight they give to different arguments and issues.

Approaching rhetorical action via *controversia* requires critics to look first to the *practice* of rhetoric while holding preexisting *theoretical* notions—the doctrine of stasis, topical reasoning, the ordering of a discourse, the language deployed, and other elements—in abeyance. All such rhetorical resources are a kind of "armamorium of flexible, responsive debating tactics, . . . a series of argumentative wrestling holds" (Struever 1983, 195) that offer judges a selection of case-building possibilities. As Michael Leff once put it, rhetorical resources are best treated "loosely as precepts that helped develop a capacity for action and performance in a particular case" (2006, 203), and as Hugh Blair reminded us centuries ago, "What is truly solid and persuasive must be drawn *ex visceribus causae*," that is, from the very viscera or guts of the case (1783, 2:391). The point is that advocates and judges are not limited to the stases, topics, organizational patterns, or linguistic suggestions outlined in classical antiquity, and those of us seeking to assess their rhetoric should not be either.

Romer v. Evans

Romer v. Evans arose in a complicated context. LGBTQ+ activists in the United States had been publicly fighting for equal rights since at least the 1920s and had intensified their efforts after the Stonewall Rebellion of 1969. Those efforts included a range of actions, from litigation attacking discriminatory laws to legislative efforts to ban discriminatory practices in housing (sales, lending, and renting), marriage, insurance coverage, health and other employment benefits, hiring and firing, public accommodation, and much more. Activists saw some of their greatest successes in cities and munici-palities where local councils were willing to pass ordinances preventing dis-crimination on the basis of sexual orientation. Such protections were crucial, as members of the LGBTQ+ community knew all too well that even into the mid-1990s there was no federal law protecting them from discrimination.[4] As Elizabeth Birch, then executive director of the Human Rights Campaign, noted in 1996, "it is still perfectly legal under Federal law to fire a person simply because he or she is gay, lesbian, or bisexual" (41).

The Supreme Court, however, had not been especially helpful to the LGBTQ+ movement. *Bowers v. Hardwick* (1986) upheld the constitutionality of Georgia's antisodomy law and encouraged and emboldened anti-gay-rights organizations. One such group, Colorado for Family Values (CFV), reacted to existing antidiscrimination ordinances in Boulder, Aspen, and Denver and a proposed ordinance in its hometown of Colorado Springs by collecting the eighty-five thousand signatures needed to qualify for the Colorado ballot. The initiative, known as Amendment 2 because of its position on the ballot, sought to invalidate all local prohibitions on discrimination based on sexual orientation, but the practical effect of the measure was to make it legal and constitutional to discriminate against people who are—or who are thought to be—LGBTQ+ by repealing existing ordinances and policies protecting such persons, by prohibiting future passage of antidiscrimination laws by state and local governments, and by preventing government bodies from considering any claim of sexual-orientation discrimination. In addition, the amendment would have changed insurance code provisions and invalidated Governor Roy Romer's executive order prohibiting discrimination in state employment. But the most far-reaching effect of Amendment 2 was to make it impossible, indeed illegal, for government to respond to existing or future discrimination toward LGBTQ+ people in Colorado by constitutionally pro-hibiting their right to make a claim.

CFV ran its campaign on a single issue—"no special rights"—that created a largely false public impression. As the *Denver Post* noted in 1993, "throughout the months of debate and public opinion sampling on Amendment Two, it has been clear that Coloradans are convinced they were voting against 'special rights' for gays and lesbians, not that they were voting against laws to protect homosexuals from discrimination" (Brown 1993). The Colorado Legal Initia-tives Project (CLIP) filed suit, and after a trial on the merits, Judge Jeffrey Bay-less of the Denver state district court found Amendment 2 unconstitutional. A year later, his ruling was upheld, on a six-to-one vote, by the Colorado Supreme Court. The US Supreme Court heard oral arguments in October 1995, just shy of the three-year anniversary of Amendment 2's passage.

Justice Kennedy Versus Justice Scalia

The Supreme Court handed down its decision in *Romer v. Evans* on May 20, 1996. Divided six to three, the Court affirmed the ruling of the Colorado Supreme Court and held that Colorado's Amendment 2 violated the Equal Protection Clause of the Fourteenth Amendment. Justice Kennedy's majority opinion was joined by Justices John Paul Stevens, Sandra Day O'Connor, David Souter, Ruth Bader Ginsburg, and Stephen Breyer. Justice Antonin Scalia's dissent was joined by Chief Justice William Rehnquist and Justice Clarence Thomas.

Controversia invites us to look first to the way Justice Kennedy and Justice Scalia frame their opinions with *pro et contra* argumentation. With this pro and con rhetorical movement, each justice seeks to map the field of relevant argument, identify what is germane and what is not, and declare what constitutional principles are at stake and what methods and standards of judgment are appropriate. These initial moves are crucial because they also allow us to see the internal dynamics of the argument, typically revealing what other principles and/or concerns might be at play and what hierarchy of judicial values is in use.

What is most striking about the *Romer* opinions is the way each begins with a profoundly rhetorical first line. Justice Kennedy writes, "One century ago, the first Justice Harlan admonished this Court that the Constitution 'neither knows nor tolerates classes among citizens'" (*Romer* 1996, 623, quoting *Plessy v. Ferguson*, 163 U.S. 537, 559 [1896], dissenting opinion). He continues, "Unheeded then, those words are now understood to state a commitment to the law's neutrality where the rights of persons are concerned" (623). Justice Kennedy thus begins with a principle embedded deep within the Fourteenth Amendment's somewhat tortured jurisprudential tradition and articulates the ground on which he believes the case is disputed: the "rights of persons." In so doing, he invokes the countermajoritarian inclination of the US constitutional rights tradition and positions the case as a traditional Equal Protection Clause question, in this instance a majoritarian statewide referendum versus the rights of a specific class of persons. He also subtly takes note of the importance of *change* with his "unheeded then, . . .

now understood" construction, acknowledging the important place change has in the Court's Fourteenth Amendment cases, even as a conservative for whom change must come incrementally and with considerable justification.

In contrast, Justice Scalia begins his dissent with, "The Court has mistaken a Kulturkampf for a fit of spite" (*Romer* 1996, 636). In a move that is not unusual in dissenting opinions, he makes the majority opinion the subject of controversy and treats the constitutional issues raised by the case within that framework. But his framing is both an exaggeration and a misrepresentation of the majority's argument. Justice Scalia's choice of the term "Kulturkampf" instead of the more prosaic "culture wars" or "culture struggle" evokes a heavy and somewhat unpleasant reference to Prussian intellectual culture and the struggle between Otto von Bismarck and the papacy. Justice Scalia's own Catholicism hovers as a specter over this line, foreshadowing his "traditional morals" argument. More importantly, Justice Scalia's first line performs what Cicero knew as a *partitio* or *divisio*, the classic first move of *controversia* in which the arguer divides the field of issues in to the germane and the nongermane. But Justice Scalia's move goes beyond that, casting the majority opinion as a "mistake" between two choices, "Kulturkampf" and "fit of spite," neither of which is germane to the constitutional question at hand. Both choices are outside the realm of the law, and in this way, he carves out the law as the space of his opinion, his reasoning.

For Justice Kennedy, the first stopping point, the first issue the case requires him to address, is the state's argument that Amendment 2 "puts gays and lesbians in the same position as other persons" and that the measure "does no more than deny homosexuals special rights" (*Romer* 1996, 626). The state's argument is an extension of CFV's "no special rights" political campaign that cast the municipal antidiscrimination ordinances as profoundly antidemocratic grants of rights to the LGBTQ+ community, rights above and beyond those guaranteed to all other Coloradans. The question allows the Court to conduct a twofold analysis, one rooted in the *status coniecturales*, or factual question (Does Amendment 2 place gays and lesbians in the same position as all others?), and the *status definitionis* (not only how an act is to be defined at trial but also what a text—in this case Amendment 2— means in practice).

Justice Kennedy's argument begins with the contention that the state's "reading of the amendment's language is implausible" (*Romer* 1996, 626). To support this claim, he advances three lines of argument. The first, an *interpretive* argument, is supported by the "authoritative" reading of the amendment by the Colorado Supreme Court, which found the amendment "invalid even on a modest reading of its implications" (626). After quoting the Colorado decision at length, Justice Kennedy concludes that the change in gay and lesbian legal status wrought by the amendment is "sweeping and comprehensive" (627). Justice Kennedy's second line of argument is *legislative*. After noting that the Fourteenth Amendment did not give Congress a "general power to prohibit discrimination in public accommodations," Justice Kennedy underscores the importance of state and municipal efforts to enact "detailed statutory schemes" to counter discrimination. He then notes, by way of example, seven states' statutory protections and focuses on the three Colorado municipalities whose ordinances prompted Amendment 2 in the first place. Their importance, he argues, lies in their enumeration of "persons or entities subject to a duty not to discriminate" as well as the "groups or persons within their ambit of protect" (628). Justice Kennedy stresses two aspects of the protections that these statutes and ordinances provide: he argues that (A) enumeration "is the essential device used to make the duty not to discriminate concrete and to provide guidance for those who must comply" (628) and (B) the state and local governments chose not to limit "antidiscrimination laws to groups that have so far been given protection of heightened equal protection scrutiny" by the Court (629). He concludes the legislative argument by noting how far beyond the common law the statutory protection has reached and the extent that the LGBTQ+ community would suffer under Amendment 2. The third line of argument, only hinted at, is *constitutional*. He writes, "At some point in the systematic administration of the laws, an official must determine whether homosexuality is an arbitrary and, thus, forbidden basis for decision. Yet a decision to that effect . . . would appear to be no more valid under Amendment 2 than" other prohibitions against discrimination. Such a result would, he notes, "compound the constitutional difficulties the law creates" (631).

In short, Justice Kennedy finds, the claim that Amendment 2 "does no more than deny homosexuals special rights" is false. To the contrary, he argues, "the amendment imposes a special disability upon those persons alone." He concludes,

> Homosexuals are forbidden the safeguards that others enjoy or may seek without constraint. They can obtain specific protection against discrimination only by enlisting the citizenry of Colorado to amend the State Constitution or perhaps, on the State's view, by trying to pass helpful law of general applicability. This is so no matter how local or discrete the harm, no matter how public and widespread the injury.

We find nothing special in the protections Amendment 2 withholds. These are protections taken for granted by most people either because they already have them or do not need them; these are protections against exclusion from an almost limitless number of transactions and endeavors that constitute ordinary civic life in a free society. (*Romer* 1996, 631)

On this first issue, then, Justice Kennedy moves through the questions related to special rights by first considering the state's argument and then offering a counterreading that considers Amendment 2's (factual) effects, as well as the interpretive, legislative, and constitutional considerations, to find the "special rights" claim worse than "implausible." The amendment has, in fact, quite the opposite result, imposing special disabilities on homosexuals alone.

Justice Kennedy's opinion then pivots to the second major stopping point, the established analysis for "even the most ordinary equal protection case," the rational basis test (*Romer* 1996, 631–32).[5] Amendment 2, Justice Kennedy finds, fails two elements of this test: it imposed a "broad and undifferentiated disability on a single named group," and "its sheer breadth is so discontinuous with the reasons offered for it that the amendment seems inexplicable by anything but animus toward the class it affects" (632).

After a two-page rationale for the Court's insistence on knowing the relation between the classification adopted and the legitimate governmental object to be attained and a quick summary of narrowly drawn laws that met the standard without much difficulty, Justice Kennedy turns to Amendment 2. In contrast to the examples he has just supplied, Amendment 2 "confounds the normal process of judicial review" because "it is at once too narrow and too broad. It identifies persons by a single trait and then denies them protection across the board" (*Romer* 1996, 633). At this point, the reader can sense Justice Kennedy's annoyance—or perhaps indignation—at what he clearly sees as the amendment's blatant disregard for judicial guidance. His language changes here (and, as we shall see, Justice Scalia pounces on that change). "It is not within our constitutional tradition to enact laws of this sort," he claims, and "a law declaring that in general it shall be more difficult for one group of citizens than for all others to seek aid from the government is itself a denial of equal protection of the laws in the most literal sense" (633). Moreover, Justice Kennedy asserts, there is no legitimate governmental interest. The inference that Amendment 2 is "inexplicable by anything but animus" toward gays and lesbians is "inevitable," he reasons, when one considers that the disadvantages imposed are not incidental. To the contrary, Amendment 2 inflicts "immediate, continuing, and real injuries that outrun and belie any legitimate justifications that may be claimed for it" (635).[6]

Viewed as a whole, Justice Kennedy's opinion enacts a judicial *controversia*, considering first the special rights claim and the arguments against it, then moving to the rational basis test, where he assesses the relation between the classification adopted and the object to be attained and then considers the legitimacy of the government interest. In each instance, he finds the state's arguments wanting and tells us why. His method, if we use that term loosely, is rhetorically transparent. His argument moves more or less systematically through the issues presented by Amendment 2 and the Equal Protection Clause, stopping at key issues (from factual and definitional questions to interpretive, legislative, and constitutional topics and then ultimately to the two-part rational basis analysis) drawn from and oriented to the particulars of the case presented and the applicable law as he understands it. Aside from the established rational basis test, he appears to follow no predetermined set of topics or issues but rather responds to questions as they arise. The argument is ordered appropriately and is articulated in a voice that only occasionally suggests exasperation or annoyance—but even then only with the sweep of Amendment 2 or the weakness of an argument in its support. He never resorts to ridicule or invective, does not target dissenting justices (only their arguments), and uses language that cultivates an ethos of rhetorical restraint and professionalism fitting to a justice of the Supreme Court rendering judgment in an important case.

In contrast to Justice Kennedy (and as noted earlier), Justice Scalia makes his dissent about the majority opinion and, ultimately, about a different *controversia*: making sound judicial judgments versus exerting political will. He takes as his task the unmasking of Justice Kennedy's majority opinion as the latter pretending to be the former. To do so, he frames the entire case in two important ways. First, his "Kulturkampf" comment is a *pro et contra* statement that begins to cast the issues as a struggle between the masses and the elites, the efforts of popular (and democratic) political effort versus the entrenched domination of the oligarchs. Set forth powerfully in the first line of the dissent, this depiction of the case is carried through to the very last line and serves a vital rhetorical function, for it makes the matter less an equal protection issue for the Court to settle and more a matter of political struggle appropriately decided where it had been—by the people of Colorado, through the ballot initiative process. Put another way, it is not government "animus" directed at a class of persons, as the majority opinion asserts, but rather a legitimate cultural battle, political in nature and appropriately contested in the democratic public sphere.

The second way in which Justice Scalia frames *Romer* is as a matter of public moral judgment of unacceptable behavior versus discriminatory state action absent legitimate purpose. This should not be a matter of judicial judgment—Justice Scalia at several points notes that it is not for the courts to take sides in the culture wars or weigh in on the morality of heterosexual monogamy or homosexual behavior—but rather a society's prerogative to disapprove of some conduct, to democratically find some behaviors "reprehensible" in light of a shared "moral heritage" (*Romer* 1996, 644). In a passage memorable for its questionable equivalencies, Justice Scalia appears to equate homosexuality with murder and other behaviors that society has found morally unacceptable, assuming that if the public can make moral judgments about one, it can make such judgments about the other (644).

Woven throughout and strengthening this framework is a not-so-subtle rhetorical act of characterizing those who are involved in or implicated by the case. Justice Scalia's rhetorical depictions gild his argument and color his rendering of the issues in the case. He paints Amendment 2 advocates, for example, as "seemingly tolerant Coloradans" and their efforts to place Amendment 2 on the ballot and then pass it during the election as "rather a modest attempt . . . to preserve traditional sexual mores" (*Romer* 1996, 636). Their "hostility reflected by Amendment 2 is the smallest conceivable," and the Court's attempt to portray them as hateful is "so false as to be comical" (645), for all they did was use the "most democratic of procedures" (647) to achieve their legitimate goals. In contrast, Justice Scalia characterizes gays and lesbians as a powerful, self-interested ruling elite. They "possess political power much greater than their numbers" and "devote this political power to achieving not merely a grudging social toleration but full social acceptance . . . of homosexuality" (646). Their influence is not limited to gay-friendly coastal metropolises such as San Francisco and New York, for they have also experienced legislative successes in the small cities and towns of Colorado. Far from being a downtrodden, politically unpopular, and threatened minority, Justice Scalia claims, the gay and lesbian community "enjoys enormous influence in American media and politics, and which, as the trial court here noted, though composing no more than 4% of the population had the support of 46% of the voters on Amendment 2"

(652). The contrast between the two groups could not be starker: in Justice Scalia's rendering, Amendment 2 advocates were David fighting Goliath, and their success was little short of a democratic miracle. The victory is snatched from their deserving hands, however, by a third group, "the lawyer class from which the Court's Members are drawn," a group thoroughly devoted to the hiring and promoting of homosexuals and apparently to taking their side "in the culture wars" (652).

These rhetorical characterizations are part of a larger stylistic choice Justice Scalia makes to underscore his argument with ridicule. It is never quite clear whether Justice Scalia's scorn is for Justice Kennedy, Justice Kennedy's opinion, or both, but the ridicule is laced throughout. The Court's finding of impermissible animus in Amendment 2 is a "mistake," and the "fit" in "fit of spite" diminishes and delegitimizes the quite serious "animus" that Justice Kennedy identifies (Romer 1996, 636). The majority's reading of the Colorado Supreme Court's interpretation "utterly fails" (637) to distinguish key portions of the opinion. Justice Kennedy engages in "hand wringing" over "the potential effect" of Amendment 2 (638), and his constitutional jurisprudence has descended into "terminal silliness" because "the world has never heard" of the principles the Court asserts (639). That is why Justice Kennedy's opinion is "so long on emotive utterance and so short on relevant legal citation" (639). Justice Kennedy's portrayal of the gay and lesbian community as at risk is "so false as to be comical" (645), and lacking "any cases" to support his position, he resorts to a "facially absurd proposition" (647) and a "novel and extravagant constitutional doctrine" (652). The opinion "has no foundation in American constitutional law and barely pretends to" (653). The ridicule is raw and untethered, and one is left wondering how such language can be reconciled with the competence, integrity, and goodwill that are traditionally associated with judicial ethos and the Court's need to maintain its institutional character and credibility. Justice Kennedy, to his credit, neither rises to the bait nor lowers himself to the dirt, and this choice marks one of the key differences between the two opinions.

Justice Scalia's framing of the issues, characterization of the parties, and ridicule of Justice Kennedy and his majority opinion so color the dissent that his arguments sometimes seem to fade from view. They are present though and highly dependent on the framing noted earlier. The most prominent line of argument is that Colorado's Amendment 2 is "an entirely reasonable provision which does not even disfavor homosexuals in any substantive sense but merely denies them preferential treatment" (Romer 1996, 653).

Framed as a viable political question, Justice Scalia's dissent dismisses the harm argument that Justice Kennedy establishes by adopting the "no special rights" language of Amendment 2's political campaign and the state's arguments before the Court, seemingly without seriously questioning it. If the voters of Colorado chose to respond to city ordinances with a statewide ballot measure, they were merely using the options offered to all citizens in a "multilevel democracy" (639).

A second justification that Justice Scalia offers in the dissent is his traditional morals argument. Working within the public moral judgment frame noted earlier, Justice Scalia seeks to characterize Amendment 2 as a reasonable limitation on *conduct* that the citizens of Colorado find reprehensible. Noting that all societies have determined some conduct to be morally reprehensible, he writes, "Of course, it is our moral heritage that one should not hate any human being or class of human beings. But I had thought that one could consider certain conduct reprehensible—murder, for example, or polygamy, or cruelty to animals—and could exhibit even 'animus' toward such conduct. Surely, that is the only sort of 'animus' at issue here: moral disapproval of homosexual conduct" (*Romer* 1996, 644). To make this point, he is at pains to distinguish *homosexual conduct* from the *class of persons identifying as homosexual* or, in his language, "individuals of homosexual 'orientation'" (643). For Justice Scalia, then, Amendment 2 is analogous to the criminal prohibition on sodomy that passed constitutional muster in *Bowers v. Hardwick* (1986) and the prohibition on voting that Idaho placed on polygamists, upheld by the Court in *Davis v. Beason* (1890). But as numerous commentators have noted, *Bowers* was more narrowly drawn, in that it focused on sodomy, not other conduct; was more broadly applicable, in that its prohibitions were not limited to homosexuals as a class but applied to heterosexual acts as well; and clearly specified conduct, which Amendment 2 did not. And Justice Scalia's reliance on *Davis* fails to engage Justice Kennedy's three-part argument distinguishing *Davis* from *Romer*, an analysis that persuasively accounts for subsequent cases and standards that render *Davis* inapplicable (see *Romer* 1996, 634).

If we peek behind these two main arguments, Justice Scalia's dissent becomes an *ad populum* case for democratically imposed traditional values. If, he reasons, a majority of voting Coloradans seek to preserve traditional sexual mores "against the efforts of a politically powerful minority" that has revised those mores through municipal ordinances, then courts should stay out of the political process and bow to the majority will. That such a result renders judicial equal protection scrutiny—even the low-level rational basis test—somewhat impotent seems fine with him.

Conclusions

Neither the majority opinion nor the dissent in *Romer* is without flaws. Justice Kennedy's decision to remain silent about *Bowers* represents at least a failure to engage a major portion of the dissent's argument and, in so doing, provided Justice Scalia an opening to exploit. More importantly, Justice Kennedy's silence on *Bowers* left lower courts and state governments to wonder exactly how to reconcile the two cases—and with what effect on existing or proposed law. Justice Kennedy also failed to explain fully his finding of animus in Amendment 2. To say only that the amendment's breadth is "inexplicable by anything but animus" begs the question of what other possible motives might be at play, what evidence of animus "inexplicability" fulfills, and why in cases alleging discrimination on sexual-orientation grounds, Justice Kennedy found animus, but when racial discrimination was the issue, he rarely did.

Justice Scalia's dissent is more problematic. The rhetorical tone of ridicule and disparagement does little to advance our understanding of the constitutional questions in the case, and his uncritical acceptance of the relatively weak "no special rights" and "no preferential treatment" arguments without at least attempting to bolster them raises questions about the integrity of his judicial rhetoric, at least in this case. Also disturbing is his heavy reliance on *Bowers* as dispositive of the questions presented in *Romer* when *Bowers* was about certain conduct across classes of persons and *Romer* is not about conduct but directed solely at a discrete and identifiable class of persons. His attempt to distinguish "homosexuals" from "homosexuality" too easily elides conduct/behavior and the state of being gay or lesbian. Merging the two in the facile manner that he does avoids doing the difficult work of judging, as does his failure to fully engage the majority's argument on *Davis v. Beason*. Finally, as Jane Schacter correctly points out, Justice Scalia's statements of neutrality on the question of the morality of gay civil rights "ring hollow" given his seeming to equate homosexuality with murder as acts a public could find equally reprehensible (1997). At the very least, these concerns raise questions about which opinion is more "an act not of judicial judgment but of political will" (*Romer* 1996, 653).

This short study of the two opinions in *Romer* also raises questions about what constitutes "judging well" if judging is seen as an art that demands the exercise of "hermeneutical and rhetorical capacities" to create nonsubjective rhetorical knowledge. Two precepts seem to emerge. From the perspective of rhetorical *controversia*, the first is the need *to engage opposing arguments and arguers fully and with integrity.* If the goal of the adversarial system is to better discern the truth between and among competing truth claims, then the direct clash of argument is essential. Both Justice Kennedy and Justice Scalia fail to meet this precept as well as they might have. A second precept is that good judging evidences *a concern for judicial ethos and the institutional character of the Court.* In the adversarial system, judges must be independent and impartial and, in contrast to the inquisitorial system, serve as adjudicators rather than inquisitors. Judicial rhetoric designed to convey competence, integrity, and goodwill—via argument, tone, and persuasive disposition—is therefore essential to the maintenance of judicial ethos. The appearance of partiality, spite, or preexisting motives and agendas erodes the institutional character of the Court and undermines public confidence in both the system and the judiciary. On this count, Justice Kennedy's majority opinion comes much closer to the mark than Justice Scalia's dissent.

Notes

1. Other decisions might include *Lawrence v. Texas,* 539 U.S. 558 (2003), *United States v. Windsor,* 570 U.S. 744 (2013), *Hollingsworth v. Perry,* 570 U.S. 693 (2013), and of course *Obergefell v. Hodges,* 576 U.S. 644 (2015).
2. For the fullest development of *controversia* as a method drawn from Cicero and used through the Renaissance, see Sloane 1997. For its reach into the nineteenth century, see O'Rourke 2007.
3. A portion of this paragraph is drawn from O'Rourke 2007, 48–50.
4. Title IX was enacted in 1972 and provided protection against harassment on the basis of sexual identity and sexual preference, but until recently its scope was limited.
5. The test is the lowest level of scrutiny in equal protection cases. In short, if a law neither burdens a fundamental right nor targets a suspect class, the Court will uphold the legislative classification so long as it bears a rational relation to some legitimate end.
6. It is worth noting, as my fellow contributor Rebecca Zietlow does in chapter 14, that Justice Kennedy is much more likely to find animus in cases alleging discriminatory intent on the basis of sexual orientation than he is in cases targeting race. This difference is, from my perspective, difficult to resolve and remains a problem in Justice Kennedy's jurisprudence.

References

Asseo, L. 1996. "High Court Dumps Anti-Gay Law." *Oregonian,* May 20, 1996, A1.
Bates, T. 1996. "Mabon: Fight Will Continue." *Oregonian,* May 20, 1996, A1.
Birch, Elizabeth. 1996. Testimony on H.R. 1863, the Employment Non-Discrimination Act. *Hearing Before the Subcommittee on Government Programs of the Committee on Small Business,* House of Representatives, 104th Congress. Vol. 4. July 17, 1996.
Blair, Hugh. 1783. *Lectures on Rhetoric and Belles Lettres.* 3 vols. Dublin: Whitestone et al.

Bostock v. Clayton County. 2020. 590 U.S. __, 140 S. Ct. 1731.

Bowers v. Hardwick. 1986. 486 U.S. 186.

Brown, Fred. 1993. "Poll: Public Sends Mixed Messages." *Denver Post*, December 15, 1993, A14.

Davis v. Beason. 1890. 133 U.S. 333.

Feldman, Noah. 2020. "The Battle over Scalia's Legacy." *New York Review of Books*, December 17, 2020, 67–69.

June Medical Services, LLC v. Russo. 2020. 591 U.S. __, 140 S. Ct. 2103.

Kilpatrick, James J. 1996. "Overturning Colorado Law on Homosexuality Was Court's 'Worst' of '96." *Oregonian*, July 26, 1996, C11.

Leff, Michael. 2006. "Up from Theory: Or I Fought the Topoi and the Topoi Won." *Rhetoric Society Quarterly* 36 (2): 203–11.

McGirt v. Oklahoma. 2020. 591 U.S. __, 140 S. Ct. 2452.

Mendelson, Michael. 2002. *Many Sides: A Protagorean Approach to the Theory, Practice, and Pedagogy of Argument.* Argumentation Library 5. Dordrecht: Kluwer.

Mootz, Francis J., III. 2018. "Judging Well." *Washington University Jurisprudence Review* 11 (1): 1–37.

O'Rourke, Sean Patrick. 2007. "The Rhetorical Dynamics of Judicial Situations: Justice Story, Ciceronian Rhetoric, and the Judicial Response to American Slavery." *Advances in the History of Rhetoric* 10:43–71.

O'Rourke, Sean Patrick, and Laura K. Lee Dellinger. 1997. "*Romer v. Evans*: The Centerpiece of the American Gay-Rights Debate." In *Anti-Gay Rights: Assessing Voter Initiatives*, edited by Stephanie L. Witt and Suzanne McCorkle, 133–39. Westport, CT: Praeger.

Romer v. Evans. 1996. 517 U.S. 620.

Rosen, Jeffrey. 2007. "Supreme Leader: On the Arrogance of Anthony Kennedy." *New Republic*, June 16, 2007. https://newrepublic.com/article/60925/supreme-leader-the-arrogance-anthony-kennedy.

Schacter, Jane S. 1997. "*Romer v. Evans* and Democracy's Domain." *Vanderbilt Law Review* 50 (2): 361–410.

Sloane, Thomas O. 1997. *On the Contrary: The Protocol of Traditional Rhetoric.* Washington, DC: Catholic University Press.

Slocum, Brian G., and Francis J. Mootz III, eds. 2019. *Justice Scalia: Rhetoric and the Rule of Law.* Chicago: University of Chicago Press.

Struever, Nancy. 1983. "Lorenzo Valla: Humanist Rhetoric and the Critique of the Classical Languages of Morality." In *Renaissance Eloquence: Studies in the Theory and Practice of Renaissance Rhetoric*, edited by James J. Murphy, 191–206. Berkeley: University of California Press.

PART 3

JUDGMENT IN CONTEMPORARY
RHETORICAL THEORY

6

CONSTRUCTING A FREE AGENT: "GOOD JUDGMENT" IN JUSTICE KENNEDY'S *LAWRENCE V. TEXAS* OPINION

Clarke Rountree

It is an indisputable yet mostly unremarked fact that appellate judicial opinions are almost exclusively concerned with discussing, describing, and character-izing actions: what litigants did that gave rise to a controversy; what lawyers, prosecutors, trial judges, juries, appellate judges, and others did to address that controversy in a case; what prior courts did in addressing similar issues in the past; what lawmakers or their delegatees did in passing constitutional provi-sions, laws, rules, and regulations; what scholars argued about the relevant law; what people did or may do in light of laws and rulings about them; how people, in general, act so that the implications of potential rulings can be assessed; and, in the midst of writing their opinions, self-descriptions of what judicial decision-makers are doing, as well as what their fellow decision-makers (in dissents, concurrences, or majority opinions) are doing (Rountree 2007, 7–10).

Because these actions are the stuff of legal opinions, their construction and characterization by opinion writers are critical to an understanding of judicial rhetoric and of judicial judgment. This chapter draws on a the-ory of action by the twentieth-century rhetorical scholar Kenneth Burke for a model of how action is constructed and shows how it applies particularly to judicial discourse, notably in assessing the quality of that discourse. That model is deployed to analyze Justice Anthony Kennedy's majority opinion in *Lawrence v. Texas* (2003), overruling the 1986 case of *Bowers v. Hardwick*.

Constructing Acts and Harmonizing Them with Related Acts

As Kenneth Burke explained in the first of his trilogy of motives, *A Grammar of Motives*, the rhetorical construction of actions builds on formal, "grammatical" relationships that prevail among the elements of action: act (what was done), scene (when and where it was done), agent (who did it), agency (by what means it was done), purpose (why it was done), and attitude (in what manner it was done, such as "cautiously") ([1945] 1969, xv, 443). Because of these formal, dramatistic relationships, the mere characterization of one of these elements carries implications for the understanding of all the other elements—no heavy rhetorical lifting required.[1] For example, if I call an agent a "firefighter," it immediately suggests acts (firefighting), scenes (burning buildings), agencies (fire hoses, ladders), purposes (putting out fires), and attitudes (courage). Burke scrutinizes such terministic relationships, such as *scene* to *act*, in pairs he calls "ratios" to track down the rhetorical implications of such characterizations (3–20). So, for example, he notes that we think of scenes as "containing" acts, whereby acts are understood as "consistent with the nature of the scene" (3). Thus, if we see someone running and screaming out of a burning house, we understand that the scene (burning house) "contained" the act (of running screaming). On the other hand, if an agent ran screaming from a perfectly sound house, we would look for other accounts of that action, such as thinking that the agent is emotionally disturbed (an agent-centered explanation), threatened by someone inside (a hidden scene), attempting to garner attention (a purpose), and so on.

Burke provides a notable illustration of the scene-act ratio from the US Supreme Court opinion in *Korematsu v. United States* (1944), decided just before his *Grammar* was published: "In a judgment written by Justice Hugo L. Black, the Supreme Court ruled that it was not 'beyond the war powers of Congress and the Executive to exclude those of Japanese ancestry from the West Coast area at the time they did [i.e., shortly after the Pearl Harbor attack].' And by implication, the scene-act ratio was invoked to substantiate the judgment: 'When under conditions of modern warfare our shores are threatened by hostile forces, the power to protect must be commensurate with the threatened danger'" (Burke [1945] 1969, 13, quoting *Korematsu* 1944, 220). What makes Justice Black's construction so powerful, then, is his characterization of the United States as "threatened by hostile [modern] forces"—a *scene* that required an *act* of commensurate power to address.

In applying Burke's dramatistic analysis to judicial and political texts, I have discovered that secondary ratios that draw on other terministic relationships greatly support such rhetorical constructions, so that more fully developed accounts of action generally create stronger arguments. Notably, in my own analysis of *Korematsu*—which involved a Japanese American arrested by military officials for failing to leave his home on the West Coast and report to a relocation center following the attack on Pearl Harbor—I concluded that "the majority did not simply have to rely on Burke's scene-act ratio to justify its decision to support Korematsu's conviction[;] it could show that the military agents undertaking this act were reasonable, that they wielded agencies crafted by the President and Congress, that they sought to protect against espionage and sabotage [a purpose], and they had a justifiably (even admirably) cautious and protective attitude" (Rountree 2001, 20). Of course, such judicial constructions of action are not created out of whole cloth; as I have noted, "The actions characterized by judges—legislative enactments, the actions of a criminal defendant, the judgments of trial and appellate courts, and so forth—are almost always prefigured by textual accounts and embodiments of those actions [in precedents, statutory preambles, trial court findings of fact, lawyer's briefs, and so forth]" (Rountree 2007, 15).

The consideration of multiple acts, as illustrated in Justice Kennedy's statements in the following sections, creates an additional challenge for opinion writers: harmonizing relationships among the various constructed acts. Although Burke said little about these inter-act relationships, my examination of judicial opinions has required that I consider the issue at length. I have noted that "the most common way relationships are constructed between different acts is through a terministic bridge connecting two acts. That is, the first act constructs an element that becomes a scene, agent, agency, purpose, or attitude in a second act" (Rountree 2017). In legal discourse, this often centers on constructing a law or precedent (an agency in Act 1) that is then applied to the case at hand (an agency in Act 2), so that one can say that one is "following the law" (through an agency-act ratio). Constructing the law might involve arguing, for example, that "this constitutional provision (act) was enacted by these people (agents) in this particular historical scene, using this language (agency) or mechanism (e.g., forbidding censorship) for this purpose, evincing a particular attitude (e.g., concern over government censorship)." Once the act is shown to yield a legal rule or principle—an agency to guide decision—it is imported into a second act as an agency of decision (in an agency-act ratio), whereby one can be shown to "follow the law." The same basic construction works for statutes and for precedent decisions, where agencies are legal provisions or holdings to be followed, respectively.

Given the centrality of act construction in appellate opinions, I believe that good judgment in those opinions requires a reasonable and artful construction (or reconstruction) of the plethora of acts relevant to a case in a way that harmonizes them so that they meet, to the fullest extent possible, three

"temporal" needs faced by judges: (1) addressing the past, by fairly considering what the law is; (2) addressing the present, by fairly considering what
justice requires for the present case and the litigants before the court; and
(3) addressing the future, by considering the implications of the decision
for those who are similarly situated, as well as for our democratic system
of government. This final consideration about our democratic system of
government goes beyond the merely legal consideration of law, cases, and
immediate justice. Ultimately, it involves a ratio that should be paramount:
act-agent. *What we do* shapes *who we are*. Inasmuch as *what we hold the law
to be* determines *what kind of people we are*, or at least aspire to be, this is a
crucial ratio. Additionally, what a court *does* determines *who* that court is in
our political system and who *we as a nation are* that would be governed by
such an institution of law. Thus does legal discourse implicate larger issues
of political order and legitimacy.

However, as Ronald Dworkin (1975) has observed, courts are often faced
with "hard cases" that are difficult to decide because the result is not dictated by a statute or precedent, as the ideal of the legal positivists would
have it. The legal realists were even more skeptical than Dworkin, insisting
that statutes and precedents put few constraints on judges wishing to interpret and apply them in different ways. They added to the consideration of
how to interpret such law—a concern with the past—the additional concern
for the future wrought by judicial decisions. They conceived of law, as Karl
Llewellyn puts it, "as a means to social ends and not as an end in itself; so
that any part needs constantly to be examined for its purpose, and for its
effect, and to be judged in the light of both and of their relation to each
other" (1931, 1236).

Since constructions of action are involved in considering the law, considering the case before the court (and its agents), and considering the future
(often drawing on possible or hypothetical actions for insight), good judgment involves carefully grappling with all the relevant acts and their pre-
figuration (by litigants, precedent courts, legal scholars, etc.), harmonizing
them to explain a decision. Often it requires one to justify ignoring one of
these temporal concerns or challenging prefigured acts (such as precedents
or standard interpretations of laws). But it can never ignore the act-agent
implications of decisions, whereby what we do determines who we are.

A focus on effective constructions of actions provides no assurance
that "good judgment" in this sense will yield good results, but it does have
the virtue of requiring one to grapple with the past, present, and future
as critical considerations and the typically prefigured acts that inform our

understanding of them. So let us consider how Justice Kennedy constructed actions and harmonized them in this case as a prelude to assessing his judgment.

Exercising "Good Judgment": Justice Kennedy in *Lawrence v. Texas*

The antisodomy statute at issue in *Lawrence*, though recent, was anachronistic, appearing as a large majority of states had eliminated antisodomy statutes or at least ignored them (*Lawrence* 2003, 570, 573). The Texas statute also expressly targeted gay people, as it allowed sodomy among heterosexuals while outlawing it for people with few alternatives for engaging in sexual intimacy. Therefore, it was not difficult for Justice Kennedy to construct as unjust the act of extracting over $300 in fines and court costs from two homosexual men for a single act of consensual sex, as well as giving them a criminal record. The same concern for future injustice if the Court allowed such legislative acts easily supported a construction of a better future and a more equitable democratic state without them. The most pressing problem was the *Bowers* precedent—a past act of interpreting the US Constitution. The principle of stare decisis required some deference to this decision, so Justice Kennedy had his hands full in showing that the *Bowers* decision was wrong and deserved to be overruled. Thus, we should not be surprised to see Justice Kennedy carefully reconstructing both this precedent decision and the law it relied on. He took pains to show that the precedent court was "mistaken" rather than malicious or stupid, lest he toss a stone inside a glass house where the current court also resided.

Justice Kennedy's most intensive work in act construction involved *Bowers*'s sweeping history of antisodomy laws and the precedent Court's act of framing the constitutional question. Justice Kennedy offers a corrective history of those innumerable acts and uses a generalized construction of human intimacy to show that the majority's act of framing was narrow and erroneous.

Justice Kennedy quotes the *Bowers* Court's assertion, "Proscriptions against that conduct [homosexual sodomy] have ancient roots" (*Lawrence* 2003, 569, quoting *Bowers* 1986, 192). Justice Byron White, writing for the majority in *Bowers*, noted that such conduct was criminalized by the common law and by US statutes from the eighteenth, nineteenth, and twentieth centuries, citing dozens of statutes (*Bowers* 1986, 192–94). Justice Kennedy does not deny that such laws existed but rather questioned what they specifically prohibited, particularly in light of how they were enforced. He begins with a simple construction of secondary law, noting that many academic writings cited in amicus briefs for *Lawrence* advanced "fundamental criticisms of the historical premises relied upon by the majority and concurring opinions in *Bowers*" (*Lawrence* 2003, 567–68). This was a counter to Justice White's own singular academic reference in *Bowers* (1986, 192). While Justice Kennedy admits that he is not "attempt[ing] to reach a definitive historical judgment" about the matter (a construction of his own action), he does insist that antisodomy statutes generally applied to both heterosexual and male homosexual sodomy:

> At the outset it should be noted that there is no longstanding history in this country of laws directed at homosexual conduct as a distinct matter. Beginning in colonial times there were prohibitions of sodomy derived from the English criminal laws passed in the first instance by the Reformation Parliament of 1533. The English prohibition was understood to include relations between men and women as well as relations between men and men. See, *e.g., King v. Wiseman*, 92 Eng. Rep. 774, 775 (K. B. 1718) (interpreting "mankind" in Act of 1533 as including women and girls). Nineteenth-century commentators similarly read American sodomy, buggery, and crime-against-nature statutes as criminalizing certain relations between men and women and between men and men. See, *e.g.,* 2 J. Bishop, Criminal Law §1028 (1858); 2 J. Chitty, Criminal Law 47–50 (5th Am. ed. 1847); R. Desty, A Compendium of American Criminal Law 143 (1882); J. May, The Law of Crimes §203 (2d ed. 1893). (*Lawrence* 2003, 568)

The *Wiseman* decision is used to interpret the foundation of antisodomy laws in the 1533 act as not limited to homosexual sodomy (noting its interpretation of "mankind" as a generic term), and the four nineteenth-century criminal law texts are used to reinforce that view.

Justice Kennedy has an explanation for why the "tradition" of antisodomy laws did not distinguish "homosexuals" specifically: "according to some scholars the concept of the homosexual as a distinct category of person did not emerge until the late 19th century" (*Lawrence* 2003, 568). He parenthetically quotes a scholarly book that insists, "The modern terms *homosexuality* and *heterosexuality* do not apply to an era that had not yet articulated these distinctions" (568). Thus, he implies, the historical scene shaped the agencies of the law. That does not fully address the fact that sodomy between two men (an act) was prohibited, even if it was not labeled as "homosexual" (i.e., focused on particular kinds of agents). Justice Kennedy strains to pull out an overarching rationale for the prohibitions against anyone engaging in sodomy by insisting that "early American sodomy laws were not directed at homosexuals as such but instead sought to prohibit nonprocreative sexual activity more generally" (568). He offers no specific support for this contention but seems to rely on the nonprocreative feature of this particular act (its *purpose* or, rather, lack of reproductive purpose) as the common ingredient for condemnation. Certainly, there were religious sources of this attitude that he could have cited, but he offered none.[2] This weakens his construction of this long-standing condemnation of sodomy. His more defensible inference is that his survey of such prohibitions "does tend to show that this particular form of conduct was not thought of as a separate category from like conduct between heterosexual persons" (568–69).

More compelling was Justice Kennedy's construction of the purposes of these antisodomy laws in light of how they were enforced (or not enforced). When prosecutors *apply* the law (an agency for convictions), one can gain insight into what the laws are *for* (purpose) through the agency-purpose ratio. Justice Kennedy notes that "laws prohibiting sodomy do not seem to have been enforced against consenting adults acting in private. A substantial number of sodomy prosecutions and convictions for which there are surviving records were for predatory acts against those who could not or did not consent, as in the case of a minor or the victim of an assault" (*Lawrence* 2003, 569).

Justice Kennedy offers a kind of reverse engineering here: looking at the acts that were subject to prosecution to figure out what the law (agency) applied by prosecutors was. The agents of the legal enactments (those who wrote the antisodomy statutes) are fairly ignored here in favor of those who applied the law or, more specifically, what they *did* with those legal agencies. In dramatistic terms, this is a complex construction involving three acts: (1) the antisodomy laws (enacted by legislatures), (2) the potentially criminal acts in question (sodomy against minors and assault victims), and (3) the acts of prosecutors in applying Act 1 to Act 2. By considering how prosecutors applied the law (Act 3) drawn from a legislative act (Act 1) to the facts of the cases (Act 2), Justice Kennedy teases out what that law (Act 1) must be without even considering legislative intent or scenic concerns (such as the Victorian setting). To paraphrase the fictitious eponymous film character Forrest Gump, we could render Justice Kennedy's argument as "the law is as the law does."

Justice Kennedy does offer an additional legislative purpose for the antisodomy statutes: "to ensure there would be no lack of coverage if a predator committed a sexual assault that did not constitute rape as defined by the criminal law" (*Lawrence* 2003, 569). To bolster this interpretation, he draws on the nineteenth-century treatise writer Joseph Chitty, who featured "model sodomy indictments" that "addressed the predatory acts of an adult man against a minor girl or minor boy" (569). Perhaps ignoring exceptions, Justice Kennedy emphasizes that such "prosecutions *typically* involved relations between men and minor girls or minor boys, relations between adults involving force, relations between adults implicating disparity in status, or relations between men and animals" (569; emphasis added).

Justice Kennedy also explains more generally why prosecutions of consensual homosexual sodomy might have been rare: because the rule of evidence in the nineteenth century "imposed a burden that would make a conviction more difficult to obtain even taking into account the problems always inherent in prosecuting consensual acts committed in private. Under then-prevailing standards, a man could not be convicted of sodomy based upon testimony of a consenting partner, because the partner was considered an accomplice" (*Lawrence* 2003, 569). On the other hand, "a partner's testimony . . . was admissible if he or she had not consented to the act or was a minor, and therefore incapable of consent" (569). So difficulties with the *means* of conviction probably determined the kind of cases prosecuted. This construction of prosecutorial motives might hurt Justice Kennedy if we assume that prosecutors *would have* gone after consensual homosexual acts if they *could have*, that is, if such acts were properly within the ambit and purposes of the law, even if they were difficult to prosecute. However, demonstrating that a law is practically impossible to apply and merely stands as a theoretical prohibition on conduct supports the idea that it was not part of what Holmes might call "the life of the law" and, thus, that it might be rejected as a serious proscription on conduct that boasts ancient roots, as Justice White would characterize it.

Though Justice Kennedy rejects Justice White's claims about the "ancient roots" of antihomosexual sodomy laws, he admits that they began appearing widely in the final third of the twentieth century (*Lawrence* 2003, 570). However, he again scrutinizes the actual prosecutions under these laws in order to characterize them as limited. Here he generalizes, urging that "the prosecution of consensual, homosexual sodomy between adults for the years 1880–1995 are not always clear in the details, but a significant number involved conduct in a public place" (570). As with his prior generalization of the bulk of cases, he uses the "significant number" characterization as a means to ignore other prosecutions as less significant to his account of the legal history here. Thus, *scene* (public places) infuses the acts in question with a bad character, perhaps removing some negative weight from the acts apart from those scenes.

Against Justice White's long list of antisodomy statutes, Justice Kennedy counters with a reduced number (nine state statutes) that prohibited same-sex sodomy specifically (*Lawrence* 2003, 570). And he lists the statutes that were prevalent in the 1970s that were now being ignored or abolished (570). The function of all these qualifications is to reject Justice White's ancient-rooted history of widespread condemnation that was the foundation for his rejection of homosexual conduct as in any way recognized as part of liberty under the Constitution. Justice White, Justice Kennedy argues, overstated the historical case that undergirded his rejection of liberty claims in *Bowers* (571). Overall, this is a simple scene-act argument where competing constructions of a scene yield different understandings of what the Fifth and Fourteenth Amendments were doing in announcing protections of liberty.

Enlarging the Substantive Interests in Personal Liberty

The majority in *Bowers* claimed in its opening to the case, "The issue presented is whether the Federal Constitution confers a fundamental right upon homosexuals to engage in sodomy and hence invalidates the laws of the many States that still make such conduct illegal and have done so for a very long time" (*Bowers* 1986, 190). Justice Kennedy rejects this focus on prohibited *acts* to suggest that such antisodomy statutes prohibit people from being particular kinds of *agents*—that they take away the liberty for self-determination in one of the most private and intimate aspects of human life. Thus, he argues, the case is not so much about human choice in *doing* so much as in *being*.

Justice Kennedy draws on a heterosexual analogy to drive his point home, insisting, "To say that the issue in *Bowers* was simply the right to engage in certain sexual conduct demeans the claim the individual put forward, just as it would demean a married couple were it to be said marriage is simply about the right to have sexual intercourse" (*Lawrence* 2003, 567). Perhaps foreshadowing his majority opinion supporting the right to gay marriage in *Obergefell v. Hodges* (2015), Justice Kennedy implicitly compares the most public and sacred heterosexual personal relationship, marriage, to homosexual relationships, which are diminished when reduced to physical intimacy alone. Thus, the status of *agents* in union overshadows the *acts* that are traditionally held to "consummate" those unions.

Justice Kennedy's focus on *agents* opens the door for his exploration of what it means to be a free human. He warns both the Court and the state to avoid trying "to define the meaning of the relationship or to set its boundaries absent injury to a person or abuse of an institution the law protects" (Lawrence 2003, 567). He draws on right-to-privacy rulings since *Griswold v. Connecticut* (1965) to show that actions within the home have received greater protection, as well as those involving private choices (*Lawrence* 2003, 564–65), concluding that "adults may choose to enter upon this relationship in the confines of their homes and their own private lives and still retain their dignity as free persons" (567). Not only does *scene* contain the *act* here, whereby acts in the home are more protected, but *agents* are converted to protected *scenes* through the metaphor of "private lives," functioning as portable scenes of individual action even outside the home, so long as it does not do public injury. Furthermore, the *act* of choosing (as an adult) is tied to a status that adheres to the *agent* as a sort of *attitudinal* status—"dignity," presumably felt by the individual and recognized by society at large.

Justice Kennedy explicitly connects the constitutionally protected choice to engage in sexual conduct with the choice to enter a personal relationship that yields individual dignity in concluding, "When sexuality finds overt expression in intimate conduct with another person, the conduct can be but one element in a personal bond that is more enduring. The liberty protected by the Constitution allows homosexual persons the right to make this choice" (*Lawrence* 2003, 567). This last argument takes for granted that there are certain types of agents—homosexuals—who then engage in acts of choice. This is the opposite of the act-agent constructions of antigay groups that claim that it is engaging in homosexual acts that creates the homosexual agent (Brummett 1979).

It is only after this rather metaphysical argument about what it means to be a free human who chooses one's personal relationships that Justice Kennedy notes that attitudes have changed on homosexuality. Making the obvious point that most people in the 2000s do not demonize homosexuals the way they did during much of the twentieth century is problematic for those who believe the Court should decide cases on either the historical grounds of constitutional history (such as what the founders intended to be protected by the Constitution) or on unchanging, objective constitutional values. On the other hand, legal scholars and judges have recognized that law fares poorly when it is too far out of step with the society to which it is applied. As Justice Oliver Wendell Holmes insisted, "The first requirement of a sound body of law is, that it should correspond with the actual feelings and demands of the community, whether right or wrong" (1881, 41). However, the appeal to such changes as a primary justification for reinterpreting the law has been problematic. First, if such changes have occurred, then that should move state legislatures to get on board and change their laws, leaving the decision to the elected branches of government. Second, adhering too closely to changes in sentiments might make the courts appear to simply blow with the social winds, tying themselves more to opinion polls than to law.

Justice Kennedy counters this concern with changeability by insisting that liberty has "manifold," if unrealized, "components," insisting, "Had those who drew and ratified the Due Process Clauses of the Fifth Amendment or the Fourteenth Amendment known the components of liberty in its manifold possibilities, they might have been more specific" (*Lawrence* 2003, 578). This hypothetical act of "knowing" serves him well to skirt the charge of blowing with the winds of social attitudes. He notes changes in legislation and model codes that reject the former antihomosexual biases of antisodomy laws (571). But instead of situating this change of heart in the public, he presents it as "an emerging awareness that liberty gives substantial protection to adult persons in deciding how to conduct their private lives in matters pertaining to sex" (572). Kenneth Burke calls this a basic strategy whereby rhetors can "translate back and forth between logical and temporal vocabularies" ([1945] 1969, 430), in this case "essentializing" the "temporal." That is, Justice Kennedy implies that adults always had constitutional liberties concerning their sex lives but that we only recently *became aware* of that fact. So a seemingly Johnny-come-lately constitutional liberty was actually always existent, though it was unrecognized; the late temporal recognition of this liberty is transformed into a logically preexistent liberty.

Even the *Bowers* Court had notice of this emergent recognition, Justice Kennedy notes, because the American Law Institute's Model Penal Code of 1955 "made clear that it did not recommend or provide for 'criminal penalties for consensual sexual relations conducted in private'" (citing American Law Institute, Model Penal Code §213.2, Comment 2 [1980], 372), and several states and foreign countries followed suit by changing their laws or refusing to enforce them (*Lawrence* 2003, 572–74).

Furthermore, Justice Kennedy notes, post-*Bowers* decisions had recognized expanded liberty involving individual privacy. Citing the abortion decision of *Planned Parenthood of Southeastern Pennsylvania v. Casey* (1992), he notes that "the Court reaffirmed the substantive force of the liberty protected by the Due Process Clause . . . [and] again confirmed that our laws and tradition afford constitutional protection to personal decisions relating to marriage, procreation, contraception, family relationships, child rearing, and education" (*Lawrence* 2003, 574, quoting *Casey* 1992, 851). He quotes a metaphysical passage about the autonomy of individuals from the plurality opinion in this case (which he coauthored with Justices David Souter and Sandra Day O'Connor), noting, "These matters, involving the most intimate and personal choices a person may make in a lifetime, choices central to personal dignity and autonomy, are central to the liberty protected by the Fourteenth Amendment. At the heart of liberty is the right to define one's own concept of existence, of meaning, of the universe, and of the mystery of human life. Beliefs about these matters could not define the attributes of personhood were they formed under compulsion of the State" (*Lawrence* 2003, 574, quoting *Casey* 1992, 851). In this passage concerning generalized human agents, the act of choosing and self-definition is central to liberty, with that act as a primary assertion by human agents (in an agent-act relationship) and those acts, in turn, defining agents as human (in an act-agent reversal).

A second post-*Bowers* decision helped Justice Kennedy more directly attack the motives of the Texas statute in question. *Romer v. Evans* (1996) involved an amendment to Colorado's constitution that deprived homosexuals, lesbians, and bisexuals (defined by "orientation, conduct, practices, or relationships") of protection from antidiscrimination laws. Justice Kennedy notes that this "class-based legislation" was deemed by the *Romer* Court as "born of animosity toward the class of persons affected" and lacking a rational relation to a legitimate governmental purpose (*Lawrence* 2003, 574, quoting *Romer* 1996, 634). Similarly, the Texas statute in *Lawrence* forbade homosexual sodomy and not sodomy in general (as *Bowers* had done), making it an easy target for claims of legislative animus (an attitude deriving from the narrow agency of the act). But instead of castigating the state directly, Justice Kennedy speaks more abstractly about such laws and their implications, noting, "If protected conduct is made criminal and the law which does so remains unexamined for its substantive validity, its stigma might remain even if it were not enforceable as drawn for equal protection reasons. When homosexual conduct is made criminal by the law of the State, that declaration in and of itself is an invitation to subject homosexual persons to discrimination both in the public and in the private spheres" (*Lawrence* 2003, 575). The damning implication that Texas was encouraging its citizens to engage in public and private discrimination is tempered by Justice Kennedy's abstract language about legal action and its impact on publics (as a legal enactment creates a scene for discriminatory acts).

But Justice Kennedy's discussion of this post-*Bowers* precedent is used to make a more standard and technical legal argument: that "the central holding of *Bowers* has been brought in question by this case, and it should be addressed" (*Lawrence* 2003, 575). That backward reference to an error in the law of *Bowers* is balanced with a reference to its implications for the future: "Its continuance as precedent demeans the lives of homosexual persons" (575). Justice Kennedy amplifies those consequences for homosexual Texans, noting that conviction under the statute creates a nontrivial stigma, including a criminal record (which typically must be reported on job applications) and the possibility of having to register as a sex criminal in some jurisdictions (575–76).

Justice Kennedy draws on another source to undermine *Bowers*, one that involves the attitudes of people outside the High Court. He notes that scholars have condemned it, that courts in five states have refused to follow it, and that European countries have eschewed it (*Lawrence* 2003, 576–77). These various acts—by scholars, states, and countries—express an attitude toward the precedent that brings into question not only the quality of the legal decision behind it but also the quality of the court that handed it down. This is an indirect, but notable, appeal to the High Court's interest in maintaining its stature. Its force comes from generalizing about others' attitudes by combining references to specific scholarly articles, specific state decisions, and specific European court decisions to amplify the negative judgment of the precedent.

Conclusion

In urging that *Bowers* was erroneous because of its faulty history and its failure to frame the constitutional issue correctly, Justice Kennedy could overcome concerns over stare decisis by noting that the principle does not represent "an inexorable command" (*Lawrence* 2003, 577, citing *Payne* 1991, 828) and that no reliance interest is at stake in reversing the precedent as there might be in property cases (*Lawrence* 2003, 577).

Justice Kennedy's majority opinion in *Lawrence* addresses the past, present, and future systematically and persuasively. He is weakest in accounting for the nonprocreative purposes behind the antisodomy history of US law, though he does well to show that such laws were not deployed frequently against homosexuals (unless they violated public decency). He is best in connecting our notions of what human freedom entails with concerns for future justice and the continuing legitimacy of the Court and the state for all people.

Justice Antonin Scalia's dissent in *Lawrence* was correct in predicting that the decision would open the way to the legalization of gay marriage (*Lawrence* 2003, 600, Scalia, J., dissenting). It is not merely precedent itself but Justice Kennedy's construction of a legal system, and the society that is governed by it, that projects a vision of the "good society." Later judgments about how to understand law and justice in particular cases may reference this vision as a goal or assumption of law. Of course, other visions compete as well, so that a rhetorical battle must be joined that invokes not only the past and the present but competing futures. Such are the implications of act construction in the law.

Notes

1. "Dramatism" is the name of his theory because these elements of action support our interpretations just as if we had staged them theatrically, with acts, scenes, agents, agencies, purposes, and attitudes all influencing the understanding of the whole.

2. For example, the Catechism of the Catholic Church includes the assertions, "Sexual pleasure is morally disordered when sought for itself, isolated from its procreative and unitive purposes" and "it is necessary that each and every marriage act remain ordered per se to the procreation of human life." Vatican, *Catechism of the Catholic Church*, 2nd ed., paragraphs 2351, 2366, accessed August 20, 2020. https://web.archive.org/web/20090304123934/https://www.vatican.va/archive/catechism/p3s2c2a6.htm.

References

Bowers v. Hardwick. 1986. 478 U.S. 186.

Brummett, Barry. 1979. "A Pentadic Analysis of Ideologies in Two Gay Rights Controversies." *Central States Speech Journal* 30:250–61.

Burke, Kenneth. (1945) 1969. *A Grammar of Motives*. Berkeley: University of California Press.

Dworkin, Ronald. 1975. "Hard Cases." *Harvard Law Review* 88 (6): 1057–109.

Griswold v. Connecticut. 1965. 381 U.S. 479.

Holmes, Oliver Wendell. 1881. *The Common Law*. Boston: Little, Brown.

Korematsu v. United States. 1944. 323 U.S. 214.

Lawrence v. Texas. 2003. 539 U.S. 558.

Llewellyn, Karl N. 1931. "Some Realism About Realism." *Harvard Law Review* 44:1222–64.

Obergefell v. Hodges. 2015. 576 U.S. 644.

Payne v. Tennessee. 1991. 501 U.S. 808.

Planned Parenthood of Southeastern Pennsylvania v. Casey. 1992. 505 U.S. 833.

Romer v. Evans. 1996. 517 U.S. 620.

Rountree, Clarke. 2001. "Instantiating 'The Law' and Its Dissents in *Korematsu v. United States*: A Dramatistic Analysis of Judicial Discourse." *Quarterly Journal of Speech* 87:1–24.

————. 2007. *Judging the Supreme Court: Constructions of Motives in* Bush v. Gore. East Lansing: Michigan State University Press.

————. 2017. "When Actions Collide: Pentadic Constructions Spanning Different Acts." *KB Journal* 12 (2). https://www.kbjournal.org/rountree_when_actions_collide.

Vatican. *Catechism of the Catholic Church.* 2nd ed. Accessed August 20, 2020. https://web.archive.org/web/20090304123934/https://www.vatican.va/archive /catechism/p3s2c2a6.htm.

7

JUSTICE KENNEDY AND NATURAL
LAW ARGUMENTATION

Francis J. Mootz III

We must never lose sight of the fact that the law has a moral foundation, and we must never fail to ask ourselves not only what the law is, but what the law should be.

—Justice Anthony M. Kennedy (Reuben 1992, 35)

In this chapter, I undertake a focused investigation that has broad implications. I argue that Justice Kennedy employed a form of natural law argumentation in some of his more notable opinions. This may be a surprising thesis in today's intellectual milieu, in which natural law generally is regarded as an anachronism. I should be clear that I am not suggesting that Justice Kennedy articulated a *consistent* natural law approach or even that he *consciously* employed natural law arguments. My narrow thesis is that at least some of his opinions are best understood by uncovering the natural law foundations for his reasoning.

One might think it is not particularly original to suggest that Justice Kennedy employed natural law arguments. Upon the announcement of his retirement, legal commentators casually noted that he used natural law and natural rights to gird his opinions (see, e.g., Rosen 2018; Turley 2018). Scholars have argued that Justice Kennedy's conception of liberty is rooted in the Enlightenment natural rights tradition that held sway at the time of the framing of the Constitution (see, e.g., Kelso and Kelso 2011). Others have pointed to his Catholic faith as a guidepost for his decisions, a faith that is deeply rooted in Aquinas's natural law philosophy (Jelliff 2013). But these general characterizations are not easily defended.

Justice Kennedy broke with core principles of classical Catholic natural law by overturning legal restrictions against gay Americans and upholding constitutional restrictions on antiabortion legislation. There is scant evidence that he adhered to a traditional theistic conception of natural law in his judging, much to the consternation of conservative Catholics (Kengor 2013, 2015, 2018). Additionally, in response to an explicit challenge by Justice David Souter in one case, Justice Kennedy emphatically disclaimed appealing to extraconstitutional natural law principles as part of his jurisprudence.[1] This corresponded to his express disavowal of a traditional natural law approach during the hearings on his nomination to the Supreme Court. "I am searching, as I think many judges are, for the correct balance in constitutional interpretation. So many of the things we are discussing here are, for me, in the nature of exploration and not the enunciation of some fixed or immutable ideas" (Knowles 2019, 3). Thus, my claim that Justice Kennedy employed natural law argumentation requires a deeper analysis that more carefully delineates the nature, so to speak, of natural law argumentation.

I develop my argument in three parts. First, I briefly review the tradition of natural law jurisprudence from classical times to the positivist present. One would be justified in assuming that legal positivism completely vanquished *natural law philosophy* in the jurisprudential debates of the previous century, but I uncover and defend the contemporary salience of *natural law argumentation* even after the hermeneutical turn. In part 2, I redefine the natural law tradition as a form of argumentation rather than a philosophy committed to moral realism, drawing on Chaïm Perelman and Lucie Olbrechts-Tyteca's controversial concept of the "universal audience." Part 3 turns to the storm of controversy over Justice Kennedy's citation to international legal materials in the course of considering the constitutional limits on the death penalty in the United States. I conclude that a more open and explicit use of the natural law argumentation that informs Justice Kennedy's rhetoric would add clarity to contemporary judicial practice. Justice Kennedy illustrates—albeit unwittingly, unsystematically, and unclearly—the important role of nontheistic, indeterminate natural law arguments.[2]

The Contemporary Rejection of Natural Law Philosophy

The great majority of legal theorists agree that the natural law tradition is irrelevant to our contemporary understanding of law. Outside religious circles, belief in abiding, determinant, and discernible principles that guide legal practice is scarcely mentioned today. As a sympathetic critic concludes, natural law today remains "a curiosity outside the mainstream, regarded mostly as a sideshow and not to be taken very seriously" (Weinreb 1996, 195; see also Soper 1992, 2394). This desuetude is appropriate, according to a well-worn tale. The phrase "natural law" brings to mind the metaphysical account that bloomed in ancient Rome, was absorbed and transmuted by the Christian tradition, reached its full expression in Aquinas, and then was secularized and rationalized as philosophy of natural rights during the Enlightenment period (Mootz 2010, 384–85). This tradition was aptly summarized by William Blackstone, who wrote that this "law of nature, being co-eval with mankind and dictated by God himself, is of course superior in obligation to any other. It is binding over all the globe, in all countries, and at all times: no human laws are of any validity, if contrary to this; and such of them as are valid derive all their force, and all their authority, mediately or immediately, from this original" (1983, 41). Natural law philosophy was recognized at the time of the founding, as demonstrated by Justice Samuel Chase's insistence, "There are certain vital principles in our free republican governments which will determine and overrule an apparent and flagrant abuse of legislative power; as to authorize manifest injustice by positive law; or to take away that security for personal liberty, or private property, for the protection whereof government was established. An act of the Legislature (for I cannot call it a law) contrary to the great first principles of the social compact, cannot be considered a rightful exercise of legislative authority" (*Calder* 1798, 388).

In time, the fundamental law of the United States was conceived in terms of natural rights, which were restated as positive law in a written Constitution that is subject to ordinary textual exegesis. The commitment to a theistic natural law subtending our practice of interpreting a written constitution was largely eradicated from our tradition by the time of the Civil War. The rationalist account of natural rights that replaced it, exemplified in the notorious *Lochner* (1905) decision, has ostensibly also been firmly rejected. The long history of natural law philosophy and the more recently developed history of natural rights are obscured today by a thoroughgoing positivist conception of legal interpretation and argumentation. It is easy to conclude that Blackstone's echoes of Ciceronian natural law are barely recognizable today and that Justice Chase's famous assertion of natural law served as a eulogy of the natural law tradition at the dawn of US jurisprudence.

The Quandary of Contemporary Legal Theory

The positivist triumph over natural law is too easily claimed. Expunging natural law philosophy has come at the cost of generating an intellectual crisis. Steven Smith (2004) concisely diagnoses "law's quandary" in the modern era (see Mootz 2008). He describes "how our understanding of law has deteriorated due to our wanton neglect (or, rather, our systematic suppression) of its ontological dimensions" (Smith 2004, ix). Put simply, the positivist revolt against natural law has left us without the conceptual ability to critique contemporary practices. When lawyers appeal to the "the law" to challenge current practices, to what are they appealing? Our legal discourse depends on something analogous to a religious ontology of natural law, but we face a quandary because we expressly disavow such a grounding in spite of the character of our practices (Smith 2004, 21). Smith concludes that there is at least "a strong *prima facie* case that modern legal discourse is operating in a sort of 'ontological gap' that divides our explicit or owned ontological commitments (which preclude us from recognizing the reality of a higher law) from the ontological assumptions not only implicit in but essential to our discourse and practice (which seem to presuppose the reality of an appeal to 'the law')" (63).

Peter Goodrich offers a similar diagnosis from the opposite side of the political and jurisprudential spectrum. The plight of contemporary legal theory, he argues, is that we have abandoned natural law foundations that were originally constructed in ecclesiastical venues only to find that the project of developing a secular legal language capable of transforming the management of social conflict into questions of technical rationality is doomed to failure (Goodrich 1996, 160–61). While Smith is wistful about the ontologically robust days of the past, Goodrich seeks a clean break from the intellectually stale tradition of positivism by embracing a new conception of law for the postmodern world. The most important question in contemporary jurisprudence is how we can face this challenge, a challenge we obstinately refuse to acknowledge.

Recuperating Natural Law for a Positivist World

My goal in this chapter is to uncover the continuing significance of natural law argumentation in contemporary legal practice. The ascendance of positivism does not settle the question, because natural law and positive law are not stark alternatives. The enactment and development of positive law are not only *consistent* with natural law but *necessary* (Helmholz 2015, 2–4). It would be implausible for judges to reason directly from general principles of the natural order to uniquely correct decisions in a particular case without the mediating effect of detailed positive law. Positive law permits a judge to justify numerous decisions, even if natural law might subtend these particular rules and occasionally provide a basis from which to critique and reject a particular provision of positive law.

Positive law and natural law may be able to coexist in principle, but the traditional natural law account of timeless and immutable principles that have been ordained by a deity or discovered by a univocal reason are no longer plausible for most commentators. Smith and Goodrich accurately describe an ontological gap in our legal practices, and the challenge now is to articulate a conception of natural law that breaks free of theistic commitments and the felt need for timeless certainty and yet is robust enough to underwrite critical leverage against accepted practices. I have argued that the "interpretive turn" of modern theory does not reject the quest for "natural" foundations for legal practice; in fact, the opposite is the case. An ontology premised on our *hermeneutical and rhetorical nature* provides the answer to law's quandary.

Our human nature promotes the generation of "rhetorical knowledge," a form of knowing that does not lay claim to the timeless certainty of divine principles, nor does it surrender to the cacophonous postmodern flow of symbols (Mootz 2006). My characterization of rhetorical knowledge begins with Hans-Georg Gadamer's philosophical hermeneutics, which teaches that understanding occurs only in the application of the text to a question in the present. I then draw on Chaïm Perelman's new rhetoric, which teaches that we can argue to an audience with integrity, even if there is no definitive answer to the question. Read together, Gadamer and Perelman describe a social process and epistemic achievement that are properly regarded as knowledge. Rhetorical knowledge is the effort of two or more persons working together creatively to refashion the linguistically structured symbols of social cohesion with the aim of motivating action of some kind. It is perhaps misleading for me to characterize rhetorical knowledge as the result of a "refashioning" to the extent that it calls to mind an image of a skilled technician adjusting the rhetorical bonds of society as one might adjust a timing belt to maximize engine performance. The distinctiveness of rhetorical knowledge is that it is not a tool to secure pregiven ends but rather consists of arguments grounded in probabilities and uncertainties that are subject to debate. Rhetorical knowledge sustains legal practice as a reasonable—even if never thoroughly rationalized—social activity.

Surveying accepted topics, norms, and opinions as resources for confronting the demands of the case at hand, rhetorical actors continually conjoin these constitutive features of themselves and their society in unique ways that serve to re-create the argumentative resources available for social discourse. The reality of rhetorical knowledge is proved not because the participants can uncover the definitive "answer" to the question posed but because they continue to develop a public discussion along new lines of argumentation that motivate justified action.

Rhetorical knowledge underwrites the activity of judgment. Judgment is an evolutionary adaptation that preceded rational analysis by millennia; consequently, it is not subject to a rational reconstruction that can be summarized in the form of a "how to" guide (Thiele 2006). Acknowledging that our refined cognitive processes build on our deep-seated capacity to judge is not a surrender to unreflective irrationalism. We posit and reflect on principles of judgment, which may take on a life of their own, circling back to influence basic assessments and evaluations. In this respect, judgments are developed and transformed by way of a "reflective equilibrium" without ever securing the status of timeless truths (Mootz 2018, 19). The practical wisdom of judging "is embodied learning mindful of its own limits," including the inability to fully rationalize or explain how a judgment is reached (Thiele 2006, 112).

Rhetorical knowledge becomes the touchstone for determining whether a judge is "judging well." If all we can aspire to in legal analysis is rhetorical knowledge, it is reasonable to ask whether this is sufficient to guide judges who must interpret the law. I have argued that the long-standing traditions of hermeneutics and rhetoric as exemplified by Gadamer and Perelman provide us with the conceptual resources to judge well in situations of verisimilitude. Before turning to Justice Kennedy, I describe the specific role of natural law argumentation in fostering rhetorical knowledge and providing a basis for ongoing critique.

The Inevitability of Natural Law Argumentation

R. H. Helmholz rejects the standard account of the irrelevance of natural law in American jurisprudence. He tracks the influence of natural law in US legal education and in legal argumentation in court, finding that although judges often decided cases according to the positive law, it was not rare for them to mention natural law (Helmholz 2015, 152). Although "arguments made on the basis of natural law were more often advanced by counsel than they were accepted by judges," the vibrancy of this practice is clear (172). Particularly in doctrinal areas such as property law and family law (152–61) and as a necessary backdrop for interpreting statutory law in the English tradition of equitable interpretation (165–68), natural law was an unacknowledged and undertheorized element of US legal practice. The jurisprudential problem is how to make sense of this persistent practice that we have disclaimed theoretically. I take guidance from Lon Fuller, who claimed that the substantive element of natural law is our nature as rhetorical and hermeneutical beings: "Communication is something more than a means of staying alive. It is a way of being alive. . . . If I were asked, then, to discern one central indisputable principle of what may be called substantive natural law—Natural Law with capital letters—I would find it in the injunction: Open up, maintain, and preserve the integrity of the channels of communication by which men convey to one another what they perceive, feel, and desire" (1964, 186). Natural law is not an eternal rulebook. Rather, it refers to our nature as argumentative beings who make appeals to a "universal audience."

Natural Law Argumentation as an Appeal to the Universal Audience

I characterize *natural law argumentation* as the practice of appealing to principles and conclusions that *should be accepted* by what Chaïm Perelman and Lucie Olbrechts-Tyteca termed the "universal audience" in their magisterial treatise *The New Rhetoric*. The universal audience is not a timeless, unchanging, and thoroughly rational audience. Quite the contrary. Natural law argumentation accepts and works within specific social settings that have a historical trajectory.

The New Rhetoric revives the classical rhetorical tradition of *persuading* an audience about matters that are only probable, in contrast to *compelling agreement* about a matter that is certain (Perelman and Olbrechts-Tyteca 1969, 26–31). The audience always is constructed by the speaker to some degree; the audience cannot be directly and perspicaciously perceived (19–23). Perelman and Olbrechts-Tyteca identify three distinct audiences: (1) one or more persons whom one wants to persuade; (2) oneself, in the manner of Plato's dialogue of the soul with itself through reflection; and (3) the "universal audience" of all reasonable, adult persons. The universal audience is never an empirical reality but rather is a construction by the rhetor with reference to an actual audience. By construing the audience as a "universal audience," the rhetor acknowledges the need to persuade the audience to accept a "universal" position rather than imposing one's will by claiming direct access to a preexisting universal norm (31–35). There is a reflexive interaction between an existing concrete audience addressed by the rhetor and the rhetor's positing of a universal audience for which the concrete audience can only serve as a temporary and incomplete stand-in (35). Ultimately, a claim that the universal audience would accept a proposition is a claim that the proposition is valid and should convince all reasonable persons, but this does not guarantee that all persons will be convinced (313).

Perelman and Olbrechts-Tyteca's rhetorical philosophy offers different ways to understand natural law argumentation. First, natural law can be used as a commonplace or line of argument, although this is rarely used today because there no longer appears to be ontological backing for such claims. To assert that "the natural law" requires a specific decision, without more, is unlikely to be persuasive to most audiences. Second, natural law can be conceived as an argumentative strategy directed to a concrete audience by appealing to that audience to rise above its parochialism.[3] This is the form of natural law argumentation employed by Justice Kennedy. Finally, we can radicalize Perelman and Olbrechts-Tyteca by "naturalizing" rhetoric as our way of being in the world. Natural law in this account is grounded in our nature of generating rhetorical knowledge. As quoted earlier, Lon Fuller concluded at the end of his productive career that natural law is just a recognition that it is our nature to engage in dialogue about questions that cannot be resolved definitively, and Perelman and Olbrechts-Tyteca demonstrate how natural law is best conceived as describing an argumentative and decisional activity rather than a pregiven moral reality.

Natural Law as Rhetorical Argumentation:
A Solution for Contemporary Theorists

My conception of the universal audience as a rhetorical construct to subtend a natural law argument provides a framework for understanding recent efforts to recuperate natural rights and natural law without becoming entangled in their traditional metaphysical trappings. For example, Jonathan Crowe insists,

> Natural law, rather than simply being posited from above, is shaped over time by both our intrinsic natures and our external environments. Principles of natural law do not arise out of nowhere but reflect the ongoing human quest to work out how best to live flourishing, fulfilling lives given the nature we have and the social worlds we inhabit.
>
> Natural law, on this view, has three key features: it is socially embodied, historically extended and dependent on facts about human nature. It is socially embodied because its content is partly derived from social institutions and practices; furthermore, we discern its content

primarily by interpreting those practices. It is historically extended because it reflects human efforts to survive and flourish in a changing natural and social environment. And it depends on human nature because it is shaped by both our biology and our social conditions. Natural law is what is good for humans given our biological, social and historical predicament. (2019, 101)

Crowe rejects moral absolutism and timeless verities, recognizing instead that natural law is a normative practice that is deeply embedded in our legal system. Among the many implications to be drawn from his account, Crowe rejects originalist methodologies (104). His impulse, shared by a number of contemporary theorists, is best sustained by my rhetorical model of legal argumentation claiming the adherence of a universal audience.

The Enlightenment effort to recast tradition natural law in terms of non-theistic natural rights has now run aground on the same shoals of indeterminacy that problematized the classical natural law tradition. Critics indict the invocation of natural rights as a cover for the imposition of Western values on traditional cultures, questioning whether the discourse of natural rights can continue to play a role in a fragmented world. Michael Ignatieff (2001) has forcefully argued that we ought to conceive of natural rights as points of political engagement rather than eternal verities to be idolized. His argument is an elegant invitation to a political rhetoric that permits an appeal to the universal audience in the development of rhetorical knowledge without assuming that this appeal in itself can ever be a conversation stopper. Ignatieff concludes that his conception of natural rights as politics is thin but sufficient (95, 173). A rhetorical account of natural law as argumentation framed for the universal audience provides the grounding for natural rights as a political achievement rather than a preexisting concept.[4]

Justice Kennedy and Natural Law Argumentation

Justice Kennedy employed natural law argumentation. He sought rhetorical knowledge in a manner that can be described as judging well. I do not suggest that Justice Kennedy expressly and consciously sought to make traditional natural law appeals. In today's political and jurisprudential climate, that would have very limited appeal and would probably undermine Justice Kennedy's ethos. I argue that he engaged in natural law argumentation despite having concluded that a traditional natural law philosophy of timeless verities could have no role in a modern constitutional democracy. As he stated in a talk, "You write an opinion differently if it's a railroad reorganization or human rights; there's a different audience" (Duehren 2015). Natural law argumentation is an appeal to a construction of the universal audience.

In *Roper v. Simmons* (2004), Justice Kennedy authored the majority opinion finding that the imposition of the death penalty for a crime committed by a juvenile violated the Eighth Amendment's ban on "cruel and unusual punishments," even though the Court had rejected this claim only fifteen years earlier.[5] Following the generative case of *Trop v. Dulles* (1958), the Court adjudicates Eighth Amendment claims in accordance with the "evolving standards of human decency," often with reference to practices in other jurisdictions. For example, five years earlier, Justice Stephen Breyer criticized the Court's refusal to hear appeals by prisoners arguing that remaining on death row for more than two decades constituted cruel and unusual punishment, quoting foreign opinions in support of the claim (*Knight* 1999, 990, Breyer, J., dissenting from denial of certiorari). This familiar doctrinal approach in Eighth Amendment cases—an area of law that most clearly embraces judgment as the search for rhetorical knowledge—did not insulate Justice Kennedy from a storm of controversy when he emphasized that the United States was an extreme outlier in the world community because it permitted states to execute persons who committed crimes as minors.

Justice Kennedy's claim that the evolving standards of human decency are confirmed by the fact that the majority of US states reject the execution of juvenile offenders was met by Justice Antonin Scalia's rebuke that the large majority of "relevant states"—those states that permit the death penalty at all—still permit the jury to decide whether to impose death for a juvenile offender (*Roper* 2004, 568, 628). Justice Kennedy, undoubtedly sensitive to the weakness of his claim that those "relevant" states had "evolved" with regard to executing persons who were minors at the time of the crime, looked to foreign decisions for judicial "confirmation" of the (recently embraced, impending?) standards within the United States (575). Given "the stark reality that the United States is the only country in the world that continues to give official sanction to the juvenile death penalty" and the provisions of the United Nations Convention on the Rights of the Child (ratified by all countries except Somalia and the United States), Justice Kennedy concludes, "The opinion of the world community, while not controlling our outcome, does provide respected and significant confirmation for our own conclusions" (575–78). By not explaining how foreign law can be "confirmatory" even if not "controlling," Justice Kennedy was open to Justice

Scalia's mendacious charge that the unstated "basic premise of the Court's argument—that American law should conform to the laws of the rest of the world—ought to be rejected out of hand" as an abuse of judicial power (624).

Justice Sandra Day O'Connor dissented, concluding that the national consensus on the moral question was far from established. However, she expressly accepted the legitimacy of looking to foreign judgments in Eighth Amendment cases because they are "neither wholly isolated from, nor inherently at odds with," the national values in the United States (*Roper* 2004, 605). Again, she provides no clear justification for looking beyond the borders of our country when assessing the development of moral sensibilities in the United States. Justice Scalia brooks no discussion of foreign law unless it is part of the rationale of the decision, and he argues that this is precisely the point, despite Justice Kennedy's "parting attempt to downplay the significance of [his] extensive discussion" (628).

We can best understand Justice Kennedy's undertheorized reasoning by recognizing that it is natural law argumentation seeking to persuade a particular concrete audience to see itself as an incarnation of the universal audience. It is clear that Justice Kennedy does not use natural law as an explicit topic, even if expunged of theistic baggage. Stalwart defenders of the holding in the case might have difficulty concluding that executing someone for their actions as a minor violates the unchanging fundamental laws of nature. Justice Kennedy explains that the world community has prohibited the execution of minors, which confirms the as-yet-unexpressed norms of our own community. He argues that we ought to confront the starkly normative question of what constitutes "cruel and unusual punishment" by looking beyond our historical practices to recognize who we are as a polity.

Justice Kennedy motivates acceptance of his argument by inviting the concrete audience of readers to regard themselves as a universal audience passing judgment on matters that should be acceptable to all reasonable persons. The United States is not *following* the world community on a question of morality and law. Instead, the world community has *anticipated* the change in understanding that we *should acknowledge* when comporting ourselves as a universal audience. It is not a coercive and oppressive Cartesian certitude from foreign lands before which Justice Kennedy bows; rather, he provokes us to recognize a new understanding of our law that we believe should be shared by the world community. Our contemporary understanding that minors have not fully formed a mature capacity for self-control puts the legal question in a new light (*Roper* 2004, 569–70). The fact that the world community has already acted merely "confirms" what we would decide as the universal audience. This is the meaning of Justice Kennedy's conclusion that it "does not lessen our fidelity to the Constitution or our pride in its origins to acknowledge that the express affirmation of certain fundamental rights by other nations and peoples simply underscores the centrality of those same rights within our own heritage of freedom" (578).

Justice Kennedy moves fluidly from a forensic inquiry into the relevant facts of the matter (juvenile capacity and responsibility) to a deliberative engagement that defines the limits of state power under constitutional doctrine. In considering the overwhelming opposition of the world community to executing minors, Justice Kennedy is doing more than offering a practical reason—that the majority is most likely correct—for choosing a course of action. He is issuing an epideictic call for the audience to see itself as the kind of polity that no longer condones the execution of minors. Traditional epideictic appeals do not seek an immediate practical response (Perelman and Olbrechts-Tyteca 1969, 52), but the judicial construction of a universal audience is epideictic inasmuch as it is formed to make a claim on a concrete audience: "We are not a people who execute child criminals, because fully informed, reasonable people would not permit such a punishment."[6]

We should not confuse recourse to natural law argumentation with following a method that generates the correct result. It is no method at all; it is a type of argument. In this volume, Elizabeth Britt, Eugene Garver, and Kathryn Stanchi justifiably criticize Justice Kennedy's opinion in *Gonzales v. Carhart* (2007), an opinion that I would interpret as his effort to invoke the universal audience's condemnation of partial birth abortion. Natural law argumentation is not always persuasive. As with all things rhetorical, the rhetor cannot avoid the obligation to argue responsibly simply by invoking the universal audience.

Justice Kennedy need not embrace the ontological claim that our nature is thoroughly rhetorical in order to successfully call on the concrete audience to see itself as participating in the construction of a universal audience that breaks free of tribal practices. Just as the sophists apparently made persuasive arguments against slavery, a justice of the Supreme Court can argue persuasively against applications of the death penalty to minors. The appeal to see oneself as part of a universal audience may not succeed—slavery continued in ancient Greece, after all—but this does not undermine the rhetorical power of such claims, claims that I call natural law argumentation in the quest for rhetorical knowledge.

Conclusion

I expect that many readers will reject my thesis because it invites an unwelcome return, however chastened, of natural law philosophy. Even if I am correctly describing Justice Kennedy's rhetoric, they would argue that the appropriate response is to eschew such rhetorical moves altogether. This critique misses my point. Justice Kennedy's opinions are persuasive to some degree because he employs natural law argumentation, which can be a source of rhetorical knowledge. No method can excise natural law argumentation from contemporary legal analysis, because it is how we address the ontological gap that defines the positivist era. Justice Kennedy cannot avoid natural law argumentation, nor can any of us. Cases will arise that call for us to break free of received understandings by calling on the audience to reconceive of itself as a universal audience. In doing so, we can generate rhetorical knowledge and responsibly mind the gap.

Notes

1. In a case upholding sovereign immunity, Kennedy emphasized that such "immunity from suit is a fundamental aspect of the sovereignty which the States enjoyed before the ratification of the Constitution and which they retain today" (*Alden* 1999, 713). He explained that this element of English political theory was wholly adopted by the founders, including Hamilton, Madison, and Marshall (713–20). Justice Souter dissented and took issue with the "majority's inherent, natural law theory of sovereign immunity," which appeared to predate and not be contained within the Constitution (795–96, Souter, J., dissenting). Justice Kennedy emphatically rejected this characterization (734). Interestingly, two years prior to this exchange, Justice Souter used natural law argumentation (as I define it in this chapter) in his concurring opinion in *Washington v. Glucksberg* (1997; see Mootz 1999, 369–78).

2. This may sound like a harsh indictment, but in this chapter, I empathize with the rhetorical situation in which Justice Kennedy judged. Justice Kennedy wrote judicial opinions about fundamental questions of human liberty and equality in a positivist world that ostensibly foreclosed natural law argumentation. This may explain what James Gardner has called Justice Kennedy's "neurotic" style (chap. 10 in this volume). Justice Kennedy simply did not have the vocabulary to describe his struggle to articulate a natural law argument in *Obergefell*.

3. This argument appears to go back to the beginning of the classical rhetorical tradition. Aristotle contends that sophists claimed that a law can be unjust as a general matter because "there is in nature a common principle of the just and unjust that all people in some way divine, even if they have no association or commerce with each other, for example . . . as Alcidamas says" (2007, 97 [1373b]). Presumably, when sophists argued that slavery was an affront to the natural dignity and equality of all men, they appealed to a specific Greek audience rooted in customary practices of slavery, but they sought to provoke this audience to recognize its membership in a broader universal audience

(Mootz 2010, 390–94). The only extant text of a sophist arguing against slavery is from Alcidamas: "God set all people free. Nature has made no one a slave" (1995, 276).

4. I would like to thank James Gardner for pointing out that democratic theory embraces this approach as well. For example, rather than viewing politicians as appealing to an audience with settled exogenous preferences, we might best view contemporary politics as the effort first to persuade the polity of its character and desires and then to claim that the speaker best serves this constructed community. Michael Saward calls this the "constitutive dimension of representation" (2010, 9).

5. In *Roper* (2004), the Court overruled *Stanford v. Kentucky* (1989) by finding that the execution of juveniles was unconstitutional. This paralleled a similar holding in *Atkins v. Virginia* (2002) that defendants who were "mentally retarded" at the time of the crime could not be put to death despite earlier precedents to the contrary.

6. Justice Thurgood Marshall provides a poignant example of the construction of the universal audience in his effort to render the death penalty unconstitutional in all cases. In *Gregg v. Georgia* (1976), he argues that the "evolving standards of decency" under the Eighth Amendment are not determined by a public opinion poll but rather by the sentiments of a hypothetical audience that is fully informed about the application of the death penalty. In his dissent, he is exhorting the public to constitute itself as a universal audience rather than a political body expressing raw and prejudicial preferences (Mootz 1988, 612–13).

References

Alcidamas. 1995. "Alcidamas." In *Early Greek Political Thought from Homer to the Sophists*, edited by Michael Gagarin and Paul Woodruff, 276–89. Cambridge: Cambridge University Press.

Alden v. Maine. 1999. 527 U.S. 706.

Aristotle. 2007. *On Rhetoric: A Theory of Civic Discourse.* Translated by George A. Kennedy. 2nd ed. Oxford: Oxford University Press.

Atkins v. Virginia. 2002. 536 U.S. 304.

Blackstone, William. 1983. *Commentaries on the Laws of England.* Vol. 1. The Legal Classic Library. Birmingham, AL: Gryphon Editions. Originally published 1765–70.

Calder v. Bull. 1798. 3 U.S. (3 Dall.) 386, 388.

Crowe, Jonathan. 2019. "Natural Law and the Nature of Law in a Nutshell." *Australasian Journal of Legal Philosophy* 44:100–105.

Duehren, Andrew M. 2015. "At Law School, Justice Kennedy Reflects on Cases, Time as Student." *Harvard Crimson*, October 23, 2015. https://www.thecrimson.com/article/2015/10/23/justice-kennedy-harvard-law.

Fuller, Lon L. 1964. *The Morality of Law.* Rev. ed. New Haven: Yale University Press.

Gonzales v. Carhart. 2007. 550 U.S. 124.

Goodrich, Peter. 1996. *Law in the Courts of Love: Literature and Other Minor Jurisprudences.* London: Routledge.

Gregg v. Georgia. 1976. 428 U.S. 153.

Helmholz, R. H. 2015. *Natural Law in Court: A History of Legal Theory in Practice.* Cambridge: Harvard University Press.

Ignatieff, Michael. 2001. *Human Rights as Politics and Idolatry.* Edited by Amy Gutmann. Princeton: Princeton University Press.

Jelliff, Anne. 2013. "Catholic Values, Human Dignity, and the Moral Law in the United States Supreme Court: Justice Anthony Kennedy's Approach to the Constitution." *Albany Law Review* 76:335–65.

Kelso, Charles D., and Randall Kelso. 2011. "The Constitutional Jurisprudence of Justice Kennedy on Liberty." *Dartmouth Law Review* 9:29–77.

Kengor, Paul. 2013. "Justice Anthony Kennedy: Poster-Boy for Failed Catechesis?" *Catholic Exchange*, July 26, 2013. https://catholicexchange.com/justice-anthony-kennedy-poster-boy-for-failed-catechesis.

———. 2015. "Kennedy Replaces the 'Laws of Nature' with His Own." *Crisis Magazine: A Voice for the Faithful Catholic Laity*, July 3, 2015. https://www.crisismagazine.com/2015/the-laws-of-nature-vs-the-laws-of-anthony-kennedy.

———. 2018. "Anthony Kennedy: Reagan's Worst Mistake." *Catholic World Report*, June 28, 2018. https://www.catholicworldreport.com/2018/06/28/anthony-kennedy-reagans-worst-mistake.

Knight v. Florida. 1999. 528 U.S. 990.

Knowles, Helen J. 2019. *The Tie Goes to Freedom: Justice Anthony M. Kennedy on Liberty.* Updated ed. Lanham, MD: Rowman and Littlefield.

Lochner v. New York. 1905. 198 U.S. 45.

Mootz, Francis J., III. 1988. "The Ontological Basis of Legal Hermeneutics: A Proposed Model of Inquiry Based on the Work of Gadamer, Habermas and Ricoeur." *Boston University Law Review* 68:523–617.

———. 1999. "Law in Flux: Philosophical Hermeneutics, Legal Argumentation, and the Natural Law Tradition." *Yale Journal of Law and the Humanities* 11:311–82.

———. 2006. *Rhetorical Knowledge in Legal Practice and Critical Legal Theory.* Tuscaloosa: University of Alabama Press.

———. 2008. "After Natural Law: A Hermeneutic Response to Law's Quandary." *Rutgers Journal of Law and Religion* 9 (2): 1–21.

———. 2010. "Perelman's Theory of Argumentation and Natural Law." *Philosophy and Rhetoric* 43:383–402.

———. 2018. "Judging Well." *Washington University Jurisprudence Review* 11 (1): 1–37.

Perelman, Chaïm, and Lucie Olbrechts-Tyteca. 1969. *The New Rhetoric: A Treatise on Argumentation.* Translated by John Wilkinson and Purcell Weaver. Notre Dame: University of Notre Dame Press.

Reuben, Richard C. 1992. "Man in the Middle." *California Lawyer* 12 (October): 34–38.

Roper v. Simmons. 2004. 543 U.S. 551.

Rosen, Jeffrey. 2018. "The Justice Who Believed in America." *Atlantic*, June 27, 2018. https://www.theatlantic.com/ideas/archive/2018/06/celebrating-anthony-kennedy/563966.

Saward, Michael. 2010. *The Representative Claim.* Oxford: Oxford University Press.

Smith, Steven D. 2004. *Law's Quandary.* Cambridge: Harvard University Press.

Soper, Philip. 1992. "Some Natural Confusions About Natural Law." *Michigan Law Review* 90:2393–423.

Stanford v. Kentucky. 1989. 492 U.S. 361.

Thiele, Leslie Paul. 2006. *The Heart of Judgment: Practical Wisdom, Neuroscience, and Narrative.* Cambridge: Cambridge University Press.

Trop v. Dulles. 1958. 356 U.S. 86.

Turley, Jonathan. 2018. "Anthony Kennedy Symbolizes Our Struggle to Find Common Ground." *The Hill*, June 28, 2018. https://thehill.com/opinion/judiciary/394603-anthony-kennedy-symbolizes-our-struggle-to-find-common-ground.

Washington v. Glucksberg. 1997. 521 U.S. 702.

Weinreb, Lloyd. 1996. "The Moral Point of View." In *Natural Law, Liberalism and Morality*, edited by Robert P. George, 195–212. Oxford, UK: Clarendon.

8

JUSTICE KENNEDY, FEDERALISM, AND THE
NONPRODUCTION OF RHETORICAL KNOWLEDGE

Darien Shanske

One reason to attend to the rhetoric of legal opinions is that the rhetoric is bound up with other problems, normative or analytic. In this volume, there are many such examples, particularly as to gender.

In this chapter, I attend to Justice Kennedy's rhetoric in order to diagnose a different problem, a failure to produce rhetorical knowledge as to federalism. Rhetorical knowledge, for my purposes, is a communal achievement of public discourse that provides refined guidance as to how to proceed, even when the knowledge is informal, because of its public, dialogic nature. The guidance provided can be to ordinary citizens, judges, lawyers, or even other justices.

Rhetorical knowledge is particularly valuable as to those areas of the law (or life!) that do not lend themselves to rules because rhetorical knowledge need not result in rules, though it is possible for rhetorical knowledge to consist of rules. Justice Kennedy seemed to recognize that federalism was such an area of the law when he repeatedly deployed the notion of a "balance" to explain the proper relationship between the state and federal governments. (And I think he was right to do so.)

Accordingly, Justice Kennedy introduced, and in other cases tried to introduce, balancing tests into federalism jurisprudence. Yet even the introduced test failed, even in the hands of Justice Kennedy, and devolved into ad hoc rules and failed to produce rhetorical knowledge about the proper balance of interests in our federation. Put another way, rather than developing the kind of nuanced federalist jurisprudence that rhetorical knowledge makes possible and Justice Kennedy thought appropriate, the Court only managed to produce rules for an area of law that would be best governed in some other manner.

This chapter can only be suggestive of broad conclusions beyond the case of Justice Kennedy and federalism, but I think that the failure to produce rhetorical knowledge here indicates the considerable preconditions of such knowledge. This knowledge is not merely informal or a knack or a hunch and cannot be the work of a solitary genius. It was not enough for Justice Kennedy to identify the right flexible norm (proportionality) for the right area of law (federalism). Rather, development of the norm required sustained—and prudent—engagement from multiple interlocutors over time.

Rhetorical Knowledge: Definition and Examples

In order to understand what it is that is lacking here I will adopt and develop Mootz's notion of "rhetorical knowledge" (Mootz 1998). What is crucial for my purposes is that rhetorical knowledge represents a collective effort—one that must be continued through time—to create a shared body of norms that can informally guide adjudicatory bodies and individuals subject to the decisions from those bodies, even if only as to how the conversation is to be continued. Rhetorical knowledge is a form of practical knowledge that is created and sustained by public discourse.

Rhetorical knowledge, as a form of practical knowledge, should be distinguished, though not absolutely, from propositional knowledge that guides exclusively by means of rules and, unlike rhetorical and other forms of practical knowledge, has content that can be fully articulated in terms of rules.[1] Justice Antonin Scalia (1989), famously, believed that the rule of law requires that we be guided by such formal rules. Rhetorical knowledge, as a category, especially within law, can and should be understood as a challenge to this way of thinking in (at least) one of two ways. First, and at a minimum, rhetorical knowledge provides an alternative way to organize legal knowledge without formal rules, one that is nevertheless still consistent with the rule of law. And, indeed, Justice Scalia himself understood that rules cannot govern every area of the law (e.g., tort law), and so he implicitly accepted that some other kind of legal knowledge is consistent with the rule of law if these unruly areas of law still manifest the rule of law (Scalia 1989, 1187). Second, more ambitiously (but I think correctly), rhetorical knowledge is a necessary supplement even to formal rules, another point Justice Scalia himself implicitly acknowledged. After all, the formal rules have to come from somewhere, and crafting the right rule for the right domain (say for tax and not for torts) would itself seem to be an exercise in rhetorical knowledge.[2]

This is pretty abstract, and so I offer a few brief examples. First, there is the example of classical Athens (generally following Gagarin 2020). Athens had relatively few written laws and limited legal professionals—no lawyers or judges as such—but there were those who made a living by knowing more about the law than others. We have little evidence as to how the Athenian legal system worked, and what evidence we have does not seem to shed a very positive light. The forensic speeches we have tend to be loaded with ad hominem attacks, for example. Given that the most famous Athenian trial ended with the death of Socrates, it has long been easy to succumb to the temptation to dismiss the Athenian legal system, with its mass democratic juries, as chaotic mob rule.

And yet for the past few decades, there has been a reconsideration. After all, the city of Athens was rather large by ancient standards and very success-ful for rather a long time (Ober 2008). Part of its success was related to its being a good place to engage in trade, but how can this be if every lawsuit was going to be a popularity contest waged before a mass of amateurs likely to favor local traders?

There is no one ingredient in the secret sauce, but the answer that the leading scholars are converging on is hidden in plain sight in these alien-seeming legal speeches. There is a relatively stable and predictable set of norms enforced through the speeches, including through the ad hominem attacks. In commercial cases, for example, it seems that the Athenians were more responsive to formalist arguments precisely because they understood how important the predictability this fostered could be for trade (Lanni 2005). In other contexts, the phenomenon of charging one's opponent with a whole litany of unrelated offenses seems to have been a way to maintain social order with a relatively light touch (Lanni 2010). That is, the Athenian polis had limited ability to monitor the behavior of individual citizens, or interest in doing so, but the citizens understood that if they should end up in litigation, a substantial possibility, then all previous offenses—real or imagined—would be used against them. The fact that the same offenses keep showing up indi-cates a fairly stable system of value that was being appealed to.

This collective knowledge of the norms, which far exceeded the few laws written, represented an example what I am calling rhetorical knowledge, a body of knowledge thick enough and alive enough to guide the behavior of hundreds of thousands of citizens of a large city for almost two hundred years. Put another way, rhetorical knowledge of this sort can be sufficient for the rule of law.[3] Federica Carrugati and colleagues call this knowledge "com-mon knowledge" (2015, 310, building on Hadfield and Weingast 2012; see also Gagarin 2020, 157), but such knowledge is far from common and does not come from—nor is it maintained from—nowhere. It comes from public discourse, from rhetoric.

Here is a more modern example and one that will be of use when we get to Justice Kennedy: the proportionality principle. The proportionality principle as a principle of constitutional law permits an abridging of a right, but only if the collective need is sufficiently important and only to the extent necessary to satisfy that need. Internationally, it is the dominant principle for adjudicating disputes as to constitutional principles. And, not to be coy about this, I think this is the right approach, and it is unfortunate that this is not how US courts address constitutional questions, at least not directly.

Within a proportionality framework, there can be and are disputes, of course. There are even "meta" disputes about the steps one takes to apply the test (Stacey 2019). Yet armed with the notion of rhetorical knowledge (and the example of Athens), we know that the seeming flexibility of a test is not a priori inconsistent with the rule of law. In fact, the proportionality principle suggests that the reverse is true. If the heart of constitutional adjudication, that is, the adjudication of clashes of fundamental rights that all must be given due, is the proportionality principle (and I think it is), then constitutional adjudication cannot do without rhetorical knowledge.

And, indeed, my understanding, as an outsider, is that constitutional courts around the world have used the proportionality principle to create rhetorical knowledge (for instance, see Jackson 2015, 3134–36). Rather than delve into an example from a foreign system, I will add an example of rhetorical knowledge from an area of US constitutional law. The US Supreme Court, in a series of federal constitutional common law decisions, established the following broad norms, or set of norms, as to the functioning of the US federal system. A state may tax the income of a multistate business—imagine Apple or, as in the original cases, a railroad—but only a proportion of that income that the state can reasonably show can be derived from the state. But how can a state do that? Where does a major national railroad derive its income? The Court decided that the standard is that the state must use a reasonable method. Over time, a lot of work had to be done by the courts to limn the limits of the reasonable. Could a simple mathematical proportion (say the ratio of sales in a state) work? Usually, but the formula cannot lead to a result that cannot be justified.[4] Could a state use a formula that was different from that of every other state? Yes, again barring an unjustifiable result (*Moorman* 1978). Without going any further with this, this area of law is providing pretty clear guidance to state legislators and officials as to how to proceed without providing them with a formal rule. This is not just a case of common law accretion, I believe, but an example of the courts collectively closing in on a sensible norm that they then illustrate by examples that legislators attend to and, on occasion, push the limits of, occasioning further cases, and so on.

To be clear about the mechanism that is producing rhetorical knowledge, the proportionality principle (or, in other cases, other informal norms) draws judges into making judgments about the balance of fundamental issues; and it forces the judges to do so as judges, and so they must provide articulate reasons to be interrogated by others, from judges to the public. If different judges used different constitutional rubrics, say, looking for formal rules, then dialogues between such judges would not produce this knowledge. A shared public rubric—or roughly shared rubric—is a precondition for the multiple rounds of discussion that can produce a body of rhetorical knowledge.[5] Just like Athenians could have a practical sense of where they stood thanks to repeated rounds of public litigation, so too do state officials as to the narrow issue of the apportionment of state taxes.

And so this brings me back to Justice Kennedy. Whatever the strengths and weaknesses of his decisions, rhetorical and otherwise, one persistent weakness, analytic and rhetorical, is that he fails to develop rhetorical knowledge in the form of the proportionality principle as to broad issues of federalism, even though he (correctly, by my lights) thinks that such knowledge would be appropriate and, in at least one case, sets up the doctrinal superstructure to produce such knowledge. This failure has multiple causes, and I will foreshadow two. First, Justice Kennedy himself is not rigorous in application of the principle, and I think more importantly, he also has few to no real interlocutors as to the project on the Court. Thus, his moves toward proportionality are either rejected outright or transformed into rules.

Federalism

Justice Kennedy's commitment to federalism was long-standing, sincere, and from where I sit in 2021 after four years of the Trump administration, prescient. Nevertheless, many of his decisions about federalism are an analytic and a rhetorical mess—if those two points are different.

To keep the issue tractable, I will simplify but I hope not oversimplify. By 1988, when Justice Kennedy came to the Court, a few broad things were true. US constitutional law had rejected the notion that there was some special zone of state autonomy. Also, US constitutional law had accepted a broad interpretation of the power of the federal government, especially under the auspices of the Commerce Clause.

Justice Kennedy clearly thought that federal power had gone too far and often speaks of the need to maintain a balance between state and federal power. Now, if the concern were with restoring the proper balance with a thumb on the scale of state and local governments, then one might think that the answer to the problem lay in adopting something like the proportionality principle, which in this guise would be known as the "subsidiarity principle." The subsidiarity principle recognizes the value of a federal system while also acknowledging the need for central power. Thus, the question to be asked is whether the "objectives of the proposed action cannot be sufficiently achieved by the [lower-level government]" (Bermann 1994, 334). Justice Kennedy—and the other four conservative justices—could have spent the 1990s (and beyond) articulating how this principle again and again indicated that the federal government had gone too far, no doubt to the intense frustration of those who would have assessed the measure differently, but, I contend, that process might have produced rhetorical knowledge. Just as state legislators have been given a rough sense as to the limits of their taxing power (at least as to apportionment formulas), and this issue calls for a flexible limit (I believe), federal legislators could have been provided with similarly appropriately rough guidance as to the limits of their power.

But that is not what Justice Kennedy and the other four justices did, and to be fair, that would have required a lot of revision to the structure of US constitutional law. Instead, as different issues and doctrines came to the Court, they crafted new rules that had in the aggregate the effect of limiting the federal government.[6]

Here are some examples. Much of the federal government's power derives from its power over "commerce"—reduce the scope of "commerce," and reduce the power of the federal government. In *United States v. Lopez* (1995), the question was whether the Gun-Free School Zones Act of 1990, which prohibited possession of a firearm in a school zone, exceeded the authority of Congress to regulate commerce. Whether guns near schools, the activity regulated, "substantially affects interstate commerce" does not seem to be the right question to this observer, on the basis of first principles. I think the question should be where the power to protect children from gun violence should reside given the subsidiarity principle. Indeed, Justice Kennedy, in his concurrence in this case, speaks of balancing, but the analysis done by the majority is about the word "commerce."[7]

Now, as the Court crafts these rules, it does argue for why the Court must be vigilant in protecting the power of the states. Is federalism a good in and of itself? At least sometimes, it appears not. As Justice Kennedy explains in his concurrence in *Lopez*, citing a key passage from Federalist No. 51, which was in turn cited by numerous other federalism decisions, "In the compound republic of America, the power surrendered by the people is first divided between two distinct governments, and then the portion allotted to each subdivided among distinct and separate departments. Hence a double security arises to the rights of the people. The different governments will control each other, at the same time that each will be controlled by itself" (*Lopez* 1995, 576). I want to pause here to note that, again writing in 2021 from California, this is not a bad argument as to the states' potential as protectors of individual rights.

But then this brings us to the Court's sovereign immunity decisions. In these cases, the basic question was whether Congress could authorize individuals to sue states for the deprivation of their rights. Viewed in the abstract, it would seem, to me at least, that the answer should be sometimes. After all, if the states are valuable, at least in part, because of the protection that they offer individuals, then sometimes it would seem that the underlying rationale for state power—individual rights—should trump the state sovereignty that is being protected in order to advance individual rights.

Yet the answer the Court eventually arrived at to the question of when the federal government could empower an individual to sue a state for money damages was virtually never. To arrive at this analysis, the Court relied on the Eleventh Amendment, even though the Eleventh Amendment does not, in fact, say what the Court needed it to say. No matter. In a particularly striking opinion by Justice Kennedy, he argued that the Eleventh Amendment only partially codified a structural principle protecting the states: "These holdings reflect a settled doctrinal understanding, consistent with the views of the leading advocates of the Constitution's ratification, that sovereign immunity derives not from the Eleventh Amendment but from the structure of the original Constitution itself" (*Alden* 1999, 728). Now, if the Court was going to imply structural principles with weak historical pedigrees, why do so in this absolutist way? Why not imply the balance that Justice Kennedy seems drawn to?[8]

In another important passage, Justice Kennedy explains, "The States thus retain 'a residuary and inviolable sovereignty.' The Federalist No. 39, at 245. They are not relegated to the role of mere provinces or political corporations, but retain the dignity, though not the full authority, of sovereignty. The generation that designed and adopted our federal system considered immunity from private suits central to sovereign dignity" (*Alden* 1999, 727). There are many things that are strange here. How can a state itself have dignity? If a state does have dignity, then how serious an offense is it to make it pay damages to its own citizens? After all, Justice Kennedy has already explained that an important reason for our federal system is the defense of individuals. Individuals would seem to be the more natural bearers of dignity, and so why is their dignity discounted?[9]

Perhaps one could square the circle here if Justice Kennedy regularly portrayed the states as zealous protectors of individual rights, but that is hardly so. Consider the dormant Commerce Clause context, where Justice Kennedy is quite wary of the states. The dormant Commerce Clause is a constitutional common law doctrine that the Supreme Court uses to strike down state and local laws that discriminate against interstate commerce. The classic example of a law struck down under this clause would be a state tax that falls more heavily on imported goods relative to locally manufactured goods.

Many cases brought to the Court involving this doctrine are much more complicated; one might have thought that Justice Kennedy would be particularly wary of bringing the full weight of federal constitutional law to bear to limit state action in close cases, but that is not so. To take one notable example, in *C&A Carbone, Inc. v. Clarkstown* (1994), Justice Kennedy found it violated the dormant Commerce Clause for a local jurisdiction to require local trash haulers to use a designated local waste-processing site that was itself (essentially) publicly financed. Justice Kennedy finds here a straightforward discrimination: "[the ordinance] hoards solid waste, and the demand to get rid of it, for the benefit of the preferred processing facility" (*Carbone* 1994, 392). Many federalism-minded justices, including Justice Sandra Day O'Connor (concurring in this case), Chief Justice William Rehnquist (dissenting in this case), and eventually Chief Justice John Roberts, who later authored a decision essentially overturning *Carbone*, did not see the action of the town as a discrimination at all. To them, it seemed much more like a public-health law that might have some incidental impact on interstate commerce. Yet, for Justice Kennedy, there was no need to probe the danger or the context: if the state or local action was close enough to a discrimination against the rights of trash haulers to participate in interstate commerce, then it was barred. This is not very dignified treatment of the states by the federal High Court.

In sum, Justice Kennedy is drawn to the figure of the balance to understand the relationship between the state and federal government. He also justifies the importance of this balance in terms of the rights of individuals. Yet when it comes to actually writing decisions, the dignity claims migrate from the individuals to the states themselves in order to defeat the rights of individuals vis-à-vis the states, and this cannot be justified by a Panglossian notion of the states, because in other contexts, Justice Kennedy is very fast to find them to be rights infringers.[10]

Balancing

In fairness, Justice Kennedy did on several occasions try to break out of doctrinal silos and apply a test more in line with his balancing conception of federalism. For instance, in his *Lopez* concurrence, he did seem to want to introduce balancing into Commerce Clause analysis.[11] In another case relating to suits against the states, he tried to introduce a kind of balancing test, an attempt that was rejected by the majority (*Idaho v. Coeur d'Alene Tribe of Idaho* 1997, 277). As to the dormant Commerce Clause, Justice Kennedy was one of the few conservative justices who retained the so-called Pike balancing test as part of the dormant Commerce Clause analysis.

But the most striking example, and the one that I think illustrates my larger point about rhetorical knowledge and how it requires sustained dialogue toward something resembling a common end, relates to the balancing test Justice Kennedy did manage to introduce: the congruence and proportionality test of *City of Boerne v. Flores* (1999). The Fourteenth Amendment explicitly gives Congress the power to enforce its provisions, and hence it appeared particularly untenable to argue as a matter of text, history, or deep structure that Congress could not enforce the Fourteenth Amendment by empowering individual lawsuits against the states. And so the Court did not say that Congress could not do so, but it did say that Congress could only do so if Congress's remedial action was congruent and proportional.

Here, then, was an opportunity for the Court to develop rhetorical knowledge as to the powers of Congress. But did it? And if not, why not? In *Board of Trustees of the University of Alabama v. Garrett* (2001), a decision written by Chief Justice Rehnquist that applies Justice Kennedy's congruent and proportional test, the Court found that Congress's attempt to give individuals a right of action against the states under the Americans with Disabilities Act (ADA) foundered because "there must be a pattern of discrimination by the States which violates the Fourteenth Amendment, and the remedy imposed by Congress must be congruent and proportional to the targeted violation" (374).

This seems, to me at least, a strange way to apply this test. There is nothing about the import of the right being vindicated or the relative impingement on the states, for example. As Justice Stephen Breyer (a fan of proportion-ality) notes in dissent, the Court is treating this constitutional question as an administrative law case, with the Court scrutinizing the record before it rather than considering broad constitutional principles.[12]

Justice Kennedy (with Justice O'Connor) concurred with the majority in *Garrett* and does so on what I would characterize as quite wooden grounds. Justice Kennedy begins his concurrence by emphatically empathizing with the purpose of the ADA: "One of the undoubted achievements of statutes designed to assist those with impairments is that citizens have an incentive, flowing from a legal duty, to develop a better understanding, a more decent perspective, for accepting persons with impairments or disabilities into the larger society. The law works this way because the law can be a teacher. So I do not doubt that the Americans with Disabilities Act of 1990 will be a milestone on the path to a more decent, tolerant, progressive society" (*Garrett* 2001, 375). And yet Justice Kennedy explains that "States can, and do, stand apart from the citizenry. States act as neutral entities, ready to take instruction and to enact laws when their citizens so demand" (375). And it is because states stand apart that "the predicate for money damages against an unconsenting State in suits brought by private persons must be a federal statute enacted upon the documentation of patterns of constitutional viola-tions committed by the State in its official capacity" (376). In other words, as the states stand apart (and indeed are bearers of their own dignity), they can only be held to account for their own wrongs. But this seems to be a case of getting caught up in one's own metaphor. There is nothing terribly wrong about using the notions of "consent" or "dignity" to communicate that state sovereignty should be accorded some weight, but, again, it is quite jarring then to have this metaphorical dignity trump the dignity of actual people whose claims Justice Kennedy is at pains to recognize (at least rhetorically).

But matters get even less satisfying. In another case in this line, *Nevada Department of Human Resources v. Hibbs* (2003), the majority opinion, writ-ten by Chief Justice Rehnquist, holds that "employees of the State of Nevada may recover money damages in the event of the State's failure to comply with the family-care provision of the Act" (725). According to Chief Justice Rehnquist, Congress *did* do its homework as to gender discrimination, and he thinks this has something to do with the fact that gender discrimination receives higher scrutiny (and thus any discrimination would be less justified) (736). So, do we have rhetorical knowledge being created? Not really. Chief Justice Rehnquist is joined by the four more liberal members of the Court, who objected to this whole approach to begin with.[13]

As for Justice Kennedy, he does not accept the idea that the heightened scrutiny that gender receives somehow changes the balance (*Hibbs* 2003, 754). As he explains, "[State sovereign] immunity cannot be abrogated without documentation of a pattern of unconstitutional acts by the States, and only then by a congruent and proportional remedy. There has been a complete failure by respondents to carry their burden to establish each of these necessary propositions" (759). The fact that this is a "complete" failure indicates, I think, that there is little to learn as to what would pass muster for Justice Kennedy.[14]

And, indeed, Justice Kennedy wrote a 2012 decision refusing to extend *Hibbs*'s reasoning from family-care leave to self-care leaves. Once again, there is primarily a resort to very strong dismissal of the evidence, no discussion of the underlying right or balancing of any kind: "The 'few fleeting references' to how self-care leave is inseparable from family-care leave fall short of what is required for a valid abrogation of States' immunity from suits for damages" (*Coleman* 2012, 41).

Conclusion

So where does this leave us as to rhetorical knowledge regarding sovereign immunity? Suppose Congress wanted to abrogate state sovereign immunity. How much evidence would it need of what kind of behavior? How proportionate need the remedy be? There have been multiple opinions on the matter from the Court, but, I would submit, they do not really converge on the kind of practical guidance that rhetorical knowledge makes possible. Most obviously, this is because many, most, of the justices are not playing the same game. More subtly, the effect of this dispersion is that there has not been the dialogue that could create this knowledge. And, finally, the absence of dialogue allowed weaker arguments, and modes of argument, to rule the day.

That all said, there is rhetorical knowledge here of a kind. I think one would be quite right to conclude that Congress is going to have a tough time abrogating sovereign immunity, because a majority of the justices on the current Court either do not believe in balancing at all (Justice Neil Gorsuch following Justice Scalia?) or would follow Justice Kennedy in applying the analysis in a manner that Congress would always fail (Justice Brett Kavanaugh, following Justice Kennedy?). But that is just a bright-line rule pretending to be something else; it is hardly a communal achievement of creating meaningful context-sensitive distinctions informally, which is what, it seemed, Justice Kennedy was (rightly) interested in developing in connection with federalism.

And this points to what I take to be the final melancholy lesson. There are some areas of the law that require non-rule-based rhetorical knowledge if they are to be done well. We need to work together in a very particular way in order to achieve this knowledge and have not yet done so as to federalism.

Notes

Many thanks to all the remarkable participants in the two days of workshops that preceded the publication of this volume for their insightful comments about this chapter and on many other topics. And special thanks to the editors of this volume, David Frank and Jay Mootz, for convening us and giving me still more remarkable feedback. I received excellent research assistance from Julianna Bramwell and Melissa Quintero.

1. This distinction is borrowed from Constable 1994, 85–95. Note that rhetorical knowledge can produce rules; it is just that it does not have to in order to be successful.

2. Scalia ends his famous essay on the rule of law with discussion of Justice Oliver Wendall Holmes's famous failure to create the right rule in a particular tort context (Scalia 1989, 1187–88). For further immanent critique of Justice Scalia's jurisprudence, see Shanske 2018.

3. Another important contribution made possible by rhetorical knowledge is that such knowledge can still provide guidance even at moments of constitutional crisis, when more traditional signposts are lacking—hence the ability of the Athenians to recover from the crises of 411 and 403 (see Shanske 2011, 2013).

4. In one of the few cases in which a state loses, it doubled the value of a railroad's property in the state while essentially conceding that the railroad's property in the state had not changed (and hence the doubling of the tax was an artifact of the formula) (*Norfolk and Western Railway Company* 1968).

5. I am far from the first to note that the proportionality principle could create rhetorical knowledge, though not using this vocabulary: "Proportionality analysis in Canada and some other jurisdictions provides a structured and transparent mode of reason-giving that produces justifications likely to be meaningful, or at least understandable, to the parties and other audiences for constitutional courts' decisions" (Jackson 2015, 3142).

6. The rules themselves do represent knowledge too, but the point is that they do not provide the flexibility that is a special possibility of rhetorical knowledge and that I think Justice Kennedy was interested in introducing into the Court's federalism jurisprudence.

7. Justice Kennedy begins his concurrence with balancing and ends with parsing the word "commerce" in the same sentence: "The statute before us upsets the federal balance to a degree that renders it an unconstitutional assertion of the commerce power, and our intervention is required" (*Lopez* 1995, 580).

8. And why not imply it in the context of the Commerce Clause, where it is sorely needed and could at least direct the courts to ask the right questions?

9. For more on the perversity of the personification here, including analogy to an earlier Court's personification of corporations, see Sherry 2000. Justice Kennedy personifies the sovereign in a similarly problematic way in the immigration context (see Saucedo, chap. 15 in this volume).

10. To be sure, one can explain this phenomenon here by noting, as Frank Colucci (2019) does, that Justice Kennedy places free markets above federalism. But note that this insight complicates but not does resolve our riddle, because *why* does Justice Kennedy put his thumb on the scale for markets and not individuals? Should the logic of the balance not suggest balancing in both cases and not nearly per se rules?

11. Another example from *Lopez*: "Absent a stronger connection or identification with commercial concerns that are central to the Commerce Clause, that interference contradicts the federal balance the Framers designed and that this Court is obliged to enforce" (1995, 583). On the one hand, the analysis here involves the notion of "commerce," but on the other is the notion of a balance. The logic of the sentence seems to be that the balance is maintained through patrolling the meaning of the word "commerce," which only works if the limits of "commerce" and the proper limits of federal power are the same, which is hard to believe. As Ash Bhagwat noted to me, the litigation involving the Affordable Care Act represented a kind of reductio of the use of "commerce" as a touchstone. In that case, as to the limits of federal power, the question whether the central government can regulate a giant portion of the national economy took a backseat to arcane arguments as to whether the insurance mandate was or was not action and, if not action, was therefore not commerce.

12. There are a lot of problems with this analogy, including that the congressional record is not an administrative record and that it is not consistent with separation-of-powers principles for the Court to treat it as such (Buzbee and Schapiro 2001).

13. There is one other case where the plaintiffs win, but that is because Justice O'Connor joined the four more liberal members. Note that at that point, Justice Scalia repents of ever joining *Boerne* and accurately sees its test as in the proportionality family: "I joined the Court's opinion in *Boerne* with some misgiving. I have generally rejected tests based on such malleable standards as 'proportionality,' because they have a way of turning into vehicles for the implementation of individual judges' policy preferences" (*Tennessee v. Lane* 2004, 556, Scalia, J., dissenting).

14. One prominent commentator (Sherry 2003) concludes that these decisions cannot be reconciled and urges the Court to move toward a proper balancing test that takes into account the importance of the rights involved and does not just involve the Court in second-guessing congressional evidence collection.

References

Alden v. Maine. 1999. 527 U.S. 706.
Bermann, George A. 1994. "Taking Subsidiarity Seriously: Federalism in the European Community and the United States." *Columbia Law Review* 94:331–456.
Board of Trustees of the University of Alabama v. Garrett. 2001. 531 U.S. 356.
Buzbee, William W., and Robert A. Schapiro. 2001. "Legislative Record Review." *Stanford Law Review* 54:87–161.
C&A Carbone, Inc. v. Clarkstown. 1994. 511 U.S. 383.
Carugati, Federica, Gillian K. Hadfield, and Barry R. Weingast. 2015. "Building Legal Order in Ancient Athens." *Journal of Legal Analysis* 7:291–324.
City of Boerne v. Flores. 1999. 521 U.S. 507.
Coleman v. Court of Appeals of Maryland. 2012. 566 U.S. 30.
Colucci, Frank. 2019. "Justice Anthony Kennedy's Federalism and the Limits of State Sovereignty." *Publius: The Journal of Federalism* 49 (3): 490–514.
Constable, Marianne. 1994. *The Law of the Other*. Chicago: University of Chicago Press.

Gagarin, Michael. 2020. *Democratic Law in Classical Athens*. Austin: University of Texas Press.

Hadfield, Gillian K., and Barry R. Weingast. 2012. "What Is Law? A Coordination Model of the Characteristics of Legal Order." *Journal of Legal Analysis* 4:471–514.

Idaho v. Coeur d'Alene Tribe of Idaho. 1997. 521 U.S. 261.

Jackson, Vicki C. 2015. "Constitutional Law in an Age of Proportionality." *Yale Law Journal*. 124:3094–3197.

Lanni, Adriaan. 2005. "Relevance in Athenian Courts." In *The Cambridge Companion to Ancient Greek Law*, edited by Michael Gagarin and David Cohen, 112–28. Cambridge: Cambridge University Press.

———. 2010. "Social Norms in the Courts of Ancient Athens." *Journal of Legal Analysis* 1:691–736.

Moorman Manufacturing Co. v. Bair. 1978. 437 U.S. 267.

Mootz, Francis J., III. 1998. "Rhetorical Knowledge in Legal Practice and Theory." *Southern California Interdisciplinary Law Journal* 6 (3): 491–547.

Nevada Department of Human Resources v. Hibbs. 2003. 538 U.S. 721.

Norfolk and Western Railway Company v. Missouri State Tax Commission. 1968. 390 U.S. 317.

Ober, Josiah. 2008. *Democracy and Knowledge: Innovation and Learning in Classical Athens*. Princeton: Princeton University Press.

Scalia, Antonin. 1989. "The Rule of Law as Law of Rules." *University of Chicago Law Review* 56:1175–88.

Shanske, Darien. 2011. "Thucydides and Lawfulness." In *Thucydides—a Violent Teacher? History and Its Representations*, edited by Georg Rechenauer and Vassiliki Pothou, 199–212. Goettingen: V&R Unipress.

———. 2013. "Thucydides and Law: A Response to Leiter." *Legal Theory* 19:282–306.

———. 2018. "Rhetoric, Jurisprudence, and the Case of Justice Scalia; or, Why Did Justice Scalia, of All Judges, Write like *That*?" In *Justice Scalia: Rhetoric and the Rule of Law*, edited by Brian G. Slocum and Francis J. Mootz III, 123–36. Chicago: University of Chicago Press.

Sherry, Suzanna. 2000. "States Are People Too." *Notre Dame Law Review* 75:1121–32.

———. 2003. "The Unmaking of Precedent." *Supreme Court Review* 203:231–68.

Stacey, Richard. 2019. "The Magnetism of Moral Reasoning and the Principle of Proportionality in Comparative Constitutional Adjudication." *American Journal of Comparative Law* 67:435–75.

Tennessee v. Lane. 2004. 541 U.S. 509.

United States v. Lopez. 1995. 514 U.S. 549.

PART 4

JUDGMENT AND
JUSTICE KENNEDY'S ETHOS

9

JUSTICE KENNEDY'S FREE SPEECH OPTIMISM

Ashutosh Bhagwat

In the thirty years that Justice Anthony M. Kennedy served on the United States Supreme Court, he was almost certainly the most free-speech-protective justice of his era (Bhagwat and Struhar 2013). He also authored a large number of extremely influential First Amendment decisions, including his separate opinion in *International Society for Krishna Consciousness v. Lee* (1992) seeking to revive the public forum doctrine; his pathbreaking (and infamous) opinion for the Court in *Citizens United v. Federal Election Commission* (2010) upholding the right of corporations to spend money to fund campaign speech; his majority opinion in *Sorrell v. IMS Health Inc.* (2011) turbocharging the commercial speech doctrine (and possibly extending First Amendment protection to data transfers); and, most recently, his opinion in *Packingham v. North Carolina* (2017) extending strong constitutional protections to speech on social media, in the course of celebrating this technology as the new epicenter for public debate and engagement. Given the importance of these opinions, there seems no doubt that Justice Kennedy's influence over free speech law will endure for decades; indeed, his influence here may be greater than any field, other than gay rights (see *Romer* 1997; *Lawrence* 2003; *Windsor* 2013; *Obergefell* 2015).

Another noteworthy feature of Justice Kennedy's free speech jurisprudence is its striking optimism about the ability of individuals to receive, process, and understand information and about the impact of speech and information on society. Especially in the political sphere, Justice Kennedy's decisions reflect a faith in human nature and societies and in the impact of technology on both (Bhagwat 2018, 1340). This chapter examines the optimistic rhetoric of Justice Kennedy's free speech opinions in the context of political speech, with the goal of teasing out what exactly he expresses optimism *about*. The chapter concludes by raising some difficult, and difficult-to-answer, questions about what the goals of the justice's expressed optimism were and what impact his expressed optimism had on his decisions.

Political Optimism: The Informed Citizen

Many of the most important recent First Amendment battles have concerned restrictions on political speech and on the places where political speech must be permitted by the government. These cases, which doctrinally range from the public forum doctrine to campaign-finance reform to more recent restrictions on online speech, all have in common one underlying question: to what extent the government should be permitted to place restrictions on speech in order to protect citizens from the distortion of public discourse by overly loud voices, or from unwanted intrusions into their lives. Resolving these cases requires the justices to determine whether citizens are best placed to make choices for themselves or whether they require shielding by the government. And on these issues, Justice Kennedy's rhetoric almost always expresses confidence in the ability of citizens to choose for themselves.

Consider in this regard the *International Society for Krishna Consciousness* case mentioned earlier. The issue in the case was whether the public, nonsecured areas of airports constitute "public forums" within which the government must broadly permit speech, subject only to narrow time, place, or manner restrictions (the case was decided almost a decade before the 9/11 attacks, when airports looked very different). The majority opinion, authored by Chief Justice William Rehnquist, rejected the public forum designation, relying in part on the burden that speech in airports imposed on travelers carrying luggage who must "alter their paths, slowing both themselves and those around them" to avoid speakers. Strikingly, the majority conceded that the resultant inconvenience "may seem small" but nonetheless concluded that it was sufficient to preclude public forum status for airports (*International Society for Krishna Consciousness* 1992, 684–85). Justice Kennedy, on the other hand, would have none of this. Here is what he had to say on the subject: "The liberties protected by our [public forum] doctrine derive from the Assembly, as well as the Speech and Press Clauses of the First Amendment, and are essential to a functioning democracy. . . . Public places are of necessity the locus for discussion of public issues, as well as protest against arbitrary government action. At the heart of our jurisprudence lies the principle that in a free nation citizens must have the right to gather and speak with other persons in public places" (696). In short, Justice Kennedy's expressed view was that the political rights and obligations of citizens trumped the more mundane concerns of travelers and airport operators. Citizens, he clearly believed, could and should cope with the inconvenience necessary to sustain our democracy.

Airports are not the only context in which Justice Kennedy has prioritized democratic debate over other concerns. In a series of cases stretching over Justice Kennedy's tenure on the Supreme Court, the Court was faced with challenges to laws and injunctions restricting antiabortion protests outside abortion clinics (see, e.g., *Madsen* 1994; *Schenck* 1997; *Hill* 2000; *McCullen* 2014). In these cases, even though Justice Kennedy had been the key, swing vote in *preserving* the constitutional right of access to abortions (see, e.g., *Casey* 1992; *Whole Women's Health* 2016), he consistently joined or authored opinions favoring free speech over other state interests, including protecting potential patients (see, e.g., *Madsen* 1994, 784–815; *Schenck* 1997, 385–95). Some of Justice Kennedy's most striking rhetoric on this topic can be found in his opinion in *Hill v. Colorado* (2000) dissenting from the majority's validation of a statute that forbade individuals from coming within eight feet of any individual near an abortion clinic for the purpose of "engaging in oral protest, education, or counseling." The majority defended the law in part on the basis of the state's interest in shielding patients from unwanted and unpleasant encounters with protesters (*Hill* 2000, 729–30). Justice Kennedy responded as follows: "The liberty of a society is measured in part by what its citizens are free to discuss among themselves. Colorado's scheme of disfavored-speech zones . . . are antithetical to our entire First Amendment tradition. To say that one citizen can approach another to ask the time or the weather forecast or the directions to Main Street but not to initiate discussion on one of the most basic moral and political issues in all contemporary discourse, a question touching profound ideas in philosophy and theology, is an astonishing view of the First Amendment" (768). As with inconvenience to travelers, then, Justice Kennedy's views reflect a singular faith in the ability of citizens, even in difficult personal circumstances, to engage in public debate and dialogue.

Another area in which Justice Kennedy has relentlessly insisted on the ability of voters to absorb and process information, and so has opposed regulatory efforts to shield them, is campaign-finance reform. First of all, in cases concerning restrictions on the size of financial contributions by individuals to political candidates, Justice Kennedy has insisted that restrictions on contributions are unnecessary and unconstitutional because disclosure laws permit citizens to judge whether politicians have been "bought" or unduly influenced by large contributions (*Randall* 2006, 264–65). Justice Kennedy's reasoning in this regard is best expressed in *Nixon v. Shrink Missouri Government PAC*, in which he dissented from a decision upholding strict limits imposed by Missouri on contributions to candidates for statewide office (2000, 405). Responding to the majority's argument that such limits were necessary to prevent the actuality or appearance of corruption, Justice Kennedy insisted that given the transparent disclosure enabled by the internet, "the public can then judge for itself whether the candidate or the officeholder has so overstepped that we no longer trust him or her to make a detached and neutral judgment" (408). And toward the end of the opinion, he posits that the Constitution requires one answer to the question of whether officeholders can act free of undue influence: "open, robust, honest, unfettered speech that the voters can examine and assess in an ever-changing and more complex environment" (409). Even more so than in *Krishna Consciousness* and *Hill*, this passage demonstrates Justice Kennedy's enduring faith in the sophistication and judgment of citizens in navigating loud, fractious, and sometimes overwhelming public debates—a faith that in his view is written into the First Amendment.

There is no question, however, that the part of election law in which Justice Kennedy has had the greatest impact, and has most strongly expressed his faith in the ability of citizens to absorb and assess multitudinous speakers, is in the area of corporate political expenditures. Very early in his career on the Supreme Court, Justice Kennedy dissented from a majority opinion upholding a Michigan state law banning corporations and unions from spending treasury funds to support or oppose political candidates (*Austin* 1990, 695). In response to the argument that such a ban was necessary to prevent large amalgamations of corporate wealth from distorting political debate, Justice Kennedy said this: "The suggestion that the government has an interest in shaping political debate by insulating the electorate from too much exposure to certain views is incompatible with the First Amendment. '[T]he people in our democracy are entrusted with the responsibility for judging and evaluating the relative merits of conflicting arguments'" (706, quoting *First National Bank of Boston* 1978, 791). But it was thirty years later, when the Court finally overruled the previously quoted decision, that Justice Kennedy made his most famous contribution to the law in this area. In *Citizens United v. Federal Election Commission* (2010), the Court was faced with a challenge to §203 of the Bipartisan Campaign Reform Act of 2002 (BCRA), better known as McCain-Feingold (2 U.S.C. §441b). This provision prohibited corporations and unions from using their general treasury funds to pay for "electioneering communications," defined as "broadcast, cable, or satellite communications" that referred by name to candidates for federal office and were made close in time to primary or general elections. The Court had upheld §203 seven years earlier in *McConnell v. Federal Election Commission* (2003), a 5–4 decision from which Justice Kennedy had dissented. In *Citizens United*, a new 5–4 majority, in an opinion authored by Justice Kennedy, struck down §203, overruling both *McConnell* and *Austin*, the 1990 Michigan case discussed earlier on which *McConnell* had relied. *Citizens United* is best remembered as the case that bestowed full First Amendment rights on corporations, including for-profit entities. But in explaining *why* corporations deserved such rights, Justice Kennedy unsurprisingly also had much to say about the audience for corporate speech, which is to say citizens and voters.

The opinion thus begins its First Amendment analysis by explaining why it is essential to protect the kind of campaign speech regulated by §203: "Speech is an essential mechanism of democracy, for it is the means to hold officials accountable to the people. The right of citizens to inquire, to hear, to speak, and to use information to reach consensus is a precondition to enlightened self-government and a necessary means to protect it. . . . For these reasons, political speech must prevail against laws that would suppress it, whether by design or inadvertence" (*Citizens United* 2010, 339–40; citations omitted). Justice Kennedy and the Court explain that the reason corporations should possess free speech rights is that failure to do so "deprive[s] the public of the right and privilege to determine for itself what speech and speakers are worthy of consideration" and later adds, "it is inherent in the nature of the political process that voters must be free to obtain information from diverse sources in order to determine how to cast their votes" (341). Finally, in rejecting the "anti-distortion" rationale for restricting corporation speech, the Court concludes, "When the government seeks to use its full power, including the criminal law, to command where a person may get his or her information or what distrusted source he or she may not hear, it uses censorship to control thought. This is unlawful. The First Amendment confirms the freedom to think for ourselves" (356). The basic message here is quite clearly that it is precisely because we rely on, and trust, voters to process and sort out information from a variety of sources that the First Amendment presumptively prohibits restrictions on political speech by disfavored speakers such as corporations.

The same theme appears later in the opinion, in Justice Kennedy's response to the argument that even independent corporate expenditures can result in corporate influence over, or access to, federal elected officials. Justice Kennedy first rejects the idea that such access or influence equates to corruption (*Citizens United* 2010, 359, citing *McConnell* 2003). Then, crucially, Justice Kennedy responds to the argument that such access or influence can create the appearance of corruption and so undermine public faith in democracy this way: "The appearance of influence or access, furthermore, will not cause the electorate to lose faith in our democracy. By definition, an independent expenditure is political speech presented to the electorate that is not coordinated with a candidate. The fact that a corporation, or any other speaker, is willing to spend money to try to persuade voters presupposes that the people have the ultimate influence over elected officials. This is inconsistent with any suggestion that the electorate will refuse 'to take part in democratic governance' because of additional political speech made by a corporation or any other speaker" (*Citizens United* 2010, 360, citing *McConnell* 2003, 140 [quoting *Nixon* 2000, 390]). As with Justice Kennedy's discussion of general First Amendment principles and his rejection of the risk of "distortion" of political debate by corporate wealth, his narrow definition of corruption—essential to the result in *Citizens United*—relies entirely on his confidence in the ability of voters to distinguish between true corruption and the unfettered workings of public discourse. Whatever the merits of that position, Justice Kennedy's opinions in this area are remarkably consistent.

Citizens United may be the most visible expression of Justice Kennedy's views on this subject, but it was neither the last nor the most sweeping. Rather, Justice Kennedy's abiding, publicly expressed faith in democratic dialogue was stated most clearly in his last important First Amendment opinion, issued in 2017, which concerned restrictions of speech on social media. The issue in *Packingham v. North Carolina* was the constitutionality of a North Carolina statute that forbade registered sex offenders from accessing "commercial social networking Web sites" that permit minors to become members (which is to say, essentially all major social networking platforms; *Packingham* 2017)—Facebook, for example, permits children thirteen and older to create accounts (Facebook, n.d.). Packingham, a registered sex offender, created a Facebook account under a false name and then posted a statement on the account about beating a traffic ticket. He was prosecuted and convicted for violating North Carolina's social media ban. The majority opinion by Justice Kennedy assumed that the law only applied to websites commonly understood to be social media, such as Facebook and Twitter (the law's poor wording could easily have been interpreted to reach websites such as Amazon; *Packingham* 2017, 1736–37), but nonetheless concluded that the statute, though content neutral, imposed an excessive burden on sex offenders' First Amendment rights (1737–38).

Striking as the result in *Packingham* is (registered sex offenders, after all, are not exactly the most popular members of our society), the reasons Justice Kennedy gives for his result are even more so. He begins by enunciating a "fundamental principle of the First Amendment . . . that *all* people have access to places where they can speak and listen, and then, after reflection, speak and listen once more" (*Packingham* 2017, 1735). He then notes that today, the key "place" where speech and debate occur "is cyberspace—the 'vast democratic forums of the internet' in general, and social media in particular" (1735, quoting *Reno* 1997, 868 [citation omitted]). Social media, he explains, permits individuals "to engage in a wide array of protected First Amendment activity on topics 'as diverse as human thought'" (1735–36, quoting *Reno* 1997, 868 [citation omitted]). He also explains in more detail what this means: "On Facebook, for example, users can debate religion and politics with their friends and neighbors or share vacation photos. On LinkedIn, users can look for work, advertise for employees, or review tips on entrepreneurship. And on Twitter, users can petition their elected representatives and otherwise engage with them in a direct manner. Indeed, Governors in all 50 states and almost every Member of Congress have set up accounts for this purpose" (1735). In short, it is precisely the ubiquity and elasticity of social media that, according to Justice Kennedy, make it such an essential forum for debate in the modern world.

It is worth taking a step back to consider the significance of these words. What jumps out first of all is Justice Kennedy's technological optimism (Bhagwat 2018, 1340).[1] He describes social media as an unqualified boon to social and political discourse, the new and supremely democratic public forum. This is despite the fact that the *Packingham* decision was announced in June 2017, in the wake of the 2016 presidential election, in which the polarizing effects of social media had become quite clear. Nor does the *Packingham* opinion touch on the complications produced by the fact that social media, unlike previous public fora, is privately owned. As with campaign-finance reform, Justice Kennedy seems to be assuming that citizens will be able to overcome these problems and harness social media to engage in meaningful and thoughtful public debate.

The other obvious lesson of the passages quoted earlier is that while Justice Kennedy recognizes (and would protect) a wide variety of online communications, his, and in his view the First Amendment's, primary focus is on public debate relevant to democratic self-governance, including both public debate regarding "religion and politics" and the ability to petition and communicate with elected officials. The assumption that the First Amendment, first and foremost, advances democratic goals may not seem surprising or controversial until one remembers that the issue in *Packingham* was the scope of First Amendment rights of *convicted and registered sex offenders.*[2] These are individuals who are as much social outcasts as any in the contemporary United States, and in many if not most states, they lack even the right to vote. Yet in the *Packingham* case, Justice Kennedy is inviting them in to join the national political debate on equal terms, going so far as to argue that "even convicted criminals—and in some instances especially convicted criminals"—deserve that right (*Packingham* 2017, 1737). This is a staggeringly optimistic—and yes, democratic—vision of a Madisonian system of government that is built on public debate that shapes and informs public opinion,[3] and it encapsulates Justice Kennedy's rhetoric of political optimism perfectly.

Cross Currents: The Corrupt Official

As the preceding section demonstrated, Justice Kennedy's judicial opinions about political speech are infused with, and driven by, particularly ambitious and optimistic views regarding the role that citizens can and should play in a constitutional democracy. One might have thought that his opinions would be equally positive about the actual workings of our democracy. In fact, however, the story here is more complicated. While Justice Kennedy certainly does not despair of democracy, his opinions do fairly consistently express concerns or doubts regarding the functioning of democratic governance, the ethics of elected officials, and especially the role of dark money in undermining both.

One example of such concerns can be found in Justice Kennedy's dissent in *Nixon v. Shrink Missouri Government PAC*, discussed earlier. Recall that in that case, Justice Kennedy objected to Missouri's relatively strict limits on campaign contributions to candidates for state office. One reason Justice Kennedy gives for opposing contribution limits is his (reasonable) view that the Supreme Court's foundational campaign-finance decision, *Buckley v. Valeo* (1976), had, by forbidding restrictions on campaign expenditures but permitting restrictions on contributions to candidates, set the stage for the entry of "covert speech" into political campaigns, via the mechanism of soft-money contributions to political parties used to fund "issue advocacy" (*Nixon* 2000, 406–7). Speech funded by direct candidate contributions, on the other hand, which the Court permits states to restrict, is "subject to full disclosure and prompt evaluation by the public" (407). Justice Kennedy then describes the need for candidates to raise soft money to counteract an opponent's soft money as "selling out to" the campaign-finance system that *Buckley* had created (407). Under this system, outsider candidates such as the one in *Nixon*, Justice Kennedy says, "cannot challenge the status quo unless he first gives into it" (407). Indeed, toward the end of his dissent, he expresses a broader thought regarding the relationship between citizens and officeholders: "Whether our officeholders can discharge their duties in a proper way when they are beholden to certain interests both for reelection and for campaign support is, I should think, of constant concern not alone to citizens but to conscientious officeholders themselves. There are no easy answers" (409). He then concludes this thought by arguing that this conundrum's solution that was adopted by the Constitution is open debate, accompanied by disclosure, through which citizens can assess and judge their representatives' conduct—but interestingly, he never says that this system will actually be *effective* in constraining representatives. Reading only slightly between the lines, the reason for this discontinuity seems to be that Justice Kennedy's optimism regarding citizens does not extend to politicians.

Nor is Justice Kennedy's opinion in *Nixon* unique in expressing these sorts of concerns. Another example is his brief concurring opinion in *Randall v. Sorrell* (2006). Though he agreed with the majority's decision to invalidate Vermont's extraordinarily strict restrictions on campaign contributions, Justice Kennedy unsurprisingly disagreed with the majority's reasoning because it continued to impose relatively relaxed scrutiny on such limits. Similarly to his views on soft money, he argued in *Randall* that the campaign-finance restrictions the Court has upheld created a "void" that has been filled by "new entities such as political action committees. . . . Those entities can manipulate the system and attract their own elite power brokers, who operate in ways obscure to the ordinary citizen" (2006, 265). Again, Justice Kennedy fears the ability of money to "manipulate the system," presumably meaning corrupt officeholders.

Finally, Justice Kennedy's majority opinion in *Citizens United* contains a particularly interesting twist on this theme. Elucidating why it is essential to protect campaign speech by corporations, he explains that corporations regularly communicate to and cooperate with government officials. Furthermore, this "cooperation may sometimes be voluntary, or it may be at the demand of a Government official who uses his or her authority, influence, and power to threaten corporations to support the Government's policies. Those kinds of interactions are often unknown and unseen," while the speech forbidden by campaign-finance laws "is public, and all can judge its content and purpose" (*Citizens United* 2010, 355). In other words, protection for corporation speech is necessary as an antidote to private corruption, as well as coercion of corporations by public officials.

Foundational Themes: Education and Aspiration

We now turn to the murky areas of meaning and motive. For what purpose did Justice Kennedy express the optimism (about citizens) and pessimism (about public officials) described in this chapter? And to what extent did Justice Kennedy actually share those views? The answers to these questions are, of course, uncertain and fundamentally unknowable. But giving attention to context and events does hint at some answers.

The opinions by Justice Kennedy quoted and discussed in this chapter span almost the entirety of Justice Kennedy's tenure on the Supreme Court, from 1990 through 2017 (Justice Kennedy served on the Court from 1988 through 2018). Consider the fact that this period was one of the most politically divisive and contentious in modern US history. Beginning with Newt Gingrich's no-holds-barred Republican Revolution of 1994, to the impeachment of President Bill Clinton in 1998, through (after a brief respite following the 9/11 attacks) the divisions over President George W. Bush's Iraq War, through the sharp, racially tinged hostility evinced by Republicans and conservatives toward President Barack Obama, culminating in the ugly and extraordinarily divisive presidency of Donald Trump, this was a time in which politicians of all stripes, and ultimately the American people, were at each other's throats. Yet this was the period in which Justice Kennedy was writing opinions extolling the ability of US citizens to objectively assess speech and engage in thoughtful debate.

Consider further that when Justice Kennedy penned perhaps his greatest paean to democratic debate, the *Citizens United* decision in 2010, conservatives around the country (including a certain then-reality-television star and real estate developer) were spreading and lapping up lies about President Obama's place of birth. Indeed, even in 2016, *72 percent* of Republicans expressed doubts about Obama's birthplace, despite his Hawaiian birth certificate being in the public record (Clinton and Roush 2016). In this atmosphere and in this time, could Justice Kennedy truly have believed in the ability of the public "to determine for itself what speech and speakers are worthy of consideration" (*Citizens United* 2010, 341)? It does seem hard to believe.

Justice Kennedy's final significant free speech opinion, in the 2017 *Packingham* decision, strongly reinforces these doubts. In *Packingham*, recall, Justice Kennedy composed an ode to the "vast democratic forums of the internet," the new public square (2017, 1735, quoting *Reno* 1997, 868). Yet this opinion was issued in June 2017, in the immediate aftermath of the 2016 election in which the internet had obviously and publicly been weaponized to spread hate, lies, and "fake news" (and, we were soon to learn, manipulated by foreign actors and governments, notably Russia; Isaac and Wakabayashi 2017). The year 2017 spelled the end, not the beginning or height, of internet utopianism. Yet the *Packingham* opinion does not even hint at these developments. In short, unless Justice Kennedy spent his entire career as a Supreme Court justice entirely cut off from the society around him, including the realities of the social impact of the internet, the gap between his rhetoric and the real world seems unbridgeable.

Why, then, the optimism? The beginning of an answer, I suggest, might be found in the fact that Justice Kennedy was first and foremost an educator. He served as an adjunct professor of constitutional law at the McGeorge School of Law in Sacramento, California, even before he was appointed to the Supreme Court, and he continued in that role throughout his time on the Court. And his role as educator did not end at the courthouse gates. Justice Kennedy's judicial opinions are notable for their rhetorical flourishes clearly directed at the public rather than a technical, legal audience, including famously his contributions to the Joint Opinion in the leading modern abortion case ("At the heart of liberty is the right to define one's own concept of existence, of meaning, of the universe, and of the mystery of human life"; *Casey* 1992, 851) and his opinion upholding a constitutional right to same-sex marriage ("the annals of human history reveal the transcendent importance of marriage. The lifelong union of a man and a woman always has promised nobility and dignity to all persons"; *Obergefell* 2015, 656). In short, Justice Kennedy very much embraced the educative role of the Court that Alexander Bickel so famously commented on (1986, 26). And to this end, Justice Kennedy sought throughout his career to convince his students and the general public that the Constitution was a force for good in our society and a source of lasting, shared values. In rhetorical terms, Justice Kennedy's opinions can be understood as a form of epideictic oratory, as characterized by Chaïm Perelman and Lucie Olbrechts-Tyteca: an effort to educate his audience members and strengthen their commitment to those common values (1971, 50–54).

And therein might lie the answer. Just as in *Obergefell v. Hodges* (2015), the same-sex marriage case, Justice Kennedy presented an aspirational (or perhaps epideictic) view of marriage, so in his free speech jurisprudence, he set forth an aspirational view of US democracy, not democracy as it actually is but democracy as the Constitution envisions it could and should be. And because the political rights of the First Amendment—not just speech but also freedoms of press, assembly, association, and petition—are essential elements of that democracy (see generally Bhagwat 2020), this also necessitates an aspirational view of those rights. The First Amendment envisions a democracy founded on free and open debate among an engaged and rational citizenry, and so that is the vision Justice Kennedy presents, instead of the rather more tawdry reality. Put differently, an aspirational view of democracy and of the role of public discourse in that democracy requires an aspirational view of the demos, the People, and that is precisely what Justice Kennedy provides in his First Amendment opinions (as Rebecca Zietlow points out in chapter 14 in this volume, Justice Kennedy's idealized vision of citizens is not restricted to free speech law). It is a form of populism, undoubtedly, but a thoroughly intellectualized version of it.

On a related note, Justice Kennedy's absolutist embrace of rights of free expression may well have necessitated his highly positive descriptions of citizens. To do otherwise, to adopt a more nuanced view of citizens' abilities, would logically have required him to consider adopting a more limited and balanced approach to First Amendment rights. But this he was clearly not willing to do, presumably because of concerns that such an approach has a tendency to end up balancing away important rights in the name of shifting social needs, including the need to manage public discourse. As an educator, Justice Kennedy may also have believed that he could bring his fellow citizens around to accepting the necessity of strong free speech rights (even for corporations) through an ongoing dialogue with the public of the sort that Bickel postulated (1986, 239–43). That he does not appear to have succeeded in that goal with respect to large segments of the public reflects the simple reality that not all dialogues accomplish their educative goals.

Finally, this understanding also explains why Justice Kennedy's free speech opinions do *not* present a particularly optimistic view of government or public officials. This is because while the US republican experiment is built on optimistic hopes about the people and their role, it most assuredly does not make the same assumptions about government. To the contrary, the fabric of the Constitution, including the separation of powers, the Bill of Rights, and the very concept of a government of limited powers, assumes the opposite: that the state, and the officials that make it up, cannot be trusted with power. There is thus no contradiction in Justice Kennedy simultaneously touting the ability of citizens to use free speech to hold public officials accountable and his concerns about those officials themselves. All of this flows directly from the Constitution of the United States, as amended.

Conclusion

This chapter argues that Justice Anthony M. Kennedy's free speech opinions present a relentlessly optimistic vision of the role of citizens in our democracy and the ability of citizens to parse and engage in public dialogue. At the same time, he is much less confident in the conduct of public officials. While the exact reasons for these consistent themes are, of course, impossible to know, the chapter concludes by suggesting one possibility. Perhaps Justice Kennedy's opinions set forth a picture of our democracy, and our citizenry, not as they actually are but as we and the Constitution aspire that they should be, in order to bolster our shared commitment to the Constitution.

Notes

1. The cited paper presents empirical evidence that Justice Kennedy was the most technology-optimistic justice of the Roberts Court across a range of free speech cases.

2. I have argued elsewhere that Justice Kennedy is quite right in equating First Amendment rights with democracy (Bhagwat 2017, 873–74).

3. "Public opinion sets bounds to every government, and is the real sovereign in every free one" (Madison 1791, 170).

References

Austin v. Michigan Chamber of Commerce. 1990. 494 U.S. 652.

Bhagwat, Ashutosh. 2017. "When Speech Is Not Speech." *Ohio State Law Journal* 78:839–85.

———. 2018. "Candides and Cassandras: Technology and Free Speech on the Roberts Court." *Washington University Law Review* 95:1327–52.

———. 2020. *Our Democratic First Amendment.* Cambridge: Cambridge University Press.

Bhagwat, Ashutosh, and Matthew Struhar. 2013. "Justice Kennedy's Free Speech Jurisprudence: A Quantitative and Qualitative Analysis." *McGeorge Law Review* 44:167–99.

Bickel, Alexander M. 1986. *The Least Dangerous Branch: The Supreme Court at the Bar of Politics.* 2nd ed. New Haven: Yale University Press.

Buckley v. Valeo. 1976. 424 U.S. 1.

Citizens United v. Federal Election Commission. 2010. 558 U.S. 310.

Clinton, Josh, and Carrie Roush. "Poll: Persistent Partisan Divide over 'Birther' Question." *NBC News*, August 10, 2016. https://www.nbcnews.com/politics/2016
-election/poll-persistent-partisan-divide-over-birther-question-n627446.

Facebook. n.d. "How Do I Report a Child Under the Age of 13 on Facebook?" Accessed July 5, 2022. https://www.facebook.com/help/157793540954833.

First National Bank of Boston v. Bellotti. 1978. 435 U.S. 765.

Hill v. Colorado. 2000. 530 U.S. 703.

International Society for Krishna Consciousness v. Lee. 1992. 505 U.S. 672.

Isaac, Mike, and Daisuke Wakabayashi. 2017. "Russian Influence Reached 126 Million Through Facebook Alone." *New York Times*, October 30, 2017. https://www.nytimes
.com/2017/10/30/technology/facebook-google-russia.html.

Lawrence v. Texas. 2003. 539 U.S. 558.

Madison, James. 1791. "Public Opinion." *National Gazette*, December 19, 1791. In *Papers of James Madison*, edited by William T. Hutchinson et al., vol. 14, 170. Charlottesville: University of Virginia Press, 1983.

Madsen v. Women's Health Center, Inc. 1994. 512 U.S. 753.

McConnell v. Federal Election Commission. 2003. 540 U.S. 93.

McCullen v. Coakley. 2014. 573 U.S. 464.

Nixon v. Shrink Missouri Government PAC. 2000. 528 U.S. 377.

Obergefell v. Hodges. 2015. 576 U.S. 644.

Packingham v. North Carolina. 2017. 582 U.S. __, 137 S. Ct. 1730.

Perelman, Chaïm, and Lucie Olbrechts-Tyteca. *The New Rhetoric: A Treatise on Argumentation*. Notre Dame: University of Notre Dame Press, 1971.

Planned Parenthood of Southeastern Pennsylvania v. Casey. 1992. 505 U.S. 833.

Randall v. Sorell. 2006. 548 U.S. 230.

Reno v. American Civil Liberties Union. 1997. 521 U.S. 844.

Romer v. Evans. 1997. 517 U.S. 620.

Schenck v. Pro-Choice Network of Western New York. 1997. 519 U.S. 357.

Sorrell v. IMS Health Inc. 2011. 564 U.S. 552.

United States v. Windsor. 2013. 570 U.S. 744.

Whole Women's Health v. Hellerstedt. 2016. 579 U.S. 582.

10

STRONGMEN AND NEUROTICS: VISIBLE STRUGGLE
AND THE CONSTRUCTION OF JUDICIAL ETHOS

James A. Gardner

Twenty years ago, on December 12, 2000, I suffered the most profound professional crisis of my career. That was the day the Supreme Court decided *Bush v. Gore* (2000). It was also the day that I became unable—deeply, viscerally, involuntarily—to take the Supreme Court of the United States seriously.

When you teach constitutional law for a living, an inability to take the Supreme Court seriously counts as a profound disability. Teachers of constitutional law, it seems to me, ought to believe that judicial decisions interpreting the Constitution comprise serious attempts by serious people to engage in a complex, genuinely engaging, and often challenging interpretational enterprise. Such teachers should not believe, with the most reductionist of political scientists, that judicial decisions are nothing more than elaborately disguised expressions of fixed ideological precommitments or, even worse, of partisan preference. They should believe that the Constitution and the body of case law interpreting it are legal objects of considerable potential coherence and integrity and that appeals to that coherence and integrity in well-crafted arguments, structured according to established disciplinary conventions, are capable of guiding self-consciously open-minded judges to the best interpretations. So I had taught my students.

In reflecting on why this decision cost me my faith in the Court, I am quite certain it was not the result. True, the result was bad and the reasoning utterly unconvincing. But anyone can, on any given occasion, reason badly to a poor decision. Who has not done so? Errors of craft may disappoint an audience, but they are rarely sufficient to alienate it entirely. My crisis was precipitated, I believe, by something else—by the ease with which the Court reached its result.

To get there, the majority had to repudiate decades of jurisprudence. The conservative justices in particular aggressively took positions that they had stood against for their entire careers. To be sure, such things are not impossible, even for a common law court committed to respect for precedent. Courts may discover unexpectedly that they have trod a false path. Judges may find they have erred; they may even find that some of their deepest commitments were mistaken and must now be revised. But when these events occur—when a court reverses course, when judges embrace positions they have previously not merely rejected but derided—a reader is entitled to assume that the path to decision was a difficult and wrenching one, that it involved, in short, some kind of struggle, and that any adequate justification for the ruling will require the court or judge to reveal and explain that struggle.

For me, then, what caused my instantaneous loss of faith in the Supreme Court was precisely the lack of evidence of any struggle. The ruling came much too easily, and the facility with which the Court repudiated itself smelled overwhelmingly of insincerity. Like the citizens of George Orwell's Oceania, the justices in the majority suddenly found themselves to have been mistaken in their belief that they were at war with Eurasia; it had been Eastasia all along (Orwell 1961, 228).

The problem, then, was not one of logos, faulty though it may have been, but of ethos: the justices in the majority showed themselves to be judges who are capable of insincerity and willing to practice it professionally and that they were therefore unworthy of credence. If a single failure of logos is easily forgiven, a single failure of ethos often is not because it reveals, suddenly and all at once, a poor character unworthy of trust and thus unworthy of belief. For judges of long tenure, it may also suggest a previous pattern of duplicity, compounding the sin.

In this chapter, I offer some reflections on the role of struggle in judging, the extent to which judges should reveal their struggles as an element of ethical self-construction, the nature of the contemporary US audience for judicial ethos, and finally, how Justice Anthony Kennedy managed—or, more to the point, neglected to manage—his own judicial ethos on those occasions when he revealed that he had struggled to reach a result, a neglect that I believe diminished the regard in which he was held by many segments of his audience.

Struggle as an Inherent Element of Judging

Although generalizations about judging may be risky, it seems safe to conclude that when judges decide cases, they will inevitably struggle in at least
some of them. Judging requires the application in concrete circumstances
of a set of skills and a body of knowledge, an inherently complex task. It is a
task that requires, as the job title clearly indicates, the exercise of judgment,
and the application of judgment cannot in every case be obvious and easy.
The very idea that "judgment" needs to be exercised in certain circumstances
implies some degree of both complexity and discretion; we do not speak of
"judgment" in cases where tasks call merely for mechanical, discretionless
administration.

If judging inherently requires struggle in at least some cases, what kind
of struggle does it entail? Most obviously, a judge's struggle might be *professional*—the kind in which the judge's professional skill, expertise, or craft
is challenged by the circumstances of decision. In our system, these might
be cases in which the judge must sift and evaluate conflicting evidence or
discern the meaning of controlling texts or precedents that are obscure and
indeterminate or sort out the interaction of principles of decision that point
unexpectedly in different directions in the circumstances of the case at hand.
One thinks, for example, of Justice Robert Jackson's influential concurrence in *Youngstown v. Sawyer* (1952), in which he expresses his "surprise[]
at the poverty of really useful and unambiguous authority applicable to concrete problems of executive power as they actually present themselves" and
laments that "just what our forefathers did envision, or would have envisioned had they foreseen modern conditions, must be divined from materials almost as enigmatic as the dreams Joseph was called upon to interpret
for Pharaoh" (634).

There is a second kind of struggle that a judge might conceivably confront: a *personal* struggle. Here, judges might encounter circumstances in
which the required application of professional judgment is so open-textured
and indeterminate as to invite them to fill the gap in authoritative decisional
principles from their own private stock of values and beliefs. Perhaps worse,
judges might in some circumstances perceive a possible conflict between
their professional duties and their personal values and must choose which
to honor. I think, for example, of Justice Felix Frankfurter's opinion in *West
Virginia v. Barnette* (1943), in which he opens his dissent to the Court's ruling
invalidating compulsory flag salutes for schoolchildren with an anguished

and almost shockingly personal cri de coeur: "One who belongs to the most vilified and persecuted minority in history is not likely to be insensible to the freedoms guaranteed by our Constitution" (646).

Here, it may be useful to refer to two images commonplace in Western iconography. One shows the exterior of a house or building at night. The dwelling is dark inside, the residents asleep or gone home, except that on an upper floor, one window is illuminated. Inside, some decision-maker is up late, pacing the floor, agonizing over a difficult yet highly consequential decision that must be taken by morning. The other image is of the Last Judgment, a frequent theme in medieval and Renaissance painting. In these images, Jesus assigns to each person who ever lived eternal bliss or damnation. Often, Mary is depicted at Jesus's side, clinging to his arm, pleading for mercy for the condemned souls. But Jesus's judgment is swift and sure. He knows precisely what each soul deserves, and indeed, no decision in this sequence, no matter how dire and permanent the consequences, can by hypothesis be difficult or challenging for the Son of God.

Most people, I assume, would prefer the first kind of judge, certainly in their own case, though what kind of judge they might prefer for *others* is a different question, to which I shall return. The legal sociologist Tom Tyler (2006) has done intriguing work suggesting that people are more likely to accept a decision, even one against them, if they feel they have gotten a fair chance to present their side. Yet in the US federal judicial system today, the propriety of judges engaging in personal struggle—and thus the legitimacy of appeals, expressly or implicitly, to their personal ideals, to their ethos—is deeply contested. Originalism and textualism, the dominant interpretational approaches advanced by the political right, are offered explicitly for the purpose of extruding personal struggle from the judicial enterprise by claiming that all problems are resolved fully by the relevant positive law, interpreted in accordance with a highly prescriptive and deliberately constraining methodology. Supreme Court justices, on this view, are not high government officials authorized to participate in complex processes of democratic self-rule; they are, on the contrary, low-level bureaucrats, automatons who, in Chief Justice John Roberts's famous phrase, merely call balls and strikes (CNN 2005). If any judgment is required of them, it is of the professional kind only.

At the same time, even if some degree of struggle is inherent in the enterprise of judging, we should not expect any judge to struggle in every case; some cases must be easy ones, even if they are not the same cases for every judge. Nevertheless, the judges of the US Supreme Court should by all rights struggle more frequently than judges of other courts do. An apex court with discretionary jurisdiction, like the Supreme Court, certainly ought to expend its limited resources on the most difficult cases, not the easiest ones. Moreover, the common law method itself should produce a docket of more rather than less complexity: as easy cases fall out of the litigation pipeline because the outcome has been settled by prior decisions, what is left should be a steady stream of cases falling in areas of remaining uncertainty.

In sum, we should expect judges to struggle in some cases, and we should expect justices of the US Supreme Court to struggle more often than most.

Should Judges Reveal Their Struggles?

To say that judges are likely to struggle some of the time, or even that occasional struggle is inherent in the job description, says nothing about the extent to which judges ought to *reveal* their struggles to those for whom they write.

Judges in our system do not merely decide cases; they issue written decisions explaining them, and the only conceivable purpose of explanation is, ultimately, persuasion. Like any rhetor, then, a judge will benefit from the cultivation of a sound and persuasive judicial ethos. Thus, in Aristotle's terminology, judges should strive to present themselves as possessing "good sense, good moral character, and goodwill" (2004, book 2, part 1) or, in Quintilian's formulation, simply as "a good man" (2001, book 1). It follows that the extent to which judges should reveal to their audiences their own internal struggles in deciding hard cases depends entirely upon the extent to which doing so will support their claim to what Aristotle called "virtues of character" (2004, book 2, part 1). This in turn depends upon contingent social understandings of what counts as a virtue of character in a judge—that is, upon whether having to struggle to reach a decision in a hard case is a quality of a good and virtuous judge. And that in turn depends on prevailing conceptions of the ideal judge. Is it the light in the window or the Last Judgment? Does the ideal judge find the act of judgment hard and complex or facile and effortless?

In the abstract, for a judge to reveal that he or she found a case difficult and struggled to reach a decision would seem to cultivate potential ethical benefits but also a certain degree of ethical risk. On the benefit side of the ledger, to reveal such a struggle may be to reveal, at bottom, one's humanity. Judges who frankly admit the difficulty or complexity of a case show themselves to be persons of conscience who desire sincerely to do the right thing and who perceive a sense of personal responsibility for doing so—they present themselves, in short, as grown-ups and thus as the right people to be in charge. In his land-mark work *The Great Chain of Being*, the intellectual historian Arthur Lovejoy described how the rise of Romanticism from the sixteenth to eighteenth centuries displaced an earlier, Enlightenment preference for "the simplification and the standardization of thought and life" in favor of the belief that "diversity itself is of the essence of excellence." On this worldview, "the glory of the imperfect" is something to be celebrated, along with efforts to "reconstruct in imagination the distinctive inner life" of other people (1936, 293). A judge's revelation of inner struggle thus might reveal his or her individual humanity in a way much appreciated in the Romantic tradition.

Similarly, judicial revelation of struggle might display a certain kind of perspicacity or wisdom: the perspicacity to distinguish genuinely difficult cases from genuinely easy ones and the wisdom to treat them differently and to do so honestly. Judicial revelation of struggle may also serve a socially and politically useful function by educating the bar and the public. It may show, in a particularly vivid and engaging way, that seemingly easy cases are in fact not so and that superficially simple issues, when examined soberly and dispassionately, reveal themselves to have multiple sides that demand respectful consideration. And perhaps most fundamentally, judicial revelation of struggle, to the extent it reflects these qualities, may help persuade key audiences to accept the validity of the ultimate rulings, thus shoring up the legitimacy and stability of judicial power.

On the other hand, a judge's display of struggle may in certain circumstances, or for certain audiences, court risk. It might reveal weakness rather than strength in circumstances where strength is highly valued. It might suggest intellectual mediocrity if the case is in fact not one that is truly difficult. If the struggle itself is more difficult or intense than justified by the circumstances, revealing it might inadvertently reveal a kind of neuroticism, an inability to make decisions—a fatal defect in a judge and one in particular that might invite not merely disbelief but contempt. A judge's struggle, if inappropriate, might show the judge to lack a sound understanding of what is truly valuable.

Yet, by the same token, the *lack* of struggle in circumstances where struggle is appropriate also carries risks. It might reveal the judge to possess an unjustified overconfidence in his or her analytic skills. It might demonstrate in the judge a certain kind of blindness to important aspects of a case and its context. It might show the judge to be inappropriately ideological or rigid or even inhumane. Judges who do not struggle when struggle is called for might reveal a lack of conscience or an inappropriate indifference to the suffering of the parties or a lack of sense of personal responsibility for his or her own actions.

It is thus impossible to say a priori whether judicial ethos will gain or suffer by revealing the existence and extent of personal or professional struggle. Much depends on the audience and the kind of character it values in its judges.

The Contemporary US Audience for Judicial Ethos

None of this would matter much were the audience for opinions of US courts relatively homogeneous in its preferences concerning judicial character. There are good reasons, however, to believe that the contemporary US audience for judicial opinions is profoundly divided on this very issue.

For decades following the conclusion of the Second World War, Americans were for the most part bound together by a strong, widely shared commitment to philosophical liberalism (Hartz 1955, 9). This commitment, concisely expressed in the Declaration of Independence, holds that all citizens are fundamentally equal, that they possess inherent dignitary rights as human beings, and that the legitimacy of government authority depends on the consent of the governed, conferred principally through free and fair democratic processes. For virtually the entirety of the second half of the twentieth century, political disagreements among Americans were for the most part best understood as intramural disagreements within liberalism.

That consensus began to erode toward the end of the twentieth century, when the commitments of the two major parties began to diverge. Although the Democratic Party has during this period moved somewhat to the left, "the Republican Party has made a much more pronounced shift toward extremism" (Pierson and Schickler 2020, 51). That shift consolidated in 2016, when Republicans nominated and then propelled into office Donald Trump, the nation's first overtly authoritarian president (Levitsky and Ziblatt 2018, 2). As leading Republicans, after initially repudiating Trump, subsequently closed ranks behind him following his election, the Republican Party departed the domain of liberalism altogether and became, in Paul Krugman's words, "an authoritarian regime in waiting" (2020, 346).

This development has significant consequences for how different segments of the public perceive their leaders, and thus for the question of ethos, because it goes to the qualities and characteristics that Americans most value in their leaders. It is unclear whether individual preferences for political systems result from socialization or innate psychological predispositions

(Stenner 2005). Nevertheless, it is perfectly clear that certain kinds of preferences travel together and that the qualities of leadership valued by those who find authoritarianism an appealing system of political organization differ from the qualities most valued by those attracted to democratic liberalism. For example, supporters of right-wing populist parties elsewhere in the world—and of Donald Trump in the United States—prefer a "strong leader" at a substantially higher rate than supporters of other parties and candidates (Diamond 2019, 151). Americans who hold racist and exclusionary views of American identity are four times as likely to endorse a "strong leader" than those who deny the importance of European heritage to national identity (Diamond 2019, 152). Supporters of Donald Trump are nine times more likely than others "to oppose congressional oversight of the president," ten times more likely to oppose "media scrutiny of the president," and five times more likely to agree that the president "should not be bound by laws or court decisions he thinks are wrong" (Diamond 2019, 153).

At the same time, those attracted to and those repelled by strongman forms of political organization respond favorably to very different kinds of appeals. The world's most pressing problems tend to be highly complex, yet successful populist authoritarians around the world typically address salient issues in simple terms and offer simple solutions. And, as Yascha Mounk has observed, "if the solutions to the world's problems are as obvious as [populist leaders] claim, then political elites must be failing to implement them for one of two reasons: either they are corrupt, or they are secretly working on behalf of outside interests" (2019, 39)—again, a neat and tidy explanation that denies complexity. More detailed studies of the language politicians use to appeal to voters at opposite ends of the political spectrum support this contention. Consistent with evidence that conservatives have a higher need than liberals for "closure, which reflects preferences for reducing ambiguity and uncertainty," politicians attempting to appeal to conservatives favor "short, unambiguous statements," while those attempting to appeal to liberals tend to use "longer compound sentences, expressing multiple points of view" (Schoovelde et al. 2019, 1).

It seems logical to conclude, then, that liberal democrats and authoritarians—and, by inference, Democrats and Republicans—value different character traits not only in their elected leaders but also in their judges, especially the highest-ranking judges. We can fill out the picture a bit simply by taking note of the fact that the Supreme Court justices most revered by the American left and right projected very different personas from the bench.

On the left, judicial heroes such as Justices William Brennan and Thurgood Marshall cultivated a judicial ethos of skepticism of power, provisionality of commitments, acknowledgment of complexity, and empathetic humanity. On the right, Justice Antonin Scalia cast himself as a supporter of strong government power, as entirely certain and self-assured in his beliefs and their application in all settings, and frequently as contemptuous of those who disagreed, often accusing them implicitly of stupidity or venality. Liberals, it seems, are more likely to prefer judges who pace the floor late into the night, while conservatives, and certainly authoritarians, seem to prefer the utter certainty and absolute self-confidence of Jesus condemning the damned—above all when those damned are members of groups other than their own (Sullivan and Transue 1999, 633).

As a result, an American judge cannot simply adopt an ethos that is in some universal sense simply the "best" or "most appropriate" ethos for a judge. On the contrary, judges must make a choice—they must choose an ethos best suited to convince the audience they aim to persuade. That audience need not be a political or a partisan one. Judges might aim to convince no one other than themselves or some ideal reader—their mother, a high school English teacher, a college roommate, or some fictional construct of an ideal reader.

On the other hand, although judges may choose their ethos, they cannot choose their audiences. Judicial opinions, especially those of the Supreme Court, are widely read, including by politicians and partisans, and the judicial ethos adopted by a judge will neither appeal to nor contribute to the persuasion of all of them. Moreover, some of these audiences—the president, Congress, lower court judges, the bar, the media, the general public— play an important role in shaping the public meaning and determining the success of judicial rulings, even if judges are not writing specifically for them. This suggests that modern American judges must do more than simply choose the ethos they think best suited to persuade the audiences they most value. If part of being a good judge means tending the institutional authority and legitimacy of your court, then judges who wish to be the best and most effective judicial officers possible must do more than simply choose an ethos upon assuming the bench; they must actively *manage* their ethos during their period of public service. They must ensure, to the extent possible, that their ethos contributes to the success—and not the undermining—of the judicial enterprise in which they and their colleagues are engaged.

Justice Kennedy and the (Mis)Management of Judicial Ethos

Whatever degree of mastery Justice Anthony Kennedy may have displayed in other domains during his thirty years on the bench, the management of judicial ethos was a skill that he did not practice with great success, above all in cases he found difficult. Like any conscientious judge, Justice Kennedy from time to time struggled to a result and often chose to reveal those struggles to his readers. But if Justice Kennedy intended his revelation of struggle to enhance the persuasiveness of his opinions, more often than not, doing so failed to produce the desired effect. Instead, Justice Kennedy's struggles often seemed unconvincing and idiosyncratic, conducted in arenas where few found the real struggles to lie, thereby frequently earning him scorn from the right and incredulity from the left.

A paradigmatic example of this clumsiness appears in Justice Kennedy's swing opinion in *Vieth v. Jubelirer*, decided in 2004, at the midpoint of his Supreme Court career. In *Vieth*, Democrats brought a challenge under the Equal Protection Clause to a grotesque partisan gerrymander enacted by the Republican-controlled Pennsylvania legislature during the 2000 redistricting cycle. Prior to enactment of the redistricting plan, Pennsylvania's US House of Representatives delegation had been evenly divided between Republicans (eleven) and Democrats (ten), reflecting with rough accuracy the close division of political opinion within the state. After redistricting (and the loss of two congressional seats), Republicans were able reliably to control thirteen or fourteen of the nineteen newly drawn districts (Anderson 2018, 103).

On only one prior occasion, in *Davis v. Bandemer* (1986), decided eighteen years earlier, had the Court adjudicated a constitutional claim of partisan gerrymandering. In a splintered and inconclusive decision, six justices had agreed that a sufficiently egregious partisan gerrymander violates the Equal Protection Clause, but the Court split decisively over how to operationalize that standard, yielding no majority opinion. During the intervening eighteen years, lower federal courts struggled badly to make sense of *Bandemer*. Indeed, despite the growing frequency and sophistication of partisan gerrymandering in the intervening two decades, not a single plaintiff had prevailed on such a claim. When the Court decided to take up *Vieth*, then, it commanded the rapt attention not merely of the legal community but of the entire political apparatus.

Observers were deeply disappointed. The Court dismissed the partisan gerrymandering claim but did so in another badly splintered opinion, one that did nothing to clear up the confusion left by *Bandemer* and indeed worsened it. A minority consisting of Justice Scalia, Chief Justice William Rehnquist, Justice Sandra Day O'Connor, and Justice Clarence Thomas ruled that all partisan gerrymandering claims should be dismissed as nonjusticiable for lack of a judicially manageable standard. A different minority, consisting of Justices John Paul Stevens, David Souter, Ruth Bader Ginsburg, and Stephen Breyer, argued in three separate opinions that partisan gerrymandering claims are justiciable, and each opinion advanced a different standard for evaluating such claims. None of these standards commanded more than two votes. That left the outcome of the case to Justice Kennedy.

Justice Kennedy clearly found this an extremely difficult case, and he revealed his struggle openly. The plaintiffs, he contended, were asking the federal courts to undertake an "unprecedented intervention in the American political process." As a result, he said, "great caution is necessary when approaching this subject" (*Vieth* 2004, 306). Precedent, he warned, offers only an "absen[ce of] sure guidance," compounded by a "dearth of helpful historical guidance" (308–9). "The impossibility of full analytical satisfaction," he concluded, "is reason to err on the side of caution" (311).

That caution, in Justice Kennedy's mind, left him with only one option: to split the difference between the two blocs. While acknowledging "weighty arguments for holding cases like these to be nonjusticiable," Justice Kennedy maintained nevertheless that such arguments "are not so compelling that they require us now to bar all future claims of injury from a partisan gerrymander" (*Vieth* 2004, 309). Although he thus refused to join the plurality in closing the door to future partisan gerrymandering claims, in the case before him, Justice Kennedy was nevertheless unwilling to affirm the prevailing *Bandemer* standard; to endorse any of the standards proposed by the litigants or by any other justice; to pluck an appealing standard from the legal or political science literature ("the parties have not shown us, and I have not been able to discover, helpful discussions on the principles of fair districting" [308]); or to propose any standard of his own design. Instead, he spent considerable space lamenting the fact that "there are yet no agreed upon substantive principles of fairness in districting" and that, as a result, "we have no basis on which to define clear, manageable, and politically neutral standards for measuring the particular burden a given partisan classification imposes on representational rights" (307–8). On the other hand, he continued, such standards may emerge in some future case, and "if workable standards do emerge, . . . courts should be prepared to order relief" (317).

In the end, then, Justice Kennedy concurred in the judgment of dismissal but took up no particular substantive position. For every other justice, the eighteen-year failure of federal courts to gain any purchase on the pressing problem of partisan gerrymandering demonstrated conclusively the need for a change of direction. For Justice Kennedy, the possibility that continued patience might be rewarded counseled staying the course: "by the timeline of the law 18 years is rather a short period" (*Vieth* 2004, 312), he proclaimed— small comfort to those deprived of meaningful political influence immediately under the new map and on into a future of unforeseeable duration.

There can be little doubt that Justice Kennedy intended his ruling to be perceived as an exercise of Solomonic wisdom. It acknowledges strength on each side, disposing of the immediate controversy on what Justice Kennedy clearly believed to be sound principles, while simultaneously holding open the possibility of a different and more considered result in the future. In this respect, however, the opinion struck most readers as a catastrophic failure. Instead of projecting an ethos of sage moderation, Justice Kennedy succeeded only in revealing himself not only as shockingly indecisive but as a model of hand-wringing neuroticism.

From the right, Justice Kennedy's opinion earned scorn and mockery. In Justice Scalia's words, Justice Kennedy's position "boils down to this: 'As presently advised, I know of no discernible and manageable standard that can render this claim justiciable. I am unhappy about that, and hope that I will be able to change my opinion in the future.'" "What," Justice Scalia added, quite accurately, "are the lower courts to make of this pronouncement?" (*Vieth* 2004, 305). From Justice Kennedy's left, his opinion was met with politely expressed incredulity. Justice Souter, for example, rejected the contention that the nearly two-decade failure of federal courts to solve the problem of partisan gerrymandering should be treated as a "counsel of despair." Instead, Justice Souter suggested, an appropriate understanding of the judicial role requires the members of the Court to take personal responsibility for devising a solution to a problem that all admit to be of constitutional dimension: "Since the Court has created the problem no one else has been able to solve, it is up to us to make a fresh start" (345). An acknowledgment of difficulty, on this view, is only the starting point: competent and responsible judges must go on to engage and overcome that difficulty; he or she should not simply wait around for someone else to solve the problem while protected constitutional rights are being actively and deliberately infringed.

What unites these critiques is their agreement that Justice Kennedy had refused to do the one thing every judge must do: decide. He had struggled but had in the end lacked the internal fortitude to resolve his struggle one way or the other; instead of mastering the judicial task, it had mastered him.

To those on the right, to whom an appropriate judicial ethos required a display of strength and certainty, this revealed Justice Kennedy to be weak and
contemptible. To those on the left, for whom an appealing judicial ethos
required not merely acknowledgment of complexity but the resolve to grind
one's way to a resolution, Justice Kennedy's opinion revealed a deep misun-
derstanding of what is important to the enterprise of judging. His struggle,
for them, occurred in a strange and inappropriate location: instead of wrestling with the merits of a difficult issue, Justice Kennedy struggled over how
to respond to complexity. Thus, from either perspective, Justice Kennedy in
Vieth revealed a judicial ethos that was poorly suited to command the respect
of—and thus to persuade—any of his colleagues or, in the end, any other
audience that Justice Kennedy might have been aiming to convince.

Conclusions

Every successful judge must adopt a professional ethos calculated to persuade, but in the twenty-first-century United States, how to do so is badly
complicated by the political polarization of the audience for judicial opinions. The right and left have gravitated not only toward distinct political
commitments but toward distinct styles of leadership. As a result, different
segments of a splintered citizenry respond favorably to different kinds of
appeals that display very different kinds of character traits. As in other areas
of politics, the middle seems to have disappeared almost entirely; respect for
those with whom we disagree seems no longer a consensual political value
(Levitsky and Ziblatt 2018; Sood and Iyengar 2016).

In this environment, contemporary Supreme Court justices may have little choice but to pick a side and cultivate an ethos suited to persuade their target audience. Perhaps enough of a middle still remains to support the hope
that displays of traditional judicial virtues—learning, impartiality, sound
legal analysis, and so forth—remain capable of commanding an audience
broader than mere copartisans and that the enterprise of judging has not yet
been irrevocably reduced in the public mind to an exercise in pure political
preference.

Justice Anthony Kennedy had the bad luck to join the Court just as the late-
twentieth-century liberal consensus, in which he had been raised as a lawyer
and a judge, was beginning to crumble. We might say that Justice Kennedy
responded in a characteristically human way: by clinging stubbornly to the
conception of judicial ethos into which he was raised even as it began to

fray. We might thus say that Justice Kennedy managed his ethos precisely by refusing to manage it, and perhaps there is some truth to that contention. Yet I think the problem ran deeper. If, as political scientists tell us, the liberal democrats of the contemporary left moved less than their counterparts who have ended up on the authoritarian right, Justice Kennedy's failure to impress the liberals on those occasions when he joined them—and in so doing to occupy a position of judicial leadership derived from his character rather than the accident of his role as the swing vote—suggests that his skills of ethos management may not have been up to the job. Justice Kennedy has his admirers, but it seems to me that they are admirers of his results more than any aspect of his judging, including the judicial character he cultivated during his time on the bench.

References

Anderson, Carol. 2018. *No Vote: How Voter Suppression Is Destroying Our Democracy*. New York: Bloomsbury.

Aristotle. *Rhetoric*. 2004. Translated by W. Rhys Roberts. New York: Dover.

Bush v. Gore. 2000. 531 U.S. 98.

CNN. 2005. "Roberts: 'My Job Is to Call Balls and Strikes and Not to Pitch or Bat.'" CNN.com, September 12, 2005. https://www.cnn.com/2005/POLITICS/09/12/roberts.statement.

Davis v. Bandemer. 1986. 478 U.S. 109.

Diamond, Larry. 2019. *Ill Winds: Saving Democracy from Russian Rage, Chinese Ambition, and American Complacency*. New York: Penguin.

Hartz, Louis. 1955. *The Liberal Tradition in America: An Interpretation of American Political Thoughts Since the Revolution*. New York: Harcourt, Brace.

Krugman, Paul. 2020. *Arguing with Zombies: Economics, Politics, and the Fight for a Better Future*. New York: Norton.

Levitsky, Steven, and Daniel Ziblatt. 2018. *How Democracies Die*. New York: Crown Books.

Lovejoy, Arthur O. 1936. *The Great Chain of Being*. Cambridge: Harvard University Press.

Mounk, Yascha. 2019. *The People vs. Democracy: Why Our Freedom Is in Danger and How to Save It*. Cambridge: Harvard University Press.

Orwell, George. 1961. *1984*. New York: Signet Classics.

Pierson, Paul, and Eric Schickler. 2020. "Madison's Constitution Under Stress: A Developmental Analysis of Political Polarization." *Annual Review of Political Science* 23:37–58.

Quintilian, Marcus Fabius. 2001. *The Orator's Education*. Translated by Donald A. Russell. Cambridge: Cambridge University Press.

Schoovelde, Martijn, Anna Brosius, Gijs Schumacher, and Bert N. Bakker. 2019. "Liberals Lecture, Conservatives Communicate: Analyzing Complexity and Ideology in 381,609 Political Speeches." *PLOS One* 14 (2): e0208450. https://doi.org/10.1371/journal.pone.0208450.

Sood, Gaurav, and Shanto Iyengar. 2016. "Coming to Dislike Your Opponents: The Polarizing Impact of Political Campaigns." Unpublished paper. https://papers.ssrn.com/sol3/papers.cfm?abstract_id=2840225.

Stenner, Karen. 2005. *The Authoritarian Dynamic.* Cambridge: Cambridge University Press.

Sullivan, J. L., and J. E. Transue. 1999. "The Psychological Underpinnings of Democracy: A Selective Review of Research on Political Tolerance, Interpersonal Trust, and Social Capital." *Annual Review of Psychology* 50:625–50.

Tyler, Tom R. 2006. *Why People Obey the Law.* Princeton: Princeton University Press.

Vieth v. Jubelirer. 2004. 541 U.S. 267.

West Virginia State Board of Education v. Barnette. 1943. 319 U.S. 624.

Youngstown Sheet & Tube Co. v. Sawyer. 1952. 343 U.S. 579.

II

THE ANTICLASSIFICATION TOPIC
AND EQUAL-LIBERTY TEMPLATE

Leslie Gielow Jacobs

Is liberty the legacy? That is the common wisdom about Justice Kennedy's impact during his many years on the Supreme Court (Knowles 2018; Colucci 2009). And it is true that, doctrinally, individual rights guaranteeing various types of liberty have been the locations for many of Justice Kennedy's most consequential opinions and that lavish appeals to liberty within some of these opinions have drawn the limelight. At first glance, it can appear that liberty is sufficient to explain the reasoning and results. But to rely solely on that first glance is to miss the equal, so to speak, or even greater part of Justice Kennedy's rhetorical legacy.

Edgar Rubin's famous optical illusion contains within it two faces or a vase, depending on which image the two lines running through it appear to create. The vase appears front and center, seemingly alone. But look longer or more closely, and the two faces on either side appear, the dual images necessarily coexisting, neither there without the other. So, too, Justice Kennedy's expositions of liberty most obviously animate his individual rights opinions. Rhetoric, however, as understood classically, is a mode of inquiry as well as of argument and persuasion (Balkin 1996; Aristotle, *Rhetoric*). Although less flashy and so less noticed, equality inspired the inquiry, the logic of the reasoning, and much of the passion of the argument in Justice Kennedy's opinions interpreting the scope of constitutional rights. Liberty and equality, often understood as embodying separate and competing ideals, mix in his opinions and stretch across doctrinal lines. In part, the mix is his innovation, but in large part, it is an adaptation of inquiry and interpretation

---

Thanks to Matt Urban for excellent cite-checking assistance.

of the scope of constitutional rights from a different era when doctrinal lines were more fluid. The move from judicial affirmation of race-based classifications soon after the post–Civil War right guarantees became a part of the Constitution to rejection of them a century later profoundly influenced how Justice Kennedy interpreted the meaning of those and other individual rights guarantees. Liberty was the loss, but unequal treatment was the outrage.

Classification and comparison are the core activities of legal reasoning. The requirement that the government treat likes alike is built into the doctrine of a number of constitutional rights. For Justice Kennedy, however, the maxim was a moral command, fundamental to constitutional meaning. This strong version of the anticlassification principle served as the rhetorical topic, or consistent starting point, for inquiry in his interpretation of the scope of constitutional rights. Of course, an equal treatment mandate is empty absent criteria for determining what is like and different (Westen 1982). Justice Kennedy supplied the substance that grounded the maxim in his inquiry as well. For him, the most supreme command across the Constitution's individual rights guarantees was that laws may not treat individuals differently with respect to their liberty to be, or to define, who they are.

Through adaptation and innovation, Justice Kennedy honed a standard two-part template to structure his reasoning and argument. The logic hinged on framing the line drawn by the law as depriving individuals of the merged equal-liberty right required by the Constitution's supreme command. Naming the government's purpose to subordinate a class of citizens or the harms experienced by those who are disadvantaged invoked emotion, urging readers to understand and embrace the fundamental injustice of the classifications that he saw the lines in laws to perpetrate. In company with the strong anticlassification topic as the guide to inquiry, this "frame-it-and-name-it" template of reasoning and persuasion, structured by equality but incorporating liberty appeals, recurred throughout Justice Kennedy's opinions interpreting the scope of constitutional rights.

The Origin of the Topic and Template in Race Classification Cases

Justice Kennedy's deep antipathy for status-based classifications is rooted in race. The first Justice John Harlan's dissent in *Plessy v. Ferguson* (1896) provided the prototype of the anticlassification topic and equal-liberty template. The Court had upheld a Louisiana statute that required railway companies to provide "equal but separate" accommodations by race as consistent with the Fourteenth Amendment's "equal protection of the laws" guarantee. The Court reasoned that the law by its terms treated Black and white citizens equally and did not "necessarily imply the inferiority of either race to the other" (*Plessy* 1896, 544). The Court's role in constitutional interpretation, according to the Court, was to defer to the state legislature's reasonable determination that the law served the comfort and convenience of passengers who preferred not to mingle with members of the other race. Justice Harlan disagreed with all of this. "Our Constitution is color-blind," he declared. "There is no caste here." The mere act of classifying citizens by race proved the law's invalidity, as he interpreted constitutional meaning. The Court's role was to see the "evil" line drawn by the law and strike it down (559–62, Harlan, J., dissenting).

While the anticlassification command drove the inquiry and dictated the result, equality and liberty merged in Justice Harlan's reasoning and argument. The Fourteenth Amendment was only a few decades old at that point, and the current doctrine of its "equal protection of the laws" and "liberty" guarantees had not solidified. The law, he argued, violated both. As to equality, establishing the premise that would prove the constitutional violation required that he reframe the purpose and effect of the law from the formal equal treatment of the races on the law's face, which was accepted by the Court. His methodology was to appeal to readers' common knowledge and experience of the social circumstances of racial prejudice that formed the background to the law. "Every one knows," he scolded the Court, that the intent of the law's creators was to keep newly freed Black citizens away from white citizens, not vice versa. "No one would be so wanting in candor as to assert the contrary" (*Plessy* 1896, 557). As to liberty, the Court had reasoned that the Constitution permitted race segregation in train cars because the activity involved a mere social, as opposed to protected political, right. Justice Harlan responded by recasting the activity's significance and emphasizing the scope of activities that would be impacted by the Court's holding. The right the law denied was unrestricted "use of a public highway" or "great thoroughfare" built for "public use and benefit," which is a "civil right[], common to all citizens" (553–54). The potential applications of such a "rule of civil conduct" were wide ranging (557), impacting "the personal liberty enjoyed by every one within the United States" (555). After framing the law as treating citizens unequally in the exercise of their common civil liberties, Justice Harlan named the purpose and effect of the classification with harsh language condemning the imposition of hierarchy. The law "proceed[ed] on

the ground that colored citizens are . . . inferior and degraded" (556), "put[]
the brand of servitude and degradation" on fellow citizens (562), and was,
quite bluntly, "sinister" (563).

Justice Kennedy confronted a race classification a few years after he joined
the Court. In *Metro Broadcasting, Inc. v. F.C.C.* (1990), the Court approved
a race-conscious plan to distribute broadcast licenses as consistent with
the equal protection guarantee, applying deferential review to the congressional action rather than the strict scrutiny review the Court had recently
held applied to state affirmative action plans. Justice Kennedy joined the primary dissenting opinion but also wrote separately. His began his dissent by
lamenting the "rank racial insult" validated by the *Plessy* Court (*Metro* 1990,
631, Kennedy, J., dissenting). He ended his short opinion by quoting the
strong anticlassification principle articulated by Justice Harlan in his *Plessy*
dissent: "The destinies of the two races . . . are indissolubly linked," and so
racial classifications in law by their very nature plant "the seeds of race hate"
(637). In between, Justice Kennedy pulled and mirrored elements of methodology, reasoning, and persuasive labels from Justice Harlan's dissent that
would inform his equal-liberty template.

Like Justice Harlan, Justice Kennedy reframed the standard for evaluating equal protection from the one adopted by the Court, appealing to background circumstances to defend his alternate framing. While the *Metro
Broadcasting* Court labeled the classifications in the law before it "benign,"
Justice Kennedy stated bluntly that it was "clear to any sensible observer
that they are not" (*Metro* 1990, 635). The Court must be "candid" about the
classifications' adverse impacts on individuals, he demanded (637). After
reframing the classification as malignant, like Justice Harlan, Justice Kennedy named its effects in terms that emphasized the unjust imposition of
hierarchy. The *Metro Broadcasting* law imposed "stigma" on the favored and
disfavored classes, provoked "animosity and discontent," and was based on
the "demeaning notion" that members of racial groups hold the same points
of view (636–37). Amid the framing and naming structure, his attitude about
the judicial role with respect to race classifications mirrored Justice Harlan's
as well. While both the *Plessy* and *Metro Broadcasting* Courts erred by being
overly certain that they, as judges, could identify some racial classifications
as harmless, like Justice Harlan, Justice Kennedy was fully confident that he
could discern the danger inherent in the line drawn by an elected branch of
government and that it was the duty of the Court, charged with interpreting
the Constitution, to invalidate it as wrong.

Full Exposition of the Topic and Template in the Gay Rights Opinions

In the series of gay rights opinions, Justice Kennedy implemented and aug-
mented the anticlassification topic and equal-liberty template and added to his
inspiration several of Chief Justice Earl Warren's opinions for the Court invalidating race-based classifications. Like Justice Harlan's dissent, Chief Justice
Warren's opinions merged equality and liberty in the reasoning with persuasive appeals. While Chief Justice Warren based his opinion in *Brown v. Board of
Education* (1954) on interpretation of the Equal Protection Clause, his reasoning hinged on the extraordinary importance of education to individuals' opportunities to exercise constitutionally guaranteed liberties. In *Loving v. Virginia*
(1960), Chief Justice Warren explicitly relied on both the Fourteenth Amendment's equality and liberty rights to invalidate a state ban on interracial marriage. And in *Bolling v. Sharpe* (1954), decided the same day as *Brown*, involving
public-school segregation in the District of Columbia, he wrote that "the concepts of equal protection and due process, both stemming from our American
ideal of fairness, are not mutually exclusive," so the Fifth Amendment's liberty
guarantee, which binds Congress, includes within it the Fourteenth Amendment's equal protection mandate, which by its words binds only the states.
The gay rights series contains a mix of cases based doctrinally on either the
Constitution's equal protection or due process liberty guarantees, culminating
in *Obergefell v. Hodges* (2015), in which Justice Kennedy, too, explicitly merged
the two doctrines. The first in the gay rights series of cases appeared almost
precisely one hundred years after *Plessy*, and the last, sixty years after *Brown*; as
Justice Kennedy noted in oral argument, the gap in years between *Brown* and
Loving was roughly the same as between Justice Kennedy's opinion invalidating a law criminalizing gay sexual conduct and the Court's consideration of the
laws that would result in the *Obergefell* decision.

   "The Constitution 'neither knows nor tolerates classes among citizens.'"
So began the opinion in *Romer v. Evans* (1996, 623), the first in the series. The
quote from Harlan's *Plessy* dissent signaled the anticlassification topic that
would drive the opinion's inquiry and the equal-liberty template that would
structure its reasoning, methodology, and persuasive appeals. The question
posed by the case was whether a Colorado initiative that prohibited subdivi-
sions of the state from implementing laws prohibiting discrimination based
on sexual orientation violated the Equal Protection Clause. Like Justice Harlan, Justice Kennedy faced the task of framing unequal treatment against a
claim by the state that the law treated people on either side of the classification
equally. Colorado, and the dissenting justices, argued that the state law simply

removed "special," and unequal, protection that gay people had received from local antidiscrimination laws. Like Justice Harlan's, Justice Kennedy's methodology asked readers to look behind the formal equality that the state claimed to be effectuated by the law to its actual operation. "We find nothing special in the protections Amendment 2 withholds" (631), he concluded after reviewing the development and content of antidiscrimination laws. Then, like Justice Harlan, he succinctly struck at readers' experiences and understanding of private prejudice in the real world to cement the correctness of the framing. The protections repealed were ones "taken for granted by most people either because they already have them or do not need them" (631).

With the unequal treatment framed, Justice Kennedy drew from Justice Harlan's dissent to navigate a doctrinal hurdle that the earlier justice had not faced. By doctrine, the Court reviewed classifications by sexual orientation under the highly deferential rational basis standard. To find a constitutional violation without adjusting the level of review, the extent of liberties impacted by a decision upholding the line drawn by the law, as employed by Justice Harlan, was the key. As Justice Harlan generalized the specific classification before the Court to the wide range of applications that would characterize the Jim Crow South, so, too, Justice Kennedy emphasized the "sweeping and comprehensive," "far-reaching," and "almost limitless" scope of the Colorado law's application to activities "that constitute ordinary civic life in a free society" (*Romer* 1996, 627, 635, 631). But for Justice Kennedy, argument emphasizing the broad scope of the loss of liberties did work within the doctrine of the Equal Protection Clause, demonstrating that disadvantaging individuals according to the single classification across such a wide range of applications could serve no legitimate policy purpose. Instead, Justice Kennedy reasoned as he named the injustice, the breadth of liberties lost by application of the law raised "the inevitable inference that the disadvantage imposed [was] born of animosity toward the class of persons affected" because of a characteristic central to who they are, a violation of the Constitution's supreme command, in Justice Kennedy's view, and an impermissible purpose under even deferential rational basis review (634).

Justice Kennedy's opinion in *Lawrence v. Texas* (2003) presented a variation in application of the topic and template. "Liberty presumes an autonomy of self that includes freedom of thought, belief, expression, and certain intimate conduct" (*Lawrence* 2003, 562). Once again, a single sentence in the opinion's introduction signaled the innovation in interpretation that would form the crux of the reasoning and the result. Equal treatment twice applied was the sleight of hand that framed the reasoning. "Certain intimate conduct," although not enumerated by those specific words, is self-defining and therefore protected as an essential "liberty" equally to the expressly guaranteed First Amendment rights of speech and religion ("thought, belief, [and] expression"), Justice Kennedy communicated in the opening salvo (562). The second equal-treatment move equated the choice to engage in "certain intimate conduct" by persons of the same sex, criminalized by the state statute, with a range of choices involving family and intimate relationships that the Court had held to be included within the scope of the Due Process Clause liberty right. "Persons in a homosexual relationship," Justice Kennedy declared, "may seek autonomy for these purposes, just as heterosexual persons do" (574). Naming the effects of the unequal treatment in strong terms calling for judgment against the imposition of hierarchy completed application of the template. The law stripped its target of their "dignity," imposed "stigma" on them, and "demean[ed] their existence" (575, 578).

Justice Kennedy's opinion for the Court in *United States v. Windsor* (2013) further integrated equality and liberty reasoning and argument within the single template. At issue was the Defense of Marriage Act (DOMA), a statute that defined "marriage" for the purpose of federal laws and distribution of benefits as limited to opposite-sex unions. Although the holding was that DOMA was "unconstitutional as a deprivation of the liberty of the person" (*Windsor* 2013, 774), the reasoning hinged on interpretation of the equal protection guarantee merged into the Fifth Amendment due process liberty right. Here, Chief Justice Warren's *Bolling* decision holding Congress to be bound by the Constitution's equality guarantee led the way. The Fifth Amendment liberty right alone, Justice Kennedy reasoned, "withdraws from Government the power to degrade or demean" (774). The equality right, incorporated within it, makes the liberty guarantee "all the more specific" (774). The framing and the naming of the unequal treatment mixed concerns of subordination of a class by law and deprivation of liberty. "DOMA singles out a class of persons deemed by a State entitled recognition and protection to enhance their own liberty," "imposes a disability" on them, instructs all who interact with them that their unions are "less worthy" and "less respected," and interferes with their "equal dignity" (774–75).

Justice Kennedy's opinion for the Court in *Obergefell* completed the gay rights series. Doctrinally, Justice Kennedy claimed the reasoning to turn primarily on interpretation of the due process liberty right, and, to be sure, appeals to liberty peppered the opinion. But once again, the question of the case was whether to interpret the Constitution to extend a right that straight people possessed to gays. So the anticlassification topic led the inquiry, and the equal-liberty template structured the opinion's logic and argument for its result. As in *Lawrence*, the unequal treatment by law was apparent. Justice Kennedy's task was to reframe the scope of liberty guaranteed by the Due Process Clause from the long-accepted standard of protecting heterosexual marriage to require equal treatment of straight people and gays. Chief Justice Warren's *Loving* opinion provided precedent for merging equality and liberty doctrine to invalidate the marriage classification. His methodology in *Brown* more extensively supplemented the template.

Both the *Brown* and *Obergefell* opinions had to acknowledge that those who wrote and ratified the Fourteenth Amendment accepted and assumed that the institutions at issue would be segregated. The *Brown* opinion related the changed nature of public education. Justice Kennedy chronicled how assumptions about the purposes of marriage and the roles of the parties to it had changed. Both opinions made appeals to the increased importance of the institutions to individual self-development and expression. The *Brown* opinion found it "doubtful that any child may reasonably be expected to succeed in life if he is denied an education" (1954, 493). Justice Kennedy's first words in *Obergefell* portrayed marriage as a liberty "that allows persons . . . to define and express their identity" (2015, 651). The *Brown* opinion asserted implicitly that race was not relevant to distribution of the benefits that education provides. In *Obergefell*, Justice Kennedy explicitly traced the reasons why marriage is a fundamental liberty right for heterosexuals and concluded that they "apply with equal force to same-sex couples" (665). After framing the equality standard, the *Brown* opinion labeled the harm of the unequal treatment as "generat[ing] a feeling of inferiority" that "affects [Black students'] motivation . . . to learn" (1954, 494). In *Obergefell*, Justice Kennedy named the injustice of the classification's effects more forcefully. It "demeans or stigmatizes" same-sex couples, "disparages their choices," "diminishes their personhood," and "disrespects and subordinates" them (672–75).

Application Across a Range of Rights

The anticlassification topic provoked the inquiry, and the equal-liberty template structured the reasoning and channeled the passion of the argument in Justice Kennedy's opinions interpreting individual rights outside the Fourteenth Amendment's equality and liberty guarantees. Equal treatment is built into the doctrine of the Free Speech Clause in the form of strict scrutiny review applied when laws classify speech according to its content. In Justice

Kennedy's early opinion concurring in *Simon & Schuster, Inc. v. Members of New York State Crime Victims Board* (1991), he signaled his strong embrace of the anticlassification principle as the guide to interpreting the free speech right. The New York statute at issue required authors and their publishers to forfeit all profits from writings in which the authors wrote about their crimes. Whereas the Court applied strict scrutiny to review the law and found the law to fail it, Justice Kennedy would not have interpreted the Constitution to permit the state to offer a justification. Justice Kennedy framed it—the law imposed "severe restrictions" on fully protected speech, using its content "as its sole criterion"—and named it: "raw censorship" (*Simon & Schuster* 1991, 124, 128, Kennedy, J., concurring). So equal treatment identified for Justice Kennedy when a law fulfilled or failed to protect the freedom of speech guarantee with "no further inquiry" required (124).

Justice Kennedy's deep commitment to the anticlassification principle was apparent, too, in his concurrence in *Texas v. Johnson* (1989), in which the Court invalidated a statute that punished a protester who burned a flag. The Court's opinion, which Justice Kennedy accepted fully, framed the law as discriminating against the protester according to the content of his speech, which led to the inevitable conclusion that "he must go free" (*Johnson* 1989, 421, Kennedy, J., concurring). Justice Kennedy's confidence in the principle and passion for it appeared as an Odysseus-style lament. Rendering decision in the case, he acknowledged, "exact[ed] its personal toll," but the responsibility could "be laid at no door but [the Court's own]" (420). Despite the respect he had for the "powerful arguments" in favor of criminalizing the "repellent" speech, he could not heed the Sirens' song, because a "pure command of the Constitution" bound him to the mast (420–21).

In two of Justice Kennedy's influential free speech opinions written for a closely divided Court, his perception of the relevant classification for analysis drove the reasoning and strong equal-liberty rhetoric urged the correctness of the result. In *Rosenberger v. Rector and Visitors of University of Virginia* (1995), the Court invalidated a university rule that prohibited disbursement of student activity funds to a Christian student group to pay for its publication. Two creative framings of the classification were required to move constitutional meaning. The first relocated the classification inquiry from the guarantee against state establishment of religion to the free speech right. The university had understood the Constitution to prohibit it from funding the evangelical publication and so had classified it as different from other student publications. Justice Kennedy reframed the funding program as creating a type of public forum for student speech, so that the excluded student group became one of many speakers who were the same in their entitlement to equal treatment. His second reframing identified the university's classification of the religious speakers as based on viewpoint, targeting their "specific motivating ideology" (*Rosenberger* 1995, 829). The university and the dissenting justices had perceived the classification of speakers as based on subject matter, segregating all viewpoints on the merits of religious belief, which would have made it permissible under existing doctrine. Justice Kennedy expressed impatience with those who urged the alternate framing. Their perception of the line drawn, he declared, was "simply wrong" (832). Naming rhetoric completed the template. The university's classification of the religious speakers, because it "cast disapproval on [their] particular viewpoints," was "egregious," "offensive," and "objectionable" (836, 829, 831).

The core logic of Justice Kennedy's dense opinion in *Citizens United v. Federal Election Commission* (2010), which invalidated a campaign-finance law that limited certain expenditures by corporations, also hinged on framing the line drawn by the law as separating similarly situated speakers. The name of the lead plaintiff was itself a rhetorical device echoed by Justice Kennedy in his explanation of why corporations possess constitutional free speech rights. Corporations are just "associations of citizens . . . that have taken on the corporate form," he reasoned (*Citizens United* 2010, 349). Strong language named the injustice of the unequal treatment as "censorship to control thought" (356). Within the *Rosenberger* and *Citizens United* opinions, liberty language appeared, emphasizing, as in Harlan's *Plessy* dissent and *Romer*, the nature and potential magnitude of the type of loss effected by the unequal treatment. Excising religious perspectives presented the "first danger to liberty," and the loss resulting from such classifications was "sweeping," affecting speakers and listeners alike (*Rosenberger* 1995, 835–36). Similarly, the censorship effected by restricting corporate speech was "vast in its reach," as it was the "electorate" that was "deprived of information," which may "advis[e] voters on which persons or entities are hostile to their interests" (*Citizens United* 2010, 354).

The topic and template drove the structure of Justice Kennedy's reasoning and argument interpreting the scope of the free exercise of religion right as well. Unlike several other justices, who would have interpreted its scope more broadly, Justice Kennedy joined the Court's opinion in *Employment Division v. Smith* (1990), establishing equal treatment by law of conduct without respect to its religious motivation as the standard for constitutional protection. Three years later, he wrote the Court's opinion invalidating a local ordinance that prohibited animal sacrifice because it violated the "general proposition" established in *Smith* and prior cases that a law burdening religious practice must be "neutral and of general applicability" to avoid strict judicial scrutiny (*Church of the Lukumi Babalu Aye* 1993, 531). With the anticlassification principle specifically embodied in the rule as the guide to inquiry, Justice Kennedy's task was to locate unequal treatment in a law that could appear, on its face, to prohibit conduct without respect to its religious motivation. His framing methodology was notable not so much for its innovation but for its vigor. While many observers might have presumed the *Smith* rule to impose a single standard, he interpreted the "neutral" and "generally applicable" requirements aggressively, to impose independent mandates. He had a Court with him as he meticulously reviewed the operation and interaction of the provisions of the ordinance to find that it failed both requirements, effectively targeting new city residents who practiced the Santeria religion. He went even further, joined by only one other justice, finding additional, or possibly sufficient, evidence of unconstitutional classification in statements made by city officials and residents exhibiting "significant hostility" toward the new residents (541). With a Court with him again, Justice Kennedy labeled the city's purpose for enacting the law "animosity" (542). In addition to framing the unequal treatment and naming its purpose as wrong, Justice Kennedy bookended the opinion with lectures. At the beginning, readers learned that city officials "did not understand, failed to perceive, or chose to ignore" the "well understood" principle that official action may not target conduct because of its religious motivation (524). At the end, government officials were told how they must conduct themselves in the future, that they should check for bias "upon even slight suspicion that proposals for state intervention stem from animosity to religion or distrust of its practices," "be resolute in resisting importunate demands," and, lest they wonder, "may not devise mechanisms, overt or disguised, designed to persecute or oppress a religion or its practices" (547). Once again liberty was at stake, but the fervor of the argument stemmed from the unequal treatment.

The anticlassification topic also structured Justice Kennedy's inquiry in cases in which his was the deciding vote striking down state death penalty rules but, with a twist, led to the conclusion that the Constitution required, rather than forbade, classification. In *Roper v. Simmons* (2005), Justice Kennedy reviewed a state law that did not differentiate between juveniles and adults in their eligibility for execution. Drawing from his supreme command, Justice Kennedy framed the equal treatment by law as an unconstitutional interference with the juvenile's liberty to engage in self-definition. "When a juvenile offender commits a heinous crime, the State can exact forfeiture of some of the most basic liberties, but the State cannot extinguish his life and his potential to attain a mature understanding of his own humanity" (*Roper* 2005, 573–74). Similarly, a state's rigid rule that relied solely on an IQ test to determine intellectual disability failed to classify capital defendants with sufficient precision and thereby risked imposing the death penalty on an intellectually disabled person, which would "violate[] his or her inherent dignity as a human being" because no valid penological purposes would be served (*Hall* 2014, 708).

Liberty When the Classification Wavers

Justice Kennedy's abortion opinions reveal that when the anticlassification conviction and the passion that flows from the equal-liberty template are lacking, liberty rights become less secure. Justice Kennedy was a late addition to the joint opinion in *Planned Parenthood of Southeastern Pennsylvania v. Casey* (1992), reaffirming that the scope of the due process liberty guarantee included the right to choose abortion prior to viability (Barnes 2019). The opinion was jointly written, so attribution of the words to any particular justice cannot be certain. Still, the description of the liberty at issue as "the right to define one's own concept of existence, of meaning, of the universe, and of the mystery of human life" is widely attributed to Justice Kennedy (*Casey* 1992, 851; Barnes 2019), and he drew from it in *Lawrence* to argue, by analogy, that acts of gay sexual intimacy are self-defining (*Lawrence* 2003, 573–74). In *Casey*, some evidence of an anticlassification inquiry and framing of abortion restrictions as implementing unequal treatment existed. The joint opinion acknowledged the "sacrifice" of pregnancy and childbirth, rejected the position that the state may implement through law "its own vision of the woman's role," and affirmed that the woman's "destiny . . . must be shaped to a large extent on her own conception of her spiritual imperatives and her place in society" (*Casey* 1992, 852). But the argument lacked the passion that exuded from full embrace of the equal-liberty template. No words made the comparative freedom of men to engage in "certain intimate conduct" free from fear of life-altering consequences explicit, and no naming of the purpose or effect of abortion restrictions as "demeaning" or "degrading" or otherwise imposing hierarchy on a "disfavored" class of citizens appeared. In place of the skepticism of regulation that characterized application of the template, Justice Kennedy, as a joint opinion participant, approved a requirement that physicians inform patients of the availability of state-created information designed to persuade them that abortion is the wrong moral choice, against claims that it violated women's liberty, and doctors' free speech, rights.

Then, when twice confronted with the question whether the woman's liberty right included the ability to choose a certain late-term abortion procedure, Justice Kennedy deployed the topic and template differently. The fetus, or "infant life," became the focus of comparative treatment, with the template deployed to validate the government-imposed restrictions (*Stenberg* 2000, Kennedy, J., dissenting; *Gonzales* 2007). As to framing the relevant equal treatment, the fetus, without prohibitions on the procedure in place, was "just as a human adult or child" in its act of dying, "bleed[ing] to death as it is torn limb from limb" (*Stenberg* 2000, 958–59). Although prompted by colleagues that "equal liberty" (*Stenberg* 2000, 920, Breyer for the Court) and "a woman's autonomy to determine her life's course, and thus to enjoy equal citizenship stature," were at stake (*Gonzales* 2007, 172, Ginsburg, J., dissenting), no words condemning, or even acknowledging, subordination of the class of citizens whose options the laws restricted appeared. Instead, readers were told, "respect for human life finds an ultimate expression in a mother's love for her child" (*Gonzales* 2007, 128). And, rather than the government classification, the regulated procedure was named with strong words calling for moral judgment. Performed by an "abortionist," it was a "shocking" and "brutal" new way to end human life (*Stenberg* 2000, 957; *Gonzales* 2007, 160).

Justice Kennedy's skepticism of government action returned when he cast the deciding vote to strike down a state law that imposed detailed and burdensome restrictions on abortion providers, which impeded women's access to their services (*Whole Woman's Health* 2016). But the weakness of the abortion right without an anticlassification grounding became apparent again when he joined the Court's opinion invalidating a California statute that required mostly faith-based pregnancy centers, formed for the purpose of persuading women against abortion but also licensed to perform medical services, to post a notice informing women seeking their free counsel and services that the state provided full and often free family-planning services, including abortion (*National Institute of Family and Life Advocates* 2018). The Court held that the abortion-availability notice requirement unconstitutionally forced the pregnancy center's medical professionals to deliver a message with which they disagreed, even though the *Casey* joint opinion had upheld the requirement that licensed abortion providers make available state-prepared antiabortion literature. The California Legislature had classified the licensed medical professionals and the pregnant clients in the pro-life pregnancy centers and in abortion clinics as the same, in the providers' susceptibility to regulation and the clients' need for state-provided information to make health decisions, and had declared itself "forward thinking" in promoting low-income women's access to information to inform reproductive choices. Justice Kennedy concurred separately, to express his outrage at the classification, which he saw as targeted to disfavor pro-life speakers by forcing them "to express a message contrary to their deepest convictions," and to reprimand the state for its "congratulatory" rhetoric. "It is forward thinking," he snapped, "to begin by reading the First Amendment" and to understand "how relentless authoritarian regimes are in their attempts to stifle free speech; and to carry those lessons onward" (*National Institute of Family and Life Advocates* 2018, 2379, Kennedy, J., concurring).

The circumstances of *Masterpiece Cakeshop, Ltd., v. Colorado Civil Rights Commission* (2018) similarly presented a clash of classifications for Justice Kennedy. The Colorado public accommodations law prohibited denial of service based on sexual orientation. The state civil rights commission found a violation when a baker, citing religious objections, refused to prepare a cake for a gay wedding. One state civil rights commissioner framed his vote as implementing the state law mandate of equal treatment with respect to sexual orientation as against the baker's reliance on "religion[, which] has been used to justify all kinds of discrimination throughout history," including slavery and the Holocaust (*Masterpiece Cakeshop* 2018, 1729). He then named "freedom of religion" as "one of the most despicable pieces of rhetoric that people can use to . . . hurt others" (1729). Justice Kennedy, once again, saw the classification that should control the outcome differently. In this opinion, he relied on the commissioner's framing-and-naming rhetoric, which some observers might perceive as not so very different from his own, as evidence that the state commission had implemented a constitutionally forbidden classification. The historical comparisons, the "despicable" label, and the description of the invocation of religion as "merely rhetorical" showed "hostility" toward the baker's "sincerely held" beliefs inconsistent with the "neutral and respectful consideration" of the claim that the Constitution required, he wrote for the Court (1729).

Conclusion

Simple lines define the dual images in Rubin's optical illusion. As with the illusion, the facts of a case inevitably depend for their legal meaning on how one sees the lines. A keen eye for classifications disadvantaging individuals in the exercise of essential liberties drove Justice Kennedy's inquiry across a

184 JUSTICE KENNEDY'S ETHOS

range of rights. As the man in the middle of nine for so many years, Justice Kennedy's framing of the equal or unequal treatment of individuals by law and his naming of government's unjust imposition of hierarchy among citizens controlled constitutional meaning. Whether the scope of an individual right would expand or contract depended critically on how Justice Kennedy saw the circumstances of a case: whether he saw the two human faces, cleaved apart by the lines in the law, or only the single inanimate vase.

References

Balkin, Jack M. 1996. "A Night in the Topics: The Reason of Legal Rhetoric and the Rhetoric of Legal Reason." In *Law Stories: Narrative and Rhetoric in the Law*, edited by Peter Brooks and Paul Gewirtz, 211–24. New Haven: Yale University Press.

Barnes, Robert. 2019. "The Last Time the Supreme Court Was Invited to Overturn *Roe v. Wade*, a Surprising Majority Was Unwilling." *Washington Post*, May 29, 2019.

Bolling v. Sharpe. 1954. 347 U.S. 497.

Brown v. Board of Education of Topeka. 1954. 347 U.S. 483.

Church of the Lukumi Babalu Aye, Inc. v. City of Hialeah. 1993. 508 U.S. 520.

Citizens United v. Federal Election Commission. 2010. 558 U.S. 310.

Colucci, Frank J. 2009. *Justice Kennedy's Jurisprudence: The Full and Necessary Meaning of Liberty*. Lawrence: University Press of Kansas.

Employment Division, Department of Human Resources of Oregon v. Smith. 1990. 494 U.S. 872.

Gonzales v. Carhart. 2007. 550 U.S. 124.

Hall v. Florida. 2014. 572 U.S. 701.

Knowles, Helen J. 2018. *The Tie Goes to Freedom: Justice Anthony M. Kennedy on Liberty*. Lanham, MD: Rowman and Littlefield.

Lawrence v. Texas. 2003. 539 U.S. 558.

Loving v. Virginia. 1960. 388 U.S. 1.

Masterpiece Cakeshop, Ltd. v. Colorado Civil Rights Commission. 2018. 584 U.S. __, 138 S. Ct. 1719.

Metro Broadcasting, Inc. v. F.C.C. 1990. 497 U.S. 547.

Obergefell v. Hodges. 2015. 576 U.S. 644.

National Institute of Family and Life Advocates v. Becerra. 2018. 585 U.S. __, 138 S. Ct. 2361.

Planned Parenthood of Southeastern Pennsylvania v. Casey. 1992. 505 U.S. 833.

Plessy v. Ferguson. 1896. 163 U.S. 537.

Romer v. Evans. 1996. 517 U.S. 620.

Roper v. Simmons. 2005. 543 U.S. 551.

Rosenberger v. Rector and Visitors of University of Virginia. 1995. 515 U.S. 819.

Simon & Schuster, Inc. v. Members of the New York State Crime Victims Board. 1991. 502 U.S. 105.

Stenberg v. Carhart. 2000. 530 U.S. 914.

Texas v. Johnson. 1989. 491 U.S. 397.

United States v. Windsor. 2013. 570 U.S. 744.

Westen, Peter. 1982. "The Empty Idea of Equality." *Harvard Law Review* 95:537–96.

Whole Woman's Health v. Hellerstedt. 2016. 579 U.S. 582.

PART 5

JUSTICE KENNEDY'S MISJUDGMENTS:
WOMEN, RACE, AND IMMIGRANTS

12

PERFORMING A "VIEW FROM NOWHERE":
JUSTICE KENNEDY'S DENIAL
OF EMBODIED KNOWLEDGE

Elizabeth C. Britt

When Justice Anthony Kennedy announced his retirement, Michele Goodwin (2018) argued in *Ms.* magazine that his legacy for feminists was complicated. Although he deserved credit for helping advance marriage equality, he was inconsistent on reproductive rights and other issues central to women. As exemplars of his complex legacy, Goodwin offered Justice Kennedy's opinions in *Obergefell v. Hodges* (2015) and *Gonzales v. Carhart* (2007). Justice Kennedy sided with the liberal members in *Obergefell*, the landmark case granting marriage rights to same-sex couples, and with the conservative members in *Gonzales*, which limited access to certain types of abortion. Kathryn Stanchi (chap. 13 in this volume) observes that these inconsistencies illustrate that for Justice Kennedy, women in same-sex relationships deserve empathy and liberty, while women seeking abortion do not.

In this chapter, I examine the rhetoric of liberty in these two cases from the perspective of feminist rhetorical theory, with the following question in mind: Despite their divergent outcomes, does Justice Kennedy make similar rhetorical moves? These opinions have been critiqued for presenting homogenizing images of marriage (see, e.g., Huntington 2015; Knouse 2018) and women as mothers (see, e.g., Resnik 2011, 231; Siegel 2008, 1769), respectively. Closer analysis reveals that Justice Kennedy makes homogenizing and totalizing statements not only when addressing the subject matter of the legal claims but also when addressing the nature of liberty and, more significantly, how one arrives at knowledge about such things in the first place, something even more evident in Justice Kennedy's majority opinion in *Lawrence v. Texas* (2003). Drawing on the philosopher of science Donna

Haraway's notion of situated knowledges, I argue that Justice Kennedy often (although not always) asserts a "view from nowhere" perspective that pretends to detach knowledge from the embodied experience of the knower. In *Gonzales*, asserting a disembodied knowledge is particularly ironic given the excruciating detail with which he describes the contested abortion procedure known as "dilation and evacuation."

Contextualizing the production of knowledge is a cornerstone of both rhetorical feminism and feminist jurisprudence. For the rhetorical theorist Cheryl Glenn, recognizing "vernaculars and experiences . . . as sources of knowledge" is a key tactic for responding to hegemonic rhetoric that seeks to dismiss or silence women and others (2018, 4). Law is one such system of hegemonic rhetoric. As explained by Kathryn Stanchi, Linda L. Berger, and Bridget J. Crawford, law's traditional idea of a "monolithic source for reason" is rejected by feminist jurisprudential methods; in its stead, feminist jurisprudence adopts feminist practical reasoning, which involves both seeking out the perspectives of people on law's margins and recognizing that all forms of reasoning are necessarily biased (2016, 15).

Justice Kennedy's decisions in *Gonzales*, *Obergefell*, and *Lawrence* fit squarely with the traditional genre of US Supreme Court opinions by exhibiting what the rhetorical theorist Katie Gibson describes as scripts of "objectivity, abstraction, and closure" (2018, 3). The script of objectivity obscures law's patriarchal bias—its roots in and commitments to masculine privilege—in favor of the "myth of the disinterested and apolitical judge" (Gibson 2018, 7). The script of abstraction promotes generalizations that ignore the lived experiences of women and others. The script of closure assumes the fixed and stable meanings of legal texts, social institutions, and cultural norms, allowing courts to resist change. Building on Gerald Wetlaufer's observation that legal rhetoric "operates through the systematic denial that it is rhetoric" (1990, 1555), Gibson argues that these scripts work together to resist critique while simultaneously upholding patriarchy as well as other structures of domination, including white privilege and heteronormativity (2018, 4). As I will illustrate, Justice Kennedy's adoption of a "view from nowhere" cuts across all three scripts.

To be clear, I argue that Justice Kennedy's adoption of this view is *performed* rather than real. However, I do not argue that Justice Kennedy performs this view intentionally or consistently. As a rhetorician, I am more interested in describing the *effects* produced by Justice Kennedy's writing than ascribing authorial intent. And while I am interested in the rhetorical moves exhibited across these three opinions, I do not claim that these are the most dominant moves or that they are notable features of his other decisions.

I also recognize that the idea that judges bring their own subjectivities to their work is not new. Since at least the nineteenth century, commentators have quipped that legal decisions result not from objective reasoning but from what a judge had for breakfast, a trope now routinely used to trivialize legal realism, especially the work of Karl Llewellyn (Priel 2020). From my perspective as a rhetorician, the actual contribution of legal realism has been to insist that law cannot be removed from its social contexts, including the experiences and worldviews of attorneys and judges.[1] Scholars of feminist legal theory and critical race studies have deepened those insights. As Patricia J. Williams explains, "much of what is spoken in so-called objective unmediated voices is in fact mired in hidden subjectivities and unexamined claims that make property of others beyond the self, all the while denying such connections" (1991, 11).

In fact, two facets of Justice Kennedy's biography have prompted commentators to speculate about how his background might affect his decisions. As the legal scholar Marie Ashe notes, all five of the justices in the *Gonzales* majority identify as Catholic, and Justice Kennedy is "invariably described as a devout Catholic" (2011, 484). According to Ashe, their religious affiliation matters because Justice Kennedy makes "moral concerns" central to the decision (485) and because the language extolling motherhood contains echoes of "theologically-confident proclamations about women's nature" from Supreme Court opinions of the previous century (487). Despite his Catholicism, however, Justice Kennedy overlooked his faith's doctrine on homosexuality when writing the decisions in gay rights cases, a departure attributed to his long friendships and comfort with gay people (Stolberg 2015).

Readers familiar with Justice Kennedy's jurisprudence may wonder why I include *Gonzales* in a discussion of his rhetoric of liberty, when that case contains no mention of the term. Justice Kennedy frames the issue in *Gonzales* primarily in terms of life rather than liberty, writing that the government's "legitimate and substantial interest in preserving and promoting fetal *life* . . . would be repudiated" if the Partial-Birth Abortion Ban Act of 2003 were declared unconstitutional (*Gonzales* 2007, 145; emphasis added). When later analyzing the government's interest in protecting the right to abortion, he adopts the point of view of physicians rather than women needing the procedure. The opinion contrasts with Justice Kennedy's coauthored opinion in *Gonzales*'s precedent *Planned Parenthood v. Casey*, whose analysis opens with the statement, "Liberty finds no refuge in a jurisprudence of doubt" (1992, 844), and which details why the right to abortion should be considered a liberty interest.

When judges frame an issue, they are not identifying the "correct" legal doctrine but making a significant rhetorical move. As the legal scholar Robert Ferguson explains, "The real creativity in a judicial decision lies in the question that judges decide to accept as the basis of their deliberations" (1990, 208). Framing is always partial and interested, favoring one way of seeing over others. The choice of legal doctrine thus functions as what the rhetorical theorist Kenneth Burke calls a "terministic screen," vocabulary that shapes how audiences perceive reality. No vocabulary can encompass every point of view; it always favors one vantage point. As Burke explains, "even if any given terminology is a *reflection* of reality, by its very nature as a terminology it must be a *selection* of reality; and to this extent it must also function as a *deflection* of reality" (1966, 45; emphasis in original). Burke likens terministic screens to photographic filters, as both alter how a represented thing is perceived.

By using the language of life and rejecting the language of liberty, Justice Kennedy reflects the reality of government interest in fetal life and deflects the reality of government interest in women's liberty. Put simply, Justice Kennedy's framing ignores a woman's right to abortion as a liberty interest. Of course, as commentators have noted, framing abortion in terms of liberty in *Casey* eroded rather than shored up the right to abortion because liberty interests require only minimal judicial review, rather than the strict scrutiny required when *Roe v. Wade* (1973) defined abortion as a fundamental right (see, e.g., Ashe 2011, 480). Essentially, the framing in *Gonzales* continues this erosion. By choosing the framing of "life," which requires strict scrutiny, Justice Kennedy deprioritizes a woman's liberty interests, which require less scrutiny. Then, by declining to call the right to abortion a "liberty interest," Justice Kennedy erases these interests from view.

Justice Kennedy's failure to mention a woman's liberty interests is particularly striking in the opening of the argument section. There he calls the government's interest in fetal life "a premise central to [*Casey's*] conclusion" (*Gonzales* 2007, 145). He does *not* say (here or later) that the other premise central to its conclusion is that women have a liberty interest in abortion, a notable rejection of the first argument presented by the respondent physicians in their brief.[2] More significant for my purposes, however, is how he frames this opening: "*Whatever one's views concerning the* Casey *joint opinion, it is evident* a premise central to its conclusion—that the government has a legitimate and substantial interest in preserving and promoting fetal life—would be repudiated were the Court now to affirm the judgments of the Courts of Appeals" (145; emphasis added). Here Justice Kennedy asserts with confidence something contradicted by evidence right in front of him: both the respondents' brief and Justice Ruth Bader Ginsburg's dissent deny that the Court's interest in fetal life would be repudiated by upholding the lower court. His claim is *not* evident to them.[3]

Although contradicted by evidence, Justice Kennedy asserts an objectivity borne of the purported ability to transcend subjective points of view. By using the phrasing "one's views" to refer to opinions about *Casey*, Justice Kennedy attaches these opinions to individuals, with the word "one" supposedly referring to individual people and the word "views" drawing on the metaphor of sight. Subsequently, the phrasing "it is evident" removes individuals entirely, asserting the possibility of a knowledge that transcends all points of view. In other words, some things are simply *evident*, not evident to a particular knower or community, a point that Eugene Garver explores more fully in chapter 2 in this volume.

Haraway calls such a move a "god trick of seeing everything from nowhere" (1988, 581). Like Burke's camera metaphor in his explanation of terministic screens, the idea that one can have "views" about an idea fits squarely within the Western philosophical tradition of associating vision with knowledge, an association that dates back to Plato but that since Descartes has been disconnected from the physical body; knowledge is linked to the "mind's eye" rather than the "body's eye" (Keller and Grontkowski 1983, 208). To reveal the god trick, Haraway reclaims the metaphor of vision as an *embodied* experience, as coming from a particular vantage point. To engage in the "conquering gaze from nowhere" is to "claim the power to see and not be seen" as a way of asserting objectivity (Haraway 1988, 581). But for Haraway, this viewpoint cannot be objective in any meaningful way because it refuses to be held accountable for its own partial vision (586). Instead, objectivity is possible only by acknowledging "particular and specific embodiment" (582). As she explains, "only partial perspective promises objective vision" (583).

Also evident to Justice Kennedy is the need to graphically describe the abortion procedure; as he explains, "The Act proscribes a particular manner of ending fetal life, so *it is necessary* . . . to discuss abortion procedures in some detail" (*Gonzales* 2007, 134; emphasis added). Although he describes the inclusion of this detail as necessary, it is certainly a choice, especially considering that he could have chosen instead (or in addition) to describe "in some detail" (or indeed in *any* detail) the various circumstances under which women choose abortion. Instead, Justice Kennedy takes seven pages in the reporter to compare two types of abortion performed in the second trimester, including the one targeted by the act. The legal scholar B. Jessie Hill characterizes his description as "having a photographic quality" that is "at once objective and objectifying" (2010, 659). Justice Kennedy's "objective" account centers the fetus rather than the woman. As Hill explains, in Justice Kennedy's account, "the female body is not so much a corporeal entity as a geographic space in which the drama plays out between the fetus and the doctor" (661).

Most of this description is detached and clinical, relying on excerpts from physician testimony. While this description is about the bodies of the woman and the fetus, it is not about embodied *knowledge*. In other words, Justice Kennedy does not ascribe knowledge to either the woman or the fetus on the basis of their particular, embodied experiences. A striking exception is when Justice Kennedy includes testimony from a nurse who had observed this procedure. Departing from the clinical description of the physician, the nurse first adopts the language of live birth, testifying that the "baby's body and the arms" were "delivered" from the "birth canal" (*Gonzales* 2007, 139). She then says that at the moment of death, "the baby's arms jerked out, like a startle reaction, like a flinch, like a baby does when he thinks he is going to fall" (139). The legal commentator Rebecca E. Ivey argues that by juxtaposing the nurse's and physician's description of the same procedure, Justice Kennedy illustrates that physicians who perform abortions are insensitive to fetal pain (2008, 1462). Significantly, the nurse's testimony also does something else: it ascribes embodied knowledge to the fetus by comparing the reaction at the moment of death to how a baby reacts "when he *thinks* he is going to fall" (emphasis added).

Justice Kennedy does not allow women the same embodied knowledge. After asserting that "it seems unexceptional to conclude that some women come to regret their choice to abort," he argues that "it is self-evident that a mother who comes to regret her choice to abort must struggle with grief more anguished and sorrow more profound *when she learns*, only after the event, what she once *did not know*: that she allowed a doctor to pierce the skull and vacuum the fast-developing brain of her unborn child, a child assuming the human form" (*Gonzales* 2007, 159–60; emphasis added). Critics have taken issue with this passage for a number of reasons, including the choice to refer to the woman as a "mother" and the fetus as an "unborn child" (Gee 2007, 987) and the assumption of a natural maternal bond (Denbow 2015, 69). The legal scholar Reva B. Siegel also notes that Justice Kennedy supports this claim by citing an amicus brief from Operation Outcry while ignoring a different amicus brief that offered the stories of more than 150 women who did *not* regret their decisions to abort (2008, 1732). Justice Ginsburg, for her part, challenges this passage not only for its language but also by reminding the majority that some pregnancies are unwanted or the result of rape (*Gonzales* 2007, 184). Commentators have also criticized Justice Kennedy for asserting that women do not understand what this procedure entails. For example, Anita Allen argues that Justice Kennedy's ideas about women in *Gonzales* are "mired in the atmospherics of maternalism and paternalism" (2009, 186), writing, "A woman whose belly is swollen with a pregnancy *knows* what lies therein (namely, a living human form), and she *knows* that there are only a limited number of ways to remove it. . . . Women generally *understand*, I would submit, that after the first trimester of pregnancy, the body of a fetus has to be physically removed or made to come out on its own through a small opening. Women *know* that physicians do not use laser beams to neatly and painlessly vaporize the unwanted unborn" (189; emphasis added). Here, Allen connects women's knowledge about abortion procedures to their embodied experience, something Justice Kennedy does not grant.

Just before Justice Kennedy asserts that his conclusion about regret is "unexceptional," he admits, "we find no reliable data to measure the phenomenon" (*Gonzales* 2007, 159). In both cases, Justice Kennedy claims a view from nowhere, deploying quasi-logical reasoning and the language of absolutism (e.g., the woman "must struggle" rather than "might struggle"). As an example of what Sanford Levinson might call the "tone of overweening confidence" common to judicial opinions (1996, 188), this unqualified language disguises that this idea is not "self-evident" but the view of particularly situated (male) writers. Justice Ginsburg lifts the veil in her dissent, writing, "Though today's majority may regard women's feelings on the matter as 'self-evident,' . . . this Court has repeatedly confirmed that '[t]he destiny of the woman must be shaped . . . on her own conception of her spiritual imperatives and her place in society'" (*Gonzales* 2007, 185).

Justice Kennedy similarly adopts the view from nowhere in *Obergefell* to discuss the nature of marriage. He opens his analysis with a lofty passage that extols its virtues, presenting it as something with a fixed and stable meaning: "From their beginning to their most recent page, the annals of human history *reveal* the *transcendent* importance of marriage. The lifelong union of a man and a woman *always has* promised nobility and dignity to all persons, without regard to their station in life. Marriage *is sacred* to those who live by their religions and offers unique fulfillment to those who find meaning in the secular realm. . . . Rising from the most basic human needs, marriage *is essential* to our most profound hopes and aspirations" (*Obergefell* 2015, 656–57; emphasis added). Moving from the present perfect tense (marriage "always has promised") to the simple present (marriage "is sacred"), this passage characterizes marriage as something unchanged over time (it is "transcendent") and required for human happiness (it is "essential"). Further, its nature stands apart from the ability of humans to understand it (it is "revealed" rather than "determined" or "constructed").

Even those who agree with the disposition of the case have taken issue with these generalizations. For example, the legal scholar Jessica Knouse "does not take issue with the result in *Obergefell* but rather with the rhetoric"; she critiques the decision not only because it favors marriage over nonmarriage but also because it presents marriage "as a universally fulfilling experience" despite its decline in popularity and relevance to Americans (2018, 611). Similarly, the legal scholar Clare Huntington admits to being "delighted" with the outcome but "unhappy" with the reasoning (2015, 23). She centers her critique on Justice Kennedy's doctrinal choices. In another striking rejection of the petitioners' framing, Justice Kennedy chose to foreground substantive due process rather than equal protection.[4] For Huntington, this choice required Justice Kennedy to say what marriage *is* and why it is important; she argues that his characterization of marriage privileges marital over nonmarital families and that his "sweeping statements about the place of marriage in legitimizing a marriage are harmful both rhetorically and substantively" (2015, 29).

Justice Kennedy's decision in *Obergefell* was chosen for revision by the editors of *Feminist Judgments: Rewritten Opinions of the United States Supreme Court*, the purpose of which was to confront the reality that judging is not neutral and to illustrate what opinions written from a feminist perspective might look like.[5] For the editors of that volume, "the situated perspective of the decision maker may drive American jurisprudence as much as—if not more than—*stare decisis* does" (Stanchi, Berger, and Crawford 2016, 5). A headnote to the revised opinion echoes the concerns of Knouse and Huntington on *Obergefell*, explaining that Justice Kennedy's rhetoric stigmatized people in nonmarital relationships and that the decision missed an opportunity to ground marriage rights in arguments about equality, which would provide greater protection against future laws enshrining traditional gender roles (Aloni 2016, 529–31). The revised feminist opinion, written by Carlos A. Ball, foregrounds the equal protection argument, making the decision more useful as a rhetorical resource for future decisions. Ball also avoids generalizing about marriage, writing that the decision is not meant to imply "that marriage is the only . . . or even the best way of ordering familial and intimate relationships" (2016, 546). Declaring marriage a fundamental right, he continues, is not the same as privileging marriage over other forms of relationships (546). Ball also explicitly critiques "law's purported objectivity and rationality" (532) and frames his own knowledge as situated, for example, by stating, "It is clear *to us*, therefore, that prohibiting two men or two women from marrying constitutes a gender-based restriction that must be subjected to heightened judicial scrutiny" (536; emphasis added).

Justice Kennedy's homogenizing statements about marriage are one form of the view from nowhere but not the only one in *Obergefell*. Perhaps more importantly for his rhetoric of liberty, Justice Kennedy adopts a distanced, totalizing stance when discussing this constitutional right. He presents liberty as something static and unchanging when he writes, "The generations that wrote and ratified the Bill of Rights and the Fourteenth Amendment *did not presume to know* the extent of freedom in all of its dimensions, and so they entrusted to future generations a charter protecting the right of all persons to enjoy liberty *as we learn its meaning*" (*Obergefell* 2015, 664; emphasis added). This narrative of epistemological progress depicts humanity as becoming ever more capable of understanding the unchanging meaning of liberty. In this narrative, liberty is a concept with an absolute meaning that can be learned, rather than a concept defined by people and changing over time.

Justice Kennedy's framing of liberty in *Obergefell* is consistent with his decision in the landmark gay rights case *Lawrence v. Texas*. He closes the majority opinion in *Lawrence* by writing, "Had those who drew and ratified the Due Process Clauses of the Fifth Amendment or the Fourteenth Amendment *known the components of liberty* in its manifold possibilities, they might have been more specific. They did not presume to have this insight. They knew *times can blind us to certain truths* and *later generations can see* that laws once thought necessary and proper in fact serve only to oppress" (2003, 578–79; emphasis added). He elsewhere describes an "emerging awareness" and "emerging recognition" of liberty evident in the "laws and tradition" governing sex (572–74). In this narrative, Justice Kennedy interpolates the framers into his own vision of epistemological progress: according to this vision, the framers knew that the full meaning of liberty was impossible for them to discern, understood that later generations would have this capacity, and deliberately used vague language to allow these later generations to act on the newly discovered meanings. Justice Kennedy draws on this narrative of progress to justify overturning *Lawrence*'s precedent *Bowers v. Hardwick* (1986). Summarizing how the *Bowers* Court framed the question presented, Justice Kennedy argues that the framing "discloses the Court's own *failure to appreciate the extent of the liberty* at stake" (*Lawrence* 2003, 567; emphasis added). Justice Kennedy positions the Court in *Lawrence* as recognizing this lack of knowledge and rectifying it, as the framers intended.

The majority opinion in *Casey* displays some of Justice Kennedy's lofty language but offers a different take on the ontological status of liberty, perhaps because Justice Kennedy coauthored it with Justices Sandra Day O'Connor and David Souter. According to a biography of Justice O'Connor, Justice Kennedy initially voted to overturn *Roe* but was convinced by Justices O'Connor and Souter to join them instead (Thomas 2019, 279). Justice O'Connor wrote the "nuts-and-bolts part of the opinion," Justice Souter tackled the discussion of precedent, and Justice Kennedy wrote the introduction (Thomas 2019, 280), opening with "Liberty finds no refuge in a jurisprudence of doubt" (*Casey* 1992, 844). Although Justice O'Connor was known for her "almost willfully dull" prose, she deferred to Justice Kennedy's opening flourish (Thomas 2019, 844). The next sentence, however, seems more grounded, reading, "Yet 19 years after our holding that the Constitution protects a woman's right to terminate her pregnancy in its early stages . . . , *that definition* of liberty is still questioned" (*Casey* 1992, 844; emphasis added), indicating a possible shift in authorship.

Although the opinion begins with Justice Kennedy's soaring generalization about liberty, the second sentence characterizes that generalization as something defined rather than discovered. Definitions can be offered as ontological certainties, but this decision instead compares a "literal reading" (which would limit liberty to procedural concerns) to how the Court has interpreted it in its precedent cases (opening up liberty to substantive concerns as well; *Casey* 1992, 846). The coauthors then assert that their own judicial role is "*to define* the liberty of all, not to mandate [their] own moral code" (850; emphasis added), a striking contrast from the judicial role imagined by Justice Kennedy in *Obergefell* and *Lawrence*. In the conclusion, the coauthors reassert this role by placing it in historical context, writing, "Our Constitution is a covenant running from the first generation of Americans to us and then to future generations. . . . We accept our responsibility not to retreat from interpreting the full meaning of the covenant in light of all of our precedents. We invoke it once again *to define the freedom* guaranteed by the Constitution's own promise, the promise of liberty" (901; emphasis added). In this narrative of living constitutionalism, liberty is something redefined as times change rather than a fixed concept that humans understand better as they evolve.

Perhaps all majority opinions of the Supreme Court make at least some of the moves associated with the view from nowhere. These moves are embedded in the genre as it has been historically constituted. For Ferguson, a judicial opinion "must appear as if forced to its inevitable conclusion by the logic of the situation and the duties of the office" rather than by the "unfettered hand" of its author (1990, 207). He links this move to the judge's status in a democratic society, arguing that judges can earn the trust of citizens only by asserting their neutrality. Judicial performance of neutrality, he writes, is therefore the result of "an innate psychological impulse" (208). But feminist legal theorists and critical legal theorists disagree that this impulse is innate, inevitable, or desirable. Instead, it is rooted in a patriarchal and white-supremacist legal culture that uses the view from nowhere to resist critique and accountability. Achieving more just and inclusive outcomes means critiquing these moves as well as offering alternatives. Williams, for example, argues that examining the simplistic taxonomies of law "as rhetorical gestures is . . . necessary for any conception of justice" (1991, 10). Similarly, some of the authors of the rewritten opinions in *Feminist Judgments* argue that their feminist visions could not be fully realized if they relied on the traditional language of neutrality (Stanchi, Berger, and Crawford 2016, 17). Indeed, this sort of rhetorical innovation marked the career of Justice Ginsburg. According to Gibson, Justice Ginsburg made important feminist challenges to law's generic commonplaces; from her influential "grandparent brief" in *Reed v. Reed* (1971) to her dissent in *Gonzales* to her majority opinion in *United States v. Virginia* (1996), her writings show a deep "commitment to context" and "shed light on the lived experiences of women" (Gibson 2018, 106).

Although not a majority opinion, Justice Sonia Sotomayor's dissent in *Utah v. Strieff* (2016) offers a more recent example of an alternative to the view from nowhere. The majority, led by Justice Clarence Thomas, considered the conduct of a police officer who ran a warrant check after stopping someone unlawfully, arguing that the stop was "an isolated instance of negligence" (*Strieff* 2016, 8). Sotomayor, in her dissent, blasts the majority for not placing the stop into a larger national context and for not considering the impact of the decision on people of color. She centers her critique on the idea that the stop was isolated, writing, "nothing about this case is isolated" (7). The man stopped by police, Edward Strieff, was white, a fact unsurprisingly not mentioned by the majority since Strieff was a member of the unmarked category against which difference is measured. Justice Sotomayor herself delays mentioning the man's race until late in her dissent. She first provides detailed evidence that such stops are routine, citing investigations by the Department of Justice into civil rights violations in Ferguson, New Orleans, and Newark and then musing that the majority failed to provide any reason why the stop of Strieff was different from those cases.

The difference, of course, is race, although Justice Sotomayor does not yet say so directly. She explains, "[I am] writing only for myself, and drawing on my professional experiences," and she describes in great detail what such stops entail, seeming to aim at a white audience without this embodied knowledge: "Although many Americans have been stopped for speeding or jaywalking, few may realize how degrading a stop can be when the officer is looking for more" (*Strieff* 2016, 10). She then places the white audience into this degrading reality with a long description (two full pages in the reporter) that directly addresses the reader, using the second-person pronoun thirty-two times in relation to what an officer might do to "your" body, including "your" arms, mouth, back, legs, feet, tongue, and genitals (11). Only then does Justice Sotomayor mention that although Strieff was white, such indignities (and worse) are disproportionately inflicted on people of color, prompting "black and brown parents" for many generations to give their children "the talk" about how to avoid becoming victim to police violence (12). Justice Sotomayor ends by naming the embodied knowledge produced by this treatment—double consciousness—and asserting that those who have this knowledge are the "canaries in the coal mine" warning everyone about how they too could lose their civil liberties or even their lives (12).

These examples from Justice Sotomayor, Justice Ginsburg, and *Feminist Judgments* are not exercises in "anything goes" relativism. They are instead examples of feminist objectivity as envisioned by Haraway, an objectivity that particularizes rather than homogenizes, grounds knowledge in embodied experience, and opens itself up to critique and accountability. We can see from their examples that a different way of judging is possible. We can see from law's continued marginalization of voices that a different way of judging is long overdue.

Notes

1. Francis J. Mootz III describes the contributions of Llewellyn in rhetorical terms, arguing that "he was principally concerned with uncovering the rhetorical nature of legal encounter with social drama" (2011, 143).

2. According to the respondents, "For over 30 years, this Court has protected the individual liberty interests of women from abortion regulations that threatened their health" (*Gonzales* 2007, Brief of Respondents 17).

3. The respondents write in their brief, "Requiring a health exception to prevent serious harm to pregnant women is not at odds with one of the central objectives of *Casey*" (*Gonzales* 2007, Brief of Respondents 19). Likewise, Ginsburg writes in her dissent, "Notably, the concerns expressed are untethered to any ground genuinely serving the Government's interest in preserving life" (181).

4. The petitioners place the equal protection argument first and the substantive due process argument second. The summary of argument from their brief begins as follows:

> Ohio's recognition bans violate the Fourteenth Amendment for all the reasons this Court struck down DOMA as unconstitutional in *Windsor*. That case invalidated DOMA because DOMA (a) was designed to treat unequally those same-sex spouses whom states, by their "marriage laws, sought to protect in personhood and dignity," 133 S. Ct. at 2696; (b) reflected a purpose to refuse recognition to existing marriages in order to make same-sex couples unequal to other married couples; (c) had the practical effect of imposing a stigma on married same-sex couples and their families by "instruct[ing] . . . all persons with whom same-sex couples interact, including their own children, that their marriage is less worthy than the marriages of others," ibid.; and (d) departed from a strong tradition of respecting marriages conferred by the states. (*Obergefell* 2015, Brief of Petitioners 18)

5. The majority opinion in *Obergefell* was also rewritten by Jack M. Balkin in an edited collection devoted to the case. The rewritten opinion rejects Kennedy's due process argument, focusing entirely on equal protection (Balkin 2020, 93).

References

Allen, Anita. 2009. "Atmospherics: Abortion Law and Philosophy." In *On Philosophy in American Law*, edited by Francis J. Mootz III, 184–204. Cambridge: Cambridge University Press.

Aloni, Erez. 2016. "Commentary on *Obergefell v. Hodges*." In *Feminist Judgments: Rewritten Opinions of the Supreme Court*, edited by Kathryn M. Stanchi, Linda L. Berger, and Bridget J. Crawford, 527–32. Cambridge: Cambridge University Press.

Ashe, Marie. 2011. "Privacy and Prurience: An Essay on American Law, Religion, and Women." *American Journal of Legal History* 51 (3): 461–504.

Balkin, Jack M. 2020. *What* Obergefell v. Hodges *Should Have Said: The Nation's Top Legal Experts Rewrite America's Same-Sex Marriage Decision*. New Haven: Yale University Press.

Ball, Carlos A. 2016. "*Obergefell v. Hodges*." In *Feminist Judgments: Rewritten Opinions of the Supreme Court*, edited by Kathryn M. Stanchi, Linda L. Berger, and Bridget J. Crawford, 532–46. Cambridge: Cambridge University Press.

Bowers v. Hardwick. 1986. 478 U.S. 186.

Burke, Kenneth. 1966. *Language as Symbolic Action: Essays on Life, Literature, and Method*. Berkeley: University of California Press.

Denbow, Jennifer M. 2015. *Governed Through Choice: Autonomy, Technology, and the Politics of Reproduction*. New York: New York University Press.

Ferguson, Robert A. 1990. "The Judicial Opinion as Literary Genre." *Yale Journal of Law and the Humanities* 2 (1): 201–20.

Gee, Graham. 2007. "Regulating Abortion in the United States After *Gonzales v Carhart*." *Modern Law Review* 70 (6): 979–92.

Gibson, Katie. 2018. *Ruth Bader Ginsburg's Legacy of Dissent: Feminist Rhetoric and the Law*. Tuscaloosa: University of Alabama Press.

Glenn, Cheryl. 2018. *Rhetorical Feminism and This Thing Called Hope*. Carbondale: Southern Illinois University Press.

Gonzales v. Carhart. 2007. 550 U.S. 124.

Goodwin, Michele. 2018. "How Feminists Should Remember Justice Kennedy." *Ms.*, June 29, 2018. https://msmagazine.com/2018/06/29/feminists-remember -justice-kennedy.

Haraway, Donna. 1988. "Situated Knowledges: The Science Question in Feminism and the Privilege of Partial Perspective." *Feminist Studies* 14 (3): 575–99.

Hill, B. Jessie. 2010. "Dangerous Terrain: Mapping the Female Body in *Gonzales v. Carhart.*" *Columbia Journal of Gender and Law* 19 (3): 649–74.

Huntington, Clare. 2015. "*Obergefell*'s Conservatism: Reifying Familiar Fronts." *Fordham Law Review* 84 (1): 23–32.

Ivey, Rebecca E. 2008. "Destabilizing Discourses: Blocking and Exploiting a New Discourse at Work in *Gonzales v. Carhart.*" *Virginia Law Review* 94 (6): 1451–508.

Keller, Evelyn Fox, and Christine Grontkowski. 1983. "The Mind's Eye." In *Discovering Reality: Feminist Perspectives on Epistemology, Metaphysics, Methodology, and Philosophy of Science*, edited by Sandra Harding and Merrill B. Hintikka, 207–24. New York: Kluwer Academic.

Knouse, Jessica. 2018. "Rhetoric Versus Reality: The Pro-Marriage Supreme Court and the Decline of Marriage." *University of Toledo Law Review* 49 (3): 605–16.

Lawrence v. Texas. 2003. 539 U.S. 558.

Levinson, Sanford. 1996. "The Rhetoric of the Judicial Opinion." In *Law's Stories: Narrative and Rhetoric in the Law*, edited by Peter Brooks and Paul Gewirtz, 187–205. New Haven: Yale University Press.

Mootz, Francis J., III. 2011. "Vico, Llewellyn, and the Task of Legal Education." *Loyola Law Review* 57 (1): 135–56.

Obergefell v. Hodges. 2015. 576 U.S. 644.

Planned Parenthood of Southeastern Pennsylvania v. Casey. 1992. 505 U.S. 833.

Priel, Dan. 2020. "Law Is What the Judge Had for Breakfast: A Brief History of an Unpalatable Idea." *Buffalo Law Review* 68 (3): 899–930.

Reed v. Reed. 1971. 404 U.S. 71.

Resnik, Judith. 2011. "The Production and Reproduction of Constitutional Norms." *New York University Review of Law and Social Change* 35 (1): 226–46.

Roe v. Wade. 1973. 410 U.S. 113.

Siegel, Reva B. 2008. "Dignity and the Politics of Protection: Abortion Restrictions Under *Casey/Carhart.*" *Yale Law Review* 117 (8): 1694–1800.

Stanchi, Kathryn M., Linda L. Berger, and Bridget J. Crawford. 2016. "Introduction to the U.S. Feminist Judgments Project." In *Feminist Judgments: Rewritten Opinions of the United States Supreme Court*, edited by Kathryn M. Stanchi, Linda L. Berger, and Bridget J. Crawford, 3–23. Cambridge: Cambridge University Press.

Stolberg, Sheryl Gay. 2015. "Justice Anthony Kennedy's Tolerance Is Seen in His Sacramento Roots." *New York Times*, June 21, 2015. httpd://www.nytimes.com/2015/06 /22/us/kennedys-gay-rights-rulings-seen-in-his-sacramento-roots.html.

Thomas, Evan. 2019. *First: Sandra Day O'Connor.* New York: Random House.

United States v. Virginia. 1996. 518 U.S. 515.

Utah v. Strieff. 2016. 579 U.S. 232.

Wetlaufer, Gerald B. 1990. "Rhetoric and Its Denial in Legal Discourse." *Virginia Law Review* 76 (8): 1545–97.

Williams, Patricia J. 1991. *The Alchemy of Race and Rights.* Cambridge: Harvard University Press.

13

WOMEN IN JUSTICE KENNEDY'S JURISPRUDENCE

Kathryn Stanchi

Justice Kennedy is known for his soaring rhetoric, particularly about humanity, dignity, and liberty. His prose style has been described as "grand," "emotional" and "poetic" (Segall et al. 2019, 909–10; Robinson 2020, 1045). His opinions in gay civil rights cases are widely lauded as showing his deep empathy for the liberty, dignity, and autonomy of gay people. But others have noted that Justice Kennedy's empathy is limited and that his empathy for some people stands in contrast to his blind spots to the suffering of other marginalized groups (Hill 2010, 660–61; Robinson 2020, 1045; Zietlow and Saucedo, chaps. 14 and 15 in this volume). Russell Robinson notably has emphasized that Justice Kennedy's empathy seems to disappear when he is confronted by legal issues about sexism, racism, and classism and the intersection of these group identities (2020, 1041, 1045, 1050).

The limits of Justice Kennedy's ability to empathize is highlighted by his opinions in which women and their civil rights are at issue. This seems particularly true in cases in which the female litigant is also marginalized by race and class or in which the legal issue typically affects women outside the mainstream white middle/upper class. A review of some of Justice Kennedy's major opinions in cases involving women's rights shows that Justice Kennedy's view of women and their place in society is, at best, conflicted.

Are Women Fully Human in Justice Kennedy's Jurisprudence?

The contrast between the portrayal of women in Justice Kennedy's abortion jurisprudence and his portrayal of people in the gay civil rights cases is stark. In abortion and other sex-bias cases, the women are often missing from the narrative or, if mentioned, are reduced to one-dimensional stock characters. By contrast, in Justice Kennedy's opinions in cases involving gay civil rights, the people depicted are more fully human, rounded characters with feelings, agency, and life. The contrast between these lines of cases raises intersecting issues of sexism, racism, and classism.

In Justice Kennedy's abortion opinions, the women are flat characters with little agency or complexity, unlike the plaintiffs in many of the gay rights opinions he wrote. Erin Daly describes the woman in the Supreme Court's abortion jurisprudence as "a phantom without substance, lurking voicelessly in the shadows, unable to assert her own interests" (1995, 98). Daly wrote those words before Justice Kennedy's opinion in *Gonzales v. Carhart* (2007), but the images of the woman in that opinion are similarly reductive. Poor women and women of color have the greatest stake in the outcome of abortion-restriction cases, so the "phantom" woman in the background of *Gonzales* is probably a poor woman of color, not a wealthy white woman (Franklin 2018, 54–60).

In *Gonzales*, for example, the woman is presented largely as a vessel for the fetus or "child" who dominates the narrative. The only time she appears more fully human is when Justice Kennedy refers to her as a "mother," and even those references are largely one-dimensional stereotypes.

Using the model provided by Anthony Amsterdam and Jerome Bruner in *Minding the Law* (2000, 143–64), I counted the number of references to "woman" and "women" and then the references to "fetus" and "child" in *Gonzales* as a way of measuring what people or entities loom largest in the narrative. In the entire opinion, the words "woman" or "women" appear a scant 38 times, as compared with the words "fetus" and "child," which dominate the narrative at 131 references. In the words of Amsterdam and Bruner, the fetus "vastly overlooms" the woman in the opinion, rendering her "inconspicuous" (152). Jessie Hill noted a similar issue, writing that in the seven pages of the opinion devoted to the abortion procedure—the part of the opinion where we would expect the woman to be fully present—the woman "barely makes an appearance, referenced only five times"; by contrast, the fetus is referenced 41 times and the doctor 31 (2010, 660). The woman is less a human being than the setting for the story—as Hill puts it, a "backdrop" for the "drama that plays out between the fetus and the doctor" (667–68).

The woman in *Gonzales*, when she is mentioned, lacks the critical human characteristics of agency and will. Using Amsterdam and Bruner's methodology, I counted the number of times in the opinion that women were the subject of an action word and how many times they were the object of a more powerful entity's action. How judges portray action impacts virtually every element of the narrative (Rountree, chap. 6 in this volume). In *Gonzales*, women rarely act; they are almost exclusively the passive recipients of the actions of others. Of the twenty-six references to "woman" singular, none are truly active. The "woman" is, for example, "placed" (2007, 188), "medicate[d]" (140), "encouraged" (160), and "burdened" (188). She "suffers" medical complications (168). Similarly, of the twelve references to "women" plural, only one is active. The one true active image of "women" in the entire majority opinion is one of the two controversial passages about women feeling "regret" about their choice to abort (and even then, the women cannot seem to regret decisively—they must *come* to it; 159–60).

The image of the abortion-seeking woman that emerges is an image of passivity and incompetence. To the extent that she appears at all, it is only to be moved about by more powerful entities. She is an object both in the grammatical sense and in the substantive sense. The federal statute in *Gonzales* can be blamed for some of this language, but Justice Kennedy's rhetoric continues and exacerbates the statute's paternalistic image of women as the uninformed, helpless victims of scheming doctors (women in *Gonzales* are "led, like horses to water"; Allen 2009, 191).

The "mothers" in Justice Kennedy's rhetoric in *Gonzales* are more fully human, in that they have feelings and life, but they are painted with the same paternalistic imagery as the "woman." The word "mother" is used fifteen times in the opinion as a substitute for "women." While some of these references are Justice Kennedy quoting the language of Congress, he chose to quote this problematic language uncritically. This rhetorical choice reduces the woman to her role as procreator and grafts onto her all the stereotypes associated with that role (Gee 2007, 988). It imposes that role on the woman seeking an abortion, who may not consider that experience to be "motherhood" (Ferree et al. 2002, 277 [noting the rhetorical difference between referring to the "pregnant woman" versus the "mother" in the abortion context]; Gee 2007, 988 [until a woman gives birth, she is not a "mother"]).

Although the "mothers" are a bit more rounded than the "women" in *Gonzales*, they also have little agency or will. In roughly half the references to "mothers," the mother appears only as part of the description of where the fetus is in space, as in "outside the body of the mother" (*Gonzales* 2007, 142, 147–48, 153, 160). The "mother" here is not a real person but simply a conduit or gateway for the fetus. In other references, the "mother" appears only as someone whose health the state must preserve or is among the parties with whom the state must foster a "dialogue" (160). The mother herself has no "personhood, no sacred self, no corporeality" and no autonomy or independence separate from the fetus (Hill 2010, 667; Resnik 2011, 235).

But as with the shadow "woman," the mother in *Gonzales* suddenly acquires a degree of humanity and agency in one passage: the second passage about regret. In that second passage, Justice Kennedy chooses the word "mother" when describing the "regret," "grief," and "sorrow" that a "mother" must "self-evident[ly]" feel when reflecting on her decision to abort (*Gonzales* 2007, 159–60). This woman—a *real* woman, a mother—outshines her one-dimensional sisters in her active emotions: her "ultimate" "bond of love" for her child. She is also the only one who receives the characteristically empathetic and florid Justice Kennedy rhetoric. The rhetoric surrounding this "mother" and her grief is like seeing a flash of color in a black-and-white movie. Justice Kennedy's description of the "mother's" tragic realization of her terrible mistake to abort is almost Shakespearean: "It is self-evident that a mother who comes to regret her choice to abort must struggle with *grief more anguished and sorrow more profound* when *she learns, only after the event, what she once did not know*: that she allowed a doctor to pierce the skull and vacuum the fast-developing brain of her unborn child, a child assuming the human form" (159–60; emphasis added).

Similarly, the minor women who seek to end their pregnancies are largely invisible and powerless in *Ohio v. Akron Center for Reproductive Health* (1990). Early in *Akron*, Justice Kennedy introduces the reader to Rachael Roe, the named minor plaintiff, but thereafter the opinion refers abstractly to "the" or "a" "minor." These references are almost exclusively passive. The minor is "required" (1990, 537), "authorized" (511), and "allowed" (507, 511–13). She almost never acts. Of the seventy-two references to minors in the majority opinion, only three are active, including the one reference to Rachael Roe. But even in these active references, the minor is a supplicant who "seeks" an abortion or who "files" an affidavit (508, 519). This abstract minor woman has no dimensionality or humanity in the opinion—no feelings, no thoughts. The reader learns little about what obstacles she faces or the impact on her life of her unplanned pregnancy. Justice Kennedy makes no mention of the burden imposed on the minor by the judicial bypass procedure or what a delay might mean for the minor with regard to finances, anxiety, or shame.

As in *Gonzales*, the rhetoric surrounding the minor woman is colorless and cold, except for one brief passage, where Justice Kennedy describes the minor as "terrified" and "lonely" (*Akron* 1990, 520). But even in this passage, the minor is the object of the actions of two more powerful entities: the state and her family. "It is rational," Justice Kennedy writes, "for the State to conclude that . . . the family will strive" to give the minor "compassionate and mature" advice (520). The state exercises its will on the minor's family, which in turn exercises its will on the minor. At least the minor has feelings in this passage, but she still has almost no personhood and dignity of her own.

The one-dimensional phantom woman is not unique to Justice Kennedy's abortion jurisprudence. Her shadowy image appears in other cases where the woman should be a central figure. In *Paroline v. United States*, for example, a woman sued for restitution because images of her being sexually abused as a child were circulated on the internet and downloaded by the defendant (2014, 439). The woman's injury, and whether it was caused by defendant, is at the center of the dispute. Although Justice Kennedy identifies the woman at the beginning of the opinion by her pseudonym "Amy," that is the last reference to "Amy" in the opinion. Thereafter, Justice Kennedy refers to her abstractly as "the victim" or the "respondent victim." Although Amy certainly is a victim (and, to be fair, "victim" is the term used by the statute at issue), Justice Kennedy's rhetorical choice to refer to her only in that way is dehumanizing and reductive.

Saying people's names is important (think of the #sayhername movement): it makes people real (using someone's name "keeps them out of the abyss of nothingness"; Sellers 2007, 273). It would seem particularly important to use even the woman's pseudonym in a case like *Paroline* because Amy is fighting to control her identity and image. As Ellen Emens writes, names are "constitutive. To have a name at all is thought to be a fundamental element of identity and dignity" (2007, 769). By contrast, a "victim subject" is a stock character: essentialized and immortalized in her trauma (Haynes 2006, 379–80). Justice Kennedy's victim in *Paroline* is denied, both doctrinally and rhetorically, the agency and power she seeks to reclaim from those who traded in her trauma.

Similarly, in Justice Kennedy's opinion in *Patterson v. McLean Credit Union* (1989), Brenda Patterson, a Black woman, lacks full humanity. Patterson sued under §1981, alleging that her employer discriminated against her on the basis of race and also racially harassed her (*Patterson* 1989, 169). As with Amy in *Paroline*, Justice Kennedy uses Brenda Patterson's name only once and thereafter refers to her as "petitioner," a one-dimensional label that reduces her to her procedural status. Indeed, in the *Patterson* opinion, a "petitioner" is all that Brenda Patterson is, and it is her whole identity; she is the flattest of flat characters, little more than a vehicle through which to explain the law (Forster 2010, 120–21). We know nothing about Brenda Patterson beyond the bare facts of her claim, nothing about how she felt about being harassed, passed over for promotion, and discharged after ten years of service for McLean.

Brenda Patterson's race, central to her identity and to the legal issue in *Patterson*, is largely erased by Justice Kennedy. The *Patterson* majority opinion makes no mention of Patterson's race after the first introduction of her as a Black woman. Among other things, for example, Patterson is asked to sweep and dust the office, an indignity that none of her white colleagues had to endure, and is told by her supervisor that "blacks are known to work slower than whites" (*Patterson* 1989, 178). Other than calling this behavior "reprehensible," Justice Kennedy does not acknowledge the historical significance, or the particular racialized injury, of asking a professional Black woman to perform housekeeping duties or the painful and enduring nature of the stereotype voiced by Patterson's supervisor (Onwuachi-Willig 2016, 308–9).

These flat characterizations of women stand in contrast to the description of the couples in *Obergefell v. Hodges* (2015) and *United States v. Windsor* (2013). In *Obergefell*, we learn about the love story of James Obergefell and James Arthur, whose life together was upended by Arthur's ALS diagnosis. Because of Arthur's deteriorating health, the couple was wed in a medical transport plane (*Obergefell* 2015, 658). We also learn about April DeBoer and Jayne Rowse, nurses with a family of special-needs children (658). Finally, we learn about Sergeant First Class Ijpe DeKoe, who "served this Nation to preserve the freedom the Constitution protects" but is stripped of his marriage rights whenever he travels (659).

Similarly, in *Windsor*, not only does Justice Kennedy refer to Edith Windsor and her partner, Thea Spyer, by name throughout the opinion, but he also shares, several times, intimate details of the couple's relationship. Justice Kennedy describes how "Windsor and Spyer longed to marry" but were denied that right (*Windsor* 2013, 763). We learn that Windsor and Spyer began their "long-term relationship" in 1963, registered as domestic partners as soon as New York gave them that right in 1993, and, "concerned about Spyer's health," journeyed to Canada to marry in 2007 (753). Justice Kennedy's thick description of the people and their experiences in *Obergefell* and *Windsor* makes the litigants and their problems real to the reader (Luban 2007, 70; Fajans and Falk 2009, 30). They are fully human: three-dimensional people with feelings, who love, yearn, suffer, and live. Justice Kennedy's description allows the reader to know them, making it much harder to deny them the dignity that all people deserve.

The analysis of *Obergefell* and *Windsor* is complicated by the fact that both cases also involved women who are portrayed three dimensionally. But in both those cases, the primary plaintiffs were white and middle or upper class (and chosen specifically for that reason; Robinson 2020, 1051–52). So it is not that Justice Kennedy portrays *all* gay people as fully human but that he portrays *some* gay people as fully human. Because in *Lawrence v. Texas* (2003), although the outcome is favorable to the litigants, Justice Kennedy glosses over—even erases—the less "mainstream" characteristics of the gay men involved (Robinson and Frost 2018, 222–23).

This raises an important question of intersectionality. Women privileged by race and class, like Edie Windsor and the *Obergefell* plaintiffs, are described as fully human. Women in cases involving legal issues primarily affecting poor women and women of color are not.

Missing Attributes of Humanity

Perhaps unsurprisingly, Justice Kennedy's flat female characters rarely possess key human attributes or rights. To examine the question of who, in Justice Kennedy's rhetoric, has dignity, autonomy, freedom, and liberty, I compared his majority opinions in two gay civil rights cases, *Obergefell v. Hodges* and *Lawrence v. Texas*, with his opinions in two abortion cases, *Gonzales v. Carhart* and *Ohio v. Akron Center for Reproductive Health*.

I counted the number of usages of "dignity," "liberty," "autonomy," and "freedom" in the opinions and examined who is the subject of the references—in other words, whom Justice Kennedy sees as possessing dignity, liberty, autonomy, and freedom (see table 13.1). The sheer number of times these concepts are mentioned in the majority opinions of the two gay civil rights cases vastly outnumbers their mention in the abortion cases. And even when Justice Kennedy does reference these concepts in the abortion cases, he rarely ascribes these attributes to women.

Table 13.1 Terms connoting humanity in Justice Kennedy's gay rights vs. abortion opinions

Case	Terms and number of references in opinion			
	"Dignity"	"Autonomy"	"Liberty"	"Freedom"
Obergefell	9	3	25	10
Lawrence	3	4	25	5
Gonzales	1	0	0	0
Akron	2	0	1	0

The concepts of "dignity," "liberty," "autonomy," and "freedom" dominate Justice Kennedy's opinions in *Obergefell* and *Lawrence*. These words appear forty-seven times in the majority opinion in *Obergefell* and thirty-seven times in *Lawrence*, for a total of eighty-four references. "Liberty" is the main concept in both opinions, with twenty-five references in both *Obergefell* and *Lawrence*. In *Obergefell*, "freedom" and "dignity" are close seconds, with ten and nine references, respectively, and "autonomy" comes in last at three references. In *Lawrence*, the references to "freedom," "dignity," and "autonomy" are roughly equal, with three references to "dignity," four to "autonomy," and five to "freedom." While the vast majority of these references are connected to abstract concepts or persons or individuals in general, the words are also frequently attached explicitly to gay people and to marriage. For example, in *Obergefell*, Justice Kennedy describes the "dignity" that inheres "in the bond between two men or two women who seek to marry and in their autonomy to make such profound choices" (2015, 666). In *Lawrence*, Justice Kennedy writes that "adults may choose to enter upon [a sexual] relationship in the confines of their homes and their own private lives and still retain their dignity as free persons" (2003, 567).

But in the abortion cases, these concepts rarely appear in Justice Kennedy's opinions, even though the right to abortion implicates women's freedom, liberty, autonomy, and dignity. That the abortion cases have a different doctrinal lens only begs the question: Why do women's civil rights have a different doctrinal lens, one that divests women of liberty, freedom, dignity, and autonomy? It was certainly not manifest, given the history of the law, that gay civil rights would be discussed in these terms, but Justice Kennedy was instrumental in bringing that lens to those cases. Given the changes in the doctrinal approaches to abortion over the course of the past few decades, why should we not expect the Court (particularly Justice Kennedy!) to discuss women's rights in these terms? A review of the briefs filed in *Gonzales v. Carhart* reveal that multiple litigants made arguments based on dignity, liberty, and autonomy. Indeed, *Planned Parenthood v. Casey* (1992), which Justice Kennedy cites in *Lawrence*, frequently references autonomy, "personal dignity," and liberty (Britt, chap. 12 in this volume).

But in *Gonzales v. Carhart*, Justice Kennedy makes only one reference to "dignity" and *zero* references to "autonomy," "freedom," or "liberty." The reference to "dignity" refers to the fetus—the "respect for the dignity of human life" (*Gonzales* 2007, 157). He does use the word "right" several times, but it is rarely attached linguistically to the woman herself; mostly it is the "constitutional" right or the "abortion" right (Resnik 2011, 235; Siegel 2008, 1773). All but one of the references to the woman's right are quotations from *Planned Parenthood v. Casey*. The one independent reference is a passive reference at the end of the opinion where Justice Kennedy finds no undue burden on the woman's right to "abortion" (*Gonzales* 2007, 168).

Similarly, in *Akron*, which involved a law requiring a minor to obtain parental or judicial consent for an abortion, Justice Kennedy makes only two references to "dignity," one reference to "liberty," and no references to "autonomy" or "freedom" (1990, 515, 520). The reference to "liberty" does not attach to the woman in *Akron* but is instead an abstract reference to what happens when the state seeks to deprive "an individual of liberty interests" (515). In the two references to "dignity" in *Akron*, only one refers to the minor woman's dignity. The other refers to the dignity of the family. Both references occur in a single paragraph at the end of the opinion, a paragraph that makes clear that any dignity the minor possesses is outweighed by the importance of the fetus and the dignity of the family. The reference to the minor's dignity is immediately qualified by a juxtaposed reference to the significance of the "human life" in the embryo: "[The minor's] decision will embrace her own destiny and personal dignity, and the origins of the other human life that lie within the embryo" (520). Moreover, directly after the reference to the minor's dignity and the "origins of the other human life" within her, Justice Kennedy states, "It would deny all dignity to the family to say that the State cannot take this reasonable step in regulating its health professions to ensure that, in most cases, a young woman will receive guidance and understanding from a parent" (520).

The Limits of Justice Kennedy's Empathy and Compassion

Justice Kennedy is frequently lauded for the empathy and compassion he shows in his often emotionally laden rhetoric. As Jamal Greene notes, even though we do not know who wrote *Planned Parenthood v. Casey*, because it is a per curiam opinion, "you can tell that the 'sweet mystery of life' [language] is Justice Kennedy" (Segall et al. 2019). Justice Kennedy's prose is often soaring and sentimental and can veer into the mawkish, such as his sentence in *Obergefell* about lonely unmarried people "call[ing] out only to find no one there" (2015, 667). Justice Kennedy tends to use intensifiers and emotionally laden language like "profound" and "transcendent." But when Justice

Kennedy writes about women in cases about their civil rights, the picture that emerges is more complicated (Kennedy "pairs soaring, aspirational language with his complicity in ongoing social stratification"; Robinson 2020, 1045). Often when Justice Kennedy confronts women, particularly those who may fall outside the white, middle/upper-class mainstream, his language can sometimes move from empathetic to contemptuous.

Obergefell and *Lawrence* both exhibit Justice Kennedy's deep empathy for the civil rights of gay people. In *Obergefell*, for example, Justice Kennedy uses the word "transcendent" twice and "profound" six times. These adjectives are attached to the marriage right but also clearly about the gay people who seek that right. He writes of "profound hopes and aspirations" and the "dignity" of making the "profound choice" to marry. He writes of the gay couples who "aspire" to the "transcendent purposes of marriage and seek fulfillment in its highest meaning" (*Obergefell* 2015, 670). The rhetoric in *Lawrence* is slightly more equivocal, as the references to "profound" beliefs and convictions refer to those who object to sodomy on religious grounds. Nevertheless, the liberty interest of gay people in *Lawrence*, like the marriage right, is "transcendent." And the word "respect" is used three times in *Lawrence* to refer to the autonomy and liberty of gay people, and the opinion concludes firmly that gay people "are entitled to respect for their private lives" (*Lawrence* 2003, 578).

But Justice Kennedy's empathetic rhetoric does not extend to women in abortion cases, a legal context in which poor and minority women are probably the most affected. In *Gonzales*, no rights, liberties, or dignities that women may possess are transcendent or profound. Justice Kennedy does use the word "respect" to mean esteem or deference seven times in the opinion but never with regard to women. Twice Justice Kennedy uses the word explicitly to describe the respect due to the life of the "unborn" or the "life within the woman," and in both instances the respect is "profound" (*Gonzales* 2007, 146, 157). The implicit references to respect for "life" and "human life" are even more telling. They very clearly refer only to the fetus, as with a reference to the state's legitimate interest in "promoting respect for human life *at all stages of the pregnancy*" (163; emphasis added). In this sentence, woman is not only excluded from the reference to "human life" but reduced to an event, an object the importance of which is only derivative of its utility to house what truly counts as human life (MacKinnon 1989, 226 [contrasting the law's approach to the fetus, "who might be a real person someday," with its treatment of women, who are "not real persons"]). Finally, Justice Kennedy also describes "respect for human life" as finding "the *ultimate expression* in the bond of love that the mother has for her child," a reference that encompasses the feeling ("bond"), not the mother herself and certainly not women as separate autonomous human beings (*Gonzales* 2007, 159).

Similarly, in *Akron*, Justice Kennedy exhibits little empathy for minor women who seek abortions. Justice Kennedy makes no mention of the potentially serious health risk to young women caused by the onerous bypass procedures in the Ohio law. He does not mention how intimidating a court procedure could be for an already frightened and ashamed young woman or how the delay inherent in Ohio's law puts particular burdens on rural, poor young women and young women of color. All of these arguments were made clearly in the briefs before the Court (*Ohio v. Akron Center for Reproductive Health*, 1989 WL 1127542, Brief of Amicus Curiae Indian Health Care Ass'n et al.; *Ohio v. Akron Center for Reproductive Health*, 1989 WL 1127539, Brief for Appellees). It is telling that the one reference to the time burdens imposed by the law regards the *physician's* schedule, which might be disrupted by the burdensome regulations (*Akron* 1990, 519).

Instead, Justice Kennedy reserves his empathy for the minor's parents, with whom he sympathizes because they confront an "event with complex philosophical and emotional dimensions" (*Akron* 1990, 519). His only reference acknowledging how fearful the young pregnant woman might be is within a sentence in which a romanticized *Father Knows Best* family "strives" to give "compassionate and mature" advice to the "lonely and terrified minor" (519). The opinion clings to this image of the family despite compelling data in the brief by the American Psychological Association referencing the prevalence of familial abuse against young girls that can be exacerbated by a pregnancy (*Ohio v. Akron Center for Reproductive Health*, 1989 WL 1127529, Brief of American Psychological Ass'n et al.).

In some cases, Justice Kennedy's language toward women can move from unempathetic to annoyed and a bit cold-hearted. A stark example of this is his rhetoric in *Ragsdale v. Wolverine World Wide, Inc.* (2002), which involved a lower-income woman disabled by cancer. In *Ragsdale*, Tracy Ragsdale sued Wolverine under the Family Medical Leave Act (FMLA) for Wolverine's failure to comply with the notification requirements of the Act's regulations. Ragsdale was a factory worker for Wolverine making six dollars an hour. She was diagnosed with cancer a year after she began work and underwent surgery and then radiation treatments. Ragsdale asked Wolverine for sick leave, and it gave her thirty weeks of unpaid leave. At the end of the thirty weeks, Ragsdale was still unable to work and asked for additional leave, which Wolverine denied. She asked to work part-time, but Wolverine refused (*Ragsdale v. Wolverine Worldwide, Inc.*, 2001 WL 1424689, Brief for

Petitioner). Wolverine then fired her when she failed to come to work (*Ragsdale* 2002, 84–85).

Ragsdale then sued, having learned that Wolverine had failed to comply with the notice requirements for FMLA leave and that therefore she was entitled to additional leave under the FMLA. Justice Kennedy, writing for the Court, struck down the notice requirement and affirmed the grant of summary judgment in favor of Wolverine, even though Wolverine conceded that it did not comply with the regulations. Here is the passage describing the issue at the very beginning of the case: "The [FMLA] encourages businesses to adopt more generous [leave] policies, and many employers have done so. Respondent Wolverine World Wide, Inc., for example, granted petitioner Tracy Ragsdale 30 weeks of leave when cancer kept her out of work in 1996. Ragsdale nevertheless brought suit under the FMLA. She alleged that because Wolverine was in technical violation of certain Labor Department regulations, she was entitled to more leave" (*Ragsdale* 2002, 84).

The vocabulary and sentence juxtapositions are subtle, but the picture they paint contrasts a magnanimous employer with an entitled and ungrateful employee. The first thing we learn, for example, is that Wolverine adopted a "more generous" leave policy than required by the FMLA. The vocabulary used to describe Wolverine is admiring: Wolverine "granted" leave to Ragsdale, making it an "example" of the "more generous" leave policies encouraged by the law. Juxtaposed against that portrayal is Ragsdale, who "nevertheless" sues this generous employer because of its "technical violation," alleging that she was "entitled" to more leave. The use of "technical" to describe the violation makes Ragsdale's request sound petty, and the use of "entitled" connotes asking for something that one does not deserve. Similarly, the use of the word "nevertheless" highlights the contrast between "generous" and "brought suit . . . [over a] technical violation." This is an example of the Court's contemptuous portrayal of poor people by, among other things, criticizing their "bad attitude[s]" and demeaning their concerns as trivial (Ross 1991, 1525, 1527).

The other noteworthy aspect of Justice Kennedy's portrayal of Tracy Ragsdale is what is missing from the opinion. Ragsdale's cancer is barely mentioned and buried midsentence, dwarfed by the emphasis on Wolverine's generous grant of sick leave. Justice Kennedy does not mention that Ragsdale's physician had advised her not to return to work to "conserve her strength to recover from the radiation treatments" (*Ragsdale v. Wolverine Worldwide, Inc.*, 2001 WL 1424689, Brief for Petitioner). Not once does Justice Kennedy make any reference to the ravages of cancer or radiation treatments on Ragsdale's body. Nor does Justice Kennedy mention the shamefully meager hourly wage the supposedly "generous" Wolverine paid Ragsdale. Finally, readers of the opinion would not know that Ragsdale had to file for bankruptcy because she became financially destitute from medical bills and loss of income. Where is the signature Justice Kennedy empathy? The rhetoric commiserating with a sick woman's attempt to recover from a deadly disease and debilitating treatments? Not in this opinion. For some reason, Tracy Ragsdale gets only Justice Kennedy's impatience and irritation.

Conclusion

No judge, regardless of superior intellect, can be wholly without bias. Bias comes with being human. But all of us, particularly those, like judges, who hold significant power over the lives of others, should confront and interrogate our biases. That will not eliminate them, but it can lessen their silent impact on our work. To that end, acknowledging personal bias and attempting to fight it is, or should be, part of judging well.

This chapter is quite critical of Justice Kennedy's apparent bias toward women as explored in the language he uses to describe them, particularly in cases where the stakes were (and are) extraordinarily high for both the woman litigants and for all women who share their plight. In these cases, Justice Kennedy's rhetoric constructs women as one-dimensional "phantoms" who do not possess the fundamental human characteristics of personhood, agency, dignity, freedom, autonomy, or liberty. Not surprisingly, these "phantom" women fail to receive the same empathetic rhetoric that Justice Kennedy lavishes on litigants in gay civil rights cases. Indeed, Justice Kennedy's conspicuously empathetic rhetoric in the gay civil rights cases highlights its absence in cases about women's civil rights. This contrast is complicated by the scholarship suggesting that the gay plaintiffs in some of the major gay civil rights cases were cherry-picked to be mainstream white and upper/middle class, whereas the cases exhibiting the bias I explore here tend to involve (and implicate) women outside that mainstream.

Justice Kennedy's rhetoric is not, in my view, evidence of intentional misogyny, classism, or racism. Rather, the language he employs demonstrates the strong and persistent influence of unexplored subconscious bias. In this, he is not alone among his brethren. But perhaps this chapter, and its criticism of Justice Kennedy, can join other scholarly voices in demonstrating the critical imperative of educating judges about implicit bias and its great potential to affect law and legal decision-making.

References

Allen, Anita. 2009. "Atmospherics: Abortion Law and Philosophy." In *On Philosophy in American Law*, edited by Francis J. Mootz III, 184–94. Cambridge: Cambridge University Press.

Amsterdam, Anthony G., and Jerome Bruner. 2000. *Minding the Law*. Cambridge: Harvard University Press.

Daly, Erin. 1995. "Reconsidering Abortion Law: Liberty, Equality, and the New Rhetoric of *Planned Parenthood v. Casey*." *American University Law Review* 45:77–150.

Emens, Elizabeth F. 2007. "Changing Name Changing: Framing Rules and the Future of Marital Names." *University of Chicago Law Review* 74:761–863.

Fajans, Elizabeth, and Mary R. Falk. 2009. "Untold Stories: Restoring Narrative to Pleading Practice." *Journal of the Legal Writing Institute* 15:3–65.

Ferree, Myra Marx, William Anthony Gamson, Jürgen Gerhards, and Dieter Rucht. 2002. *Shaping Abortion Discourse: Democracy and the Public Sphere in the United States and Germany*. Cambridge: Cambridge University Press.

Forster, E. M. 2010. *Aspects of the Novel*. New York: Rosetta Books.

Franklin, Cary. 2018. "The New Class Blindness." *Yale Law Journal* 127:2–98.

Gee, Graham. 2007. "Regulating Abortion in the United States After *Gonzales v Carhart*." *Modern Law Review* 70:979–92.

Gonzales v. Carhart. 2007. 550 U.S. 124.

Haynes, Dina Francesca. 2006. "Client-Centered Human Rights Advocacy." *Clinical Law Review* 13:379–416.

Hill, B. Jessie. 2010. "Dangerous Terrain: Mapping the Female Body in *Gonzales v. Carhart*." *Columbia Journal of Gender and Law* 19:649–74.

Lawrence v. Texas. 2003. 539 U.S. 558.

Luban, David. 2007. *Legal Ethics and Human Dignity*. Cambridge: Cambridge University Press.

MacKinnon, Catharine A. 1989. *Toward a Feminist Theory of State*. Cambridge: Harvard University Press.

Obergefell v. Hodges. 2015. 576 U.S. 644.

Ohio v. Akron Center for Reproductive Health. 1990. 497 U.S. 502.

Onwuachi-Willig, Angela. 2016. "Rewritten Opinion in *Meritor Savings Bank v. Vinson*." In *Feminist Judgments: Rewritten Opinions of the United States Supreme Court*, edited by Kathryn M. Stanchi, Linda L. Berger, and Bridget J. Crawford, 297–321. Cambridge: Cambridge University Press.

Paroline v. United States. 2014. 572 U.S. 434.

Patterson v. McLean Credit Union. 1989. 491 U.S. 164.

Planned Parenthood of Southeastern Pennsylvania v. Casey. 1992. 505 U.S. 833.

Ragsdale v. Wolverine World Wide, Inc. 2002. 535 U.S. 81.

Resnik, Judith. 2011. "The Production and Reproduction of Constitutional Norms." *New York University Review of Law and Social Change* 35:226–46.

Robinson, Russell K. 2020. "Justice Kennedy's White Nationalism." *UC Davis Law Review* 53:1027–72.

Robinson, Russell K., and David M. Frost. 2018. "The Afterlife of Homophobia." *Arizona Law Review* 60:213–89.

Ross, Thomas. 1991. "The Rhetoric of Poverty: Their Immorality, Our Helplessness." *Georgetown Law Journal* 79:1499–1547.

Segall, Eric, Eric Berger, Michael Dorf, and Jamal Greene. 2019. "Panel 2: Justice Kennedy's Prose-Style and Substance." *Georgia State University Law Review* 35:907–35.

Sellers, Susan. 2007. *A History of Feminist Literary Criticism*. Cambridge: Cambridge University Press.

Siegel, Reva B. 2008. "Dignity and the Politics of Protection: Abortion Restrictions Under *Casey/Carhart*." *Yale Law Journal* 117:1694–1800.

United States v. Windsor. 2013. 570 U.S. 744.

14

JUSTICE KENNEDY'S ANTICLASSIFICATION DOCTRINE: NOT JUDGING WELL

Rebecca E. Zietlow

What does it mean to judge well? Along with the many thoughtful and enlightening observations of my colleagues in this book, I propose the following: judging well requires attempting to understand the effect of the law on people's lives, especially on those who have historically been marginalized and disenfranchised by our laws. Thus, judging well requires balancing rules to guide future courts with empathy toward the parties in the case at hand. During Justice Anthony Kennedy's time on the Court, he demonstrated considerable empathy toward parties challenging restrictions on the equality rights of members of the LGBTQ community and established a fluid doctrine enforcing liberty and equality principles (Camper, O'Rourke, and Jacobs, chaps. 3, 5, and 11 in this volume). In cases such as *Romer v. Evans* (1996) and *Obergefell v. Hodges* (2015), Justice Kennedy eschewed the formalism of legal categories such as suspect class and fundamental rights. Instead, Justice Kennedy empathetically focused on the impact that laws restricting intimate relations and engaging in the political process had on the actual lives of members of the LGBTQ community. By contrast, in race-equality cases, Justice Kennedy applied a rigidly formalistic anticlassification approach that left little room for empathy and imposed barriers to achieving substantive equality. Justice Kennedy attempted to strike a middle ground in his race-discrimination jurisprudence between his colleagues on the right and left. However, like Justice Kennedy's "First Amendment optimism" (Bhagwat, chap. 9 in this volume), Justice Kennedy's anticlassification race jurisprudence reflected either a naivete about how racism functions in our law and society or a deliberate willingness to ignore that reality.

During Justice Kennedy's professional life, it appeared that our country was making progress in eradicating racial discrimination. In 1954, the year that Justice Kennedy graduated from high school, the Supreme Court issued its landmark decision in *Brown v. Board of Education*, holding that racial segregation in public schools violates the Equal Protection Clause of the Fourteenth Amendment. Justice Kennedy attended law school and began his practice at the height of the civil rights movement, as the Court and Congress outlawed racial segregation in employment, education, and public accommodations and removed racial barriers to voting rights. While Justice Kennedy was on the Supreme Court, Barack Obama was elected our nation's first Black president, and many commentators proclaimed that our country was entering a postracial era. However, those claims overlooked the fact that racial injustice is still deeply embedded in our law and society, the result of centuries of discriminatory state and private action. People of color lag behind whites in virtually every economic indicator and are disproportionately likely to be imprisoned and to be subjected to violence by law enforcement officials. Schools are as segregated now as they were at the time of *Brown*, due largely to residential segregation caused by state and private action. These are just some indicators of the racial inequality that persists to this day.

On the Court, Justice Kennedy condemned racially facial classifications, arguing that identity-based classifications violate the "dignity of individuals in our society" (*Parents Involved* 2007, 797). In his opinions, Justice Kennedy often cited Justice John Marshall Harlan's dissent in the 1896 case of *Plessy v. Ferguson* to support his anticlassification views (Jacobs, chap. 11 in this volume). In *Plessy*, the Court upheld a Louisiana law that required the racial segregation of railroad cars because "separate but equal" state facilities did not violate the Equal Protection Clause. For the majority, Justice Henry Brown opined, "We consider the underlying fallacy of the plaintiff's argument to consist in the assumption that the enforced separation of the two races stamps the colored race with a badge of inferiority. If this be so, it is not by reason of anything found in the act, but solely because the colored race chooses to put that construction upon it" (*Plessy* 1896, 551). Justice Harlan responded in his dissent, "Everyone knows that the statute in question had its origin in the purpose, not so much to exclude white persons from railroad cars occupied by blacks, as to exclude colored people from coaches occupied by or assigned to white persons" (557). For that reason, Justice Harlan argued, the law violated the Equal Protection Clause. Justice Harlan explained, "In view of the constitution, in the eye of the law, there is in this country no superior, dominant, ruling class of citizens. There is no caste here. Our constitution is color-blind" (559). Unlike the majority, Justice Harlan recognized how the law affected people's lives.

To Justice Kennedy, Justice Harlan's dissent epitomized the anticlassification doctrine. Justice Kennedy viewed Justice Harlan's color-blind language as an aspirational goal. He explained, "The enduring hope is that race should not matter; the reality is that too often it does" (*Parents Involved* 2007, 787, Kennedy, J., concurring). Justice Kennedy argued that this goal could best be achieved by limiting the capacity of government to take race into account, even when remedying racial harms. According to Justice Kennedy, "To be forced to live under a state-mandated racial label is inconsistent with the dignity of individuals in our society" (*Parents Involved* 2007, 797). However, Justice Kennedy privileged the ideology of dignity over the lived experience of racial injustice. Justice Kennedy's rule-bound approach to racial classifications left little room for empathy and understanding of how people of color experience the law in their lives.

Moreover, neither Justice Harlan's dissent in *Plessy* nor the Court's ruling in *Brown* required the rejection of racial classifications that aided racial minorities. An alternative reading of Justice Harlan's dissent in *Plessy* focuses on his admonition that there is "no superior, dominant, ruling class of citizens." In contrast to anticlassification, an anticaste approach to race requires courts to inquire into how the law actually works on the ground. Does the law oppress racial minorities, regardless of whether it is facially based on race? Does a law that classifies based on race oppress or empower racial minorities? These questions were relatively easy to answer in the Jim Crow South, where racial classifications perpetuated a caste system in which Blacks were denied basic civil rights. The Warren Court struck down facially discriminatory laws because they enforced a racial caste system that limited the opportunities of racial minorities and treated them as second-class citizens (Schmidt 2008, 227). Because classification enforced caste, anticlassification rulings opened opportunities for racial minorities and promoted a more equal society (Siegel 2003). Like Justice Harlan's *Plessy* dissent, the *Brown* Court relied on both anticlassification and anticaste reasoning.

In 1975, when Justice Kennedy was first appointed to the federal bench, the Court's rulings and federal civil rights legislation had mostly dismantled the facial racial segregation of the Jim Crow South. The new battles over racial equality concerned laws that did not facially classify based on race but had a disproportionate impact on racial minorities. When considering racially disparate impact, federal courts were forced to choose between an anticaste approach to racial equality, which would have addressed deeply embedded systemic racism brought about by intentional and unintentional discrimination, and an anticlassification approach to racial equality, focused only on laws that facially classified based on race (Fiss 1976). The courts had to make the same choice when ruling on affirmative action policies that used facially racial classifications to dismantle the caste system (Siegel 2003).

Justice Harlan's anticaste rationale suggested that courts should reject laws that reinforce racial caste, regardless of whether they facially classified based on race. In Justice Harlan Stone's influential footnote 4 to *United States v. Carolene Products* (1938), he suggested that federal courts should subject laws that discriminated against "discrete and insular minorities" to heightened scrutiny (151). Numerous scholars have argued that countermajoritarian courts should protect minorities against the tyranny of the majority (Ely 1980). *Carolene Products'* footnote 4 justified the use of judicial review to strike down not only laws that classified based on race but also those that reflected the failure of the political process to protect racial minorities, regardless of whether they were facial classifications (Karst 1977). Because of the history of racial animus in our society and law, courts should view laws that have a racially disparate impact with skepticism (Gotanda 1991). Nonetheless, when Justice Kennedy joined the Supreme Court in 1988, the Court had largely chosen the anticlassification approach, requiring a showing of discriminatory intent to allege a cause of action for race discrimination and imposing the highest level of scrutiny on race-based affirmative action programs. Justice Kennedy joined with his conservative colleagues to impose a rigid, rules-bound anticlassification approach, rejecting disparate-impact claims and applying strict scrutiny to affirmative action measures.

In addition, and perhaps most importantly, Justice Kennedy wrote opinions limiting Congress's authority to remedy race discrimination by subjecting legislation enforcing the Fourteenth and Fifteenth Amendments to rigorous scrutiny. The enforcement clause cases limit Congress to the Court's cramped reading of the Equal Protection Clause, eviscerating its effectiveness as a weapon against race discrimination. In the area of race, then, Justice Kennedy and his colleagues on the Court turned *Carolene Products'* footnote 4 on its head. Instead of empathy toward plaintiffs of color, Justice Kennedy adopts a "view from nowhere," turning a blind eye toward the reality of their lives (Britt, chap. 12 in this volume).

Justice Kennedy's race jurisprudence differs markedly from his empathetic attitude toward people alleging discrimination on the basis of sexual orientation. For example, in *Romer v. Evans*, Justice Kennedy wrote the opinion for the Court as it struck down a Colorado constitutional amendment that prohibited all legislative, judicial, and executive action designed to prohibit discrimination based on sexual orientation. Justice Kennedy began his opinion quoting Justice Harlan's anticaste language in *Plessy*. "One century ago," said Justice Kennedy, "the first Justice Harlan admonished this Court that the Constitution 'neither knows nor tolerates classes among citizens'" (*Romer* 1996, 623). Justice Kennedy accurately described the effect of the law on people's lives. "The amendment withdraws from homosexuals, but no others, specific legal protection from the injuries caused by discrimination, and it forbids reinstatement of these laws and policies" (627).

Justice Kennedy refused in his opinion in *Romer* to follow the Court's equal protection doctrine, although he did not identify sexual orientation as a suspect class and purported to apply rational basis review but scrutinized the purpose behind the law in a manner that is inconsistent with rational basis review. The Colorado amendment was enacted via a referendum process, and it is virtually impossible to determine what motivated the voters who approved the amendment. Nonetheless, Justice Kennedy held that the voters must have been motivated by animus. He opined that the amendment's "sheer breadth is so discontinuous with the reasons offered for it that the amendment seems inexplicable by anything but animus toward the class it affects" (*Romer* 1996, 632).

In *Romer*, Justice Kennedy showed his distrust of laws that classify based on an immutable aspect of one's identity (Bhagwat 2016). However, the discrepancy between his attitude toward laws that harm racial minorities and those that harm members of the LGBTQ community places form before substance. Given the long (and continued) history of discrimination based on sexual orientation, Justice Kennedy is probably correct that a significant number of Colorado voters were motivated by anti-LGBTQ bias. However, there is an even longer well-documented history of discrimination based on race. The Court has repeatedly acknowledged the history of race discrimination, which is the basis for applying strict scrutiny to race-based classifications. As Kathryn Stanchi notes, Justice Kennedy's "empathy for some people stands in contrast to his blind spots to the suffering of other marginalized groups," including people of color (chap. 13 in this volume).

Considering Justice Kennedy's anticlassification doctrine as a topos that "organize(s) or constitute(s) our imagining of social life" may aid in understanding the appeal of the doctrine to Justice Kennedy (Cintron 2010, 101). In his time on the Court, Justice Kennedy championed liberty and dignity as fundamental human rights, and he viewed his race jurisprudence as promoting those ideals (Bhagwat 2016, 392; Jacobs, chap. 11 in this volume). Justice

Kennedy hoped that his rhetoric would generate those ideals. Anticlassification is an effective rhetorical device because it is a common topos, an idea present in the common culture, and arguably has no connection to material resources (Cintron 2010, 106). Anticaste, on the other hand, is a special topos without a simple universal resonance. Anticaste forces the judge to face the fact that resources are limited and requires the redistribution of those resources, something Justice Kennedy was unwilling to do. However, as Clarke Rountree points out, "Once the act is shown to yield a legal rule or principle—an agency to guide decision—it is imported into a second act as an agency of decision" (chap. 6 in this volume). Once imported into the Court's doctrine, anticlassification did not generate equality, as Justice Kennedy hoped it would. Instead, it imposes barriers to those who are seeking to achieve equality.

The Requirement of Showing Discriminatory Intent

In the 1976 case of *Washington v. Davis*, the Court held that government practices that merely have a racially disparate impact are not racial classifications warranting a heightened level of scrutiny. Thus, plaintiffs alleging race discrimination must show that the government officials who made the allegedly discriminatory decision were motivated by discriminatory intent. Requiring a showing of discriminatory intent treats race discrimination as exceptional rather that the norm, a few bad actors marring what is primarily a fair and unbiased system. Unfortunately, numerous governmental policies, from housing to criminal justice, social welfare to health care, affect communities of color disproportionately negatively. Unconscious bias can also influence government officials to adopt policies that have a disproportionately disparate impact on racial minorities, even if those policies do not facially classify based on race (Lawrence 1987). Racial inequality is "woven into our social fabric, rather than placed on top of it" (Banks 2001, 1122). The discriminatory-intent requirement poses a significant hurdle for plaintiffs alleging race discrimination and makes it virtually impossible to use litigation to address systemic racism that permeates our society. During Justice Kennedy's time on the Supreme Court, he not only reinforced the Court's requirement of discriminatory intent but also wrote opinions making it harder for plaintiffs to prove that intent.

For example, in *Hernandez v. New York* (1991), Justice Kennedy wrote a plurality opinion rejecting a Latino criminal defendant's challenge to the prosecutor's use of peremptory jury challenges to exclude Latino jurors. The defendant, victim, and witnesses in the case were all Latino, and some testimony was expected to be in Spanish. The prosecutor argued that he had sought to exclude Spanish-speaking Latino jurors because he was uncertain whether they would be able to listen to and follow the court interpreter (*Hernandez* 1991, 356). Hernandez argued that the prosecutor's challenge was based on race, violating the Equal Protection Clause. Justice Kennedy acknowledged that the prosecutor's reasoning would have a disproportionate impact on Latino jurors. "But even if we knew that a high percentage of bilingual jurors would hesitate in answering questions like these and, as a consequence, would be excluded under the prosecutor's criterion, that fact alone would not cause the criterion to fail the race-neutrality test. . . . An argument relating to the impact of a classification does not alone show its purpose" (362). Because Justice Kennedy was persuaded that the prosecutor had a nondiscriminatory justification for his actions, he held that the defendant had failed to state a claim.

Similarly, in *Ashcroft v. Iqbal* (2009), Justice Kennedy wrote the majority opinion for the Court rejecting the claim of a Muslim Pakistani pretrial detainee that government officials, including the attorney general and the director of the FBI, had adopted an unconstitutional policy to subject him to harsh conditions on account of his race, religion, or national origin. In his complaint, Iqbal alleged that he was one of thousands of Muslim men detained after 9/11 because of their race, religion, and national origin (*Iqbal* 2009, 668). According to Iqbal's complaint, he was held in a special prison unit where he was subjected to unjustified strip and body-cavity searches, called a "terrorist" and "Muslim killer," and deprived of adequate food. Iqbal further claimed that prison staff interfered with his attempts to pray and engage in religious study (668, 689). Iqbal further alleged that the attorney general and FBI director knew, or should have known, about their subordinates' actions.

Federal Rule of Civil Procedure 8(a) requires plaintiffs merely to state "a short and plain statement of the claim showing that the pleader is entitled to relief." Well-established case law provides that when a judge is evaluating a defendant's motion to dismiss for failure to state a claim, a judge must "accept as true all of the factual allegations contained in the complaint" (*Erickson* 2007, 93). In *Iqbal*, however, the Court imposed a new pleading requirement—plaintiff's claims must be "plausible"—and held that Iqbal's claims were not.

According to Justice Kennedy, Iqbal had pleaded no more than a disparate-impact case, and his allegations of discriminatory intent were not plausible. Justice Kennedy opined, "The September 11 attacks were perpetrated by 19

Arab Muslim hijackers who counted themselves members in good standing of al Qaeda, an Islamic fundamentalist group. . . . It should come as no surprise that a legitimate policy directing law enforcement to arrest and detain individuals because of their suspected link to the attacks would produce a disparate, incidental impact on Arab Muslims, even though the purpose of the policy was to target neither Arabs nor Muslims" (*Iqbal* 2009, 682). Again, Justice Kennedy held that disproportionate impact was insufficient to prove racial discrimination. Moreover, Justice Kennedy and his colleagues disregarded credible evidence of discriminatory intent.

The heightened pleading standard in *Iqbal* imposes an additional burden for plaintiffs alleging that government officials discriminated against them on the basis of race. Plaintiffs often lack evidence of a defendant's intent before discovery, which is unavailable to plaintiffs responding to motions to dismiss. The *Iqbal* standard allows federal judges, who themselves may be unconsciously biased, more discretion to evaluate and reject civil rights claims. Many judges are skeptical of those claims. Indeed, "dismissals of employment discrimination and civil rights claims have risen significantly in the wake of *Iqbal*" (Reinert 2015, 2122).

Justice Kennedy's skepticism of the plaintiffs in *Hernandez* and *Iqbal* contrasts markedly from his willingness to identify animus in *Romer*. Also contrasting with his skepticism in most cases alleging civil rights violations, Justice Kennedy was solicitous of the white plaintiffs who alleged race discrimination in the case of *Ricci v. DeStefano* (2009), finding that the defendant intentionally discriminated based on race, overturning the lower courts' holding that the defendant's conduct was racially neutral. The town of New Haven required firefighters seeking a promotion to take a written exam, which nonwhite candidates failed at a significantly higher proportion than white candidates. After the disproportionate results were announced, city officials feared that if they promoted based on the exam, it would subject the city to liability under Title VII of the 1964 Civil Rights Act, which prohibits employment practices that have a disparate impact based on race. The city decided not to certify the results. A group of white firefighters who would have been promoted based on the exam results sued the city for race discrimination under Title VII and the Equal Protection Clause. The district court judge rejected the suit, holding that the city had not acted because of discriminatory animus toward the white firefighters because "all applicants took the same test, and the result was the same for all because the test results were discarded and nobody was promoted" (*Ricci* 2009, 576). The court of appeals affirmed in a one-paragraph per curiam opinion.

For the Court, Justice Kennedy disagreed and held that the city's decision was in fact based on racial animus. Justice Kennedy explained, "All the evidence demonstrates that the City chose not to certify the examination results because of the statistical disparity based on race" (*Ricci* 2009, 579). The Court also ruled that the city's good-faith effort to avoid liability under Title VII was not a sufficient defense since that belief was not based on sufficient evidence. In stark contrast to Justice Kennedy's lack of empathy toward the minority firefighters, he empathized with the plaintiff white firefighters. Justice Kennedy noted that the named plaintiff, Frank Ricci, had "several learning disabilities, including dyslexia," had spent $1,000 to purchase study materials, and had studied eight to thirteen hours a day to prepare for the test (567–68). Apparently without grasping the irony of his statement, Justice Kennedy noted, "our decision must be consistent with the important purpose of Title VII—that the workplace be an environment free of race discrimination, where race is not a barrier to opportunity," before ruling that the city was required under law to use a test that imposed a significant barrier to the opportunity of racial minorities (580).

Strict Scrutiny of Affirmative Action

Requiring discriminatory intent and heightened pleading requirements are barriers to remedying race discrimination through litigation. Justice Kennedy also made it more difficult for political actors to remedy race discrimination by insisting that race-based affirmative action is subject to a stringent application of strict scrutiny review. At the time that Justice Kennedy joined the Court, its members were still engaged in a debate over the level of scrutiny that should apply to "benign" racial measures such as affirmative action in education and racial preferences. Some members of the Court argued that they should be subjected to a lower level of scrutiny than the laws intended to harm racial minorities. Others insisted that all racial classifications should be subjected to strict scrutiny, regardless of whether they hurt or helped racial minorities. Affirmative action measures classify based on race to dismantle the racial caste system. These cases thus pit anticlassification against anticaste theories of equal protection. Justice Kennedy embraced the latter view, anticlassification. Unlike his most conservative colleagues, Justice Kennedy refused to adopt a blanket racial-blindness rule, but he enforced strict scrutiny diligently against affirmative action measures while he was on the Court.

In the 1990 case of *Metro Broadcasting v. F.C.C.*, the Court upheld an order of the Federal Communications Commission awarding preferences for minority ownership in applications for new licenses. Writing for the majority, Justice William Brennan applied intermediate scrutiny and held that the preference was justified by the important government purpose of promoting diversity of viewpoints in broadcasting. In dissent, Justice Kennedy accused the Court of making the same "fundamental errors in *Plessy*, its standard of review and its validation of rank racial insult by the State" (*Metro* 1990, 632). Citing Justice Harlan's dissent in *Plessy*, Justice Kennedy argued that like the Louisiana law at issue in that case, the FCC program also plants the "seeds of race hate under the sanction of law" (635). Justice Kennedy thus equated Justice Brennan's decision upholding a law that benefited minority communities with the majority opinion in *Plessy*, upholding a classification that marginalized and dehumanized minority communities.

Only a few years later, in *Adarand v. Pena* (1995), Justice Kennedy joined the majority opinion as the Court overruled *Metro Broadcasting* and held that all racial classifications are subject to strict scrutiny. Under *Adarand*, all race-based affirmative action programs must be narrowly tailored to achieve a compelling government interest. In *Grutter v. Bollinger* (2003), the Court upheld the Michigan Law School's race-based affirmative action plan, which was similar to the Harvard plan that Justice Lewis Powell had extolled in *Regents of the University of California v. Bakke* (1978). Writing for the Court, Justice Sandra Day O'Connor purported to apply strict scrutiny but deferred to the university's arguments that racial diversity was a compelling interest, because of its educational benefits and because it helped to prepare students for their careers in a diverse workplace. Dissenting from the ruling, Justice Kennedy agreed that universities could take race into account in narrowly tailored affirmative action policies but argued that Justice O'Connor had not actually applied strict scrutiny to the Michigan program and argued that the program was not narrowly tailored to achieve diversity. In his majority opinions in the more recent cases of *Fisher v. University of Texas* (2013, 2016), Justice Kennedy continued to insist on a rigorous application of strict scrutiny to university affirmative action admissions programs. However, he rejected his conservative colleagues' calls for a race-blind approach that would foreclose all race-based affirmative action.

Justice Kennedy explained his views on affirmative action in particular and race discrimination in general in his concurrence to *Parents Involved v. Seattle* (2007), in which the Court struck down race-conscious measures of local school boards to prevent racial segregation. Writing for four justices,

Chief Justice John Roberts declined to rule whether the school districts' goal of achieving racial diversity was a compelling government interest. Chief Justice Roberts's plurality opinion held that the school assignment program was not narrowly tailored because race was a decisive factor in school assignment. He concluded, "The way to stop discrimination on the basis of race is to stop discriminating on the basis of race" (*Parents Involved* 2007, 748).

In Justice Kennedy's concurrence, he toed a middle line between the Roberts plurality and the four justices in dissent. On the one hand, Justice Kennedy lauded the school districts' goal of "teach[ing] that our strength comes from people of different races, creeds, and cultures uniting in commitment to the freedom of all" (*Parents Involved* 2007, 782). Justice Kennedy agreed with the four dissenters that "diversity, depending on its meaning and definition, is a compelling educational goal a school district may pursue" (783). Justice Kennedy disagreed with Chief Justice Roberts's race-blind reasoning and his famous conclusion. According to Justice Kennedy, "as an aspiration, Justice Harlan's axiom [that the constitution is "color blind"] must command our assent. In the real world, it is regrettable to say, it cannot be a universal constitutional principle" (788). However, Justice Kennedy agreed with Justice Roberts that what he called the "sweeping race-based classifications" that the school districts adopted to achieve their goal were not narrowly tailored (790).

In Justice Kennedy's concurrence in *Parents Involved*, he conceded that "from the standpoint of the victim, it is true, an injury stemming from racial prejudice can hurt as much when the demeaning treatment based on race identity stems from bias masked deep within the social order as when it is imposed by law" (*Parents Involved* 2007, 795). However, when the government intentionally distinguishes between people based on race, it reduces "an individual to an assigned racial identity," which "is among the most pernicious actions our government can undertake" (795). The city of Seattle used only two racial classifications (white and Black), even though it also had a large proportion of Asian and Latino students. In this case, the school boards of Louisville and Seattle believed that it was necessary to take race into account when assigning students to schools in order to prevent the segregation (Louisville) or resegregation (Seattle) of their schools, but they were not sufficiently careful in tailoring their programs. According to Justice Kennedy, protecting the dignity of the individual justified striking down group-based remedies to group-based harms. In this case, he presented himself as a realist with a nod to the perspective of the victim, yet once again, he privileged formalism over substance, creating more barriers to achieving racial justice.

Limits on Congress's Remedial Power

Section 5 of the Fourteenth Amendment authorizes Congress to enact "appropriate" measures to enforce the amendment, and the Fifteenth Amendment
contains nearly identical language. The Warren Court deferred to Congress
and upheld all of the civil rights measures that Congress enacted (Zietlow
2008). Since the Reconstruction era, Congress has had a constitutional obligation to protect the rights of minorities, including racial minorities, and
Congress has played a leading role in protecting those rights (Zietlow 2006).
However, under the leadership of Justice Kennedy, the Court cut back on this
congressional enforcement power, greatly restricting its authority to legislate
to protect minority rights. In his opinions on section 5, Justice Kennedy privileged judicial supremacy and state sovereignty over the interests of people
who would benefit from federal civil rights laws.

When evaluating federal civil rights legislation, the Warren Court applied
a deferential rational basis review to uphold congressional power. For
example, the Court upheld provisions of the 1965 Voting Rights Act that
prohibited states' use of literacy tests even when no court had found that
the state intentionally discriminated on the basis of race. This was notable
because a previous Court ruling held that literacy tests did not violate the
Equal Protection Clause absent evidence that states used those tests to discriminate intentionally. In *Katzenbach v. Morgan* (1966), the Court held that
Congress itself could make that determination. Speaking for the Court, Justice Brennan opined, "It is not for us to review the congressional resolution
of these factors. It is enough that we be able to perceive a basis upon which
the Congress might resolve this conflict as it did" (653). Brennan's ruling
in *Katzenbach* stopped just short of acknowledging a congressional role in
defining constitutional meaning. Justice Brennan's rationale left Congress
room to develop an anticaste approach to racial equality, even if the Court
confined itself to anticlassification.

Thirty years later, however, in *City of Boerne v. Flores* (1997), Justice Kennedy wrote an opinion for the Court greatly restricting congressional power
to enforce the Fourteenth Amendment. At issue was the constitutionality
of a provision of the 1996 Religious Freedom Restoration Act that required
states to show a compelling interest to justify any law or policy that had
an incidental impact on an individual's free exercise of religion. Congress
enacted the law in response to the Court's ruling in *Employment Division v.
Smith* (1990) that such laws did not violate the Free Exercise Clause. According to Justice Kennedy, Congress unconstitutionally usurped the power of

the Court when enacting the law. Justice Kennedy explained, "Congress does not enforce a constitutional right by changing what that right is. It has been given the power 'to enforce,' not the power to determine what constitutes a constitutional violation" (*Boerne* 1997, 519). Justice Kennedy also expressed concern for state sovereignty, noting that the law imposed a "considerable congressional intrusion into the States' traditional prerogatives and general authority for the health and welfare of their citizens" (534).

To prevent Congress from usurping the Court's power again, Justice Kennedy articulated a new stringent test on congressional authority under section 5. To be constitutional, "there must be a congruence and proportionality between the injury to be prevented or remedied and the means adapted to that end" (*Boerne* 1997, 520). In a series of cases, the Court applied the congruence and proportionality test to strike down numerous civil rights measures (*Garrett* 2001; *Morrison* 2000; *Kimel* 2000). At the same time, Justice Kennedy and his colleagues expanded the doctrine of sovereign immunity to limit suits by individual plaintiffs suing states for violating their rights. For example, in the case of *Alden v. Maine* (1999), Justice Kennedy wrote the opinion for the Court dismissing a case brought by state prison guards to recover unpaid overtime owed them under the Federal Fair Labor Standards Act. Referring to the prison guards as "judgment creditors," Justice Kennedy opined that allowing them to sue their state employer would unconstitutionally infringe on the "sovereign dignity" of the state (*Alden* 1999, 715). The unpaid prison guards, whose federal case was dismissed under the Court's Eleventh Amendment doctrine, were left entirely without a remedy. Justice Kennedy's lack of empathy for the guards was striking, but the dignity of the state of Maine was preserved.

In *Board of Trustees of the University of Alabama v. Garrett* (2001), the Court struck down a provision of the Americans with Disabilities Act that authorized state employees to sue states for disability discrimination. Justice Kennedy noted in his concurring opinion, "prejudice, we are beginning to understand, arises not from malice or hostile animus alone," conceding that prejudice against people with disabilities can be motivated by "indifference or insecurity as well as malicious ill will" (*Garrett* 2001, 374–75). Nonetheless, Justice Kennedy argued that Congress exceeded its section 5 power when it imposed liability on state officials for engaging in facially neutral acts that had a disparate impact on people with disabilities. Justice Kennedy explained, "It is a most serious charge to say a State has engaged in a pattern or practice designed to deny its citizens the equal protection of the laws, particularly where the accusation is based not on hostility but instead on the failure to act or the omission to remedy. States can, and do, stand apart from the citizenry" (376). Again, Justice Kennedy's concern about state sovereignty trumped his empathy for the civil rights plaintiffs.

While neither *Alden* nor *Garrett* was about race equality, Justice Kennedy's *Boerne* opinion has ominous implications for the future of federal civil rights laws. In *Shelby County v. Holder* (2013), Justice Kennedy joined Chief Justice Roberts in a 5–4 opinion striking down the preclearance provision of the 1965 Voting Rights Act. Imposing the rigid scrutiny of *Boerne*, Chief Justice Roberts observed, "The [Fifteenth] Amendment is not designed to punish for the past; its purpose is to ensure a better future" (*Shelby* 2013, 554). Almost immediately after the Court's opinion in *Shelby*, states that had been subjected to Department of Justice preclearance reenacted restrictive voting-rights laws that the Department of Justice had previously rejected. *Boerne* could also prove to be the death knell of disparate-impact causes of action under federal civil rights laws, such as Title VII of the 1964 Civil Rights Act, which impose broader liberty than the Court's equal protection doctrine. Like the requirement of discriminatory intent and the strict scrutiny test for affirmative action, Justice Kennedy's rigid congruence and proportionality test hamstrings political actors who seek to protect their constituents' rights to racial equality.

Conclusion

Recent years have revealed the errors of those who proclaimed the end of racism in our society. People of color lag behind whites in virtually all economic indicators, especially in their acquisition of wealth. The death of George Floyd in 2020 and the Black Lives Matter movement uncovered the widespread racial disparity in law enforcement systems. The disproportionate impact of the COVID pandemic on communities of color has revealed racial disparities in health and economic security. Prominent politicians have resorted to overt racism, and violent white supremacists started an insurrection in our nation's capital in January 2021. At the time of the writing of this chapter, state legislatures throughout the country are considering restrictive measures, including restrictions on early voting and absentee voting, that would have a disproportionate impact on racial minorities. But it is not clear whether equal-protection-based challenges to these laws could prevail. Challengers will need to prove that state legislatures adopted the measures because of, not in spite of, the racial discriminatory impact, and they will confront the procedural barriers imposed by Justice Kennedy's opinion in *Iqbal*.

These developments reveal the extent to which our country is still plagued by racial prejudice, economic exploitation, and years of government condoning practices, such as redlining, which limited economic opportunities of people of color. Activists and lawmakers seeking to remedy this discrimination will confront Supreme Court doctrine that limits their authority to address racial discrimination. In the past thirty years, much of that doctrine was written by Justice Kennedy. In his time on the Court, Justice Kennedy imposed significant barriers to minorities alleging race discrimination and limited government actors from adopting affirmative measures to remedy that discrimination. In the field of racial equality, Justice Kennedy showed no empathy, only rules that disadvantage racial minorities. This is not judging well.

References

Adarand v. Pena. 1995. 515 U.S. 200.

Alden v. Maine. 1999. 527 U.S. 706.

Ashcroft v. Iqbal. 2009. 556 U.S. 662.

Banks, R. Richard. 2001. "Race-Based Suspect Selection and Colorblind Equal Protection Doctrine and Discourse." *UCLA Law Review* 48:1075–124.

Bhagwat, Ashutosh. 2016. "Liberty or Equality?" *Lewis & Clark Law Review* 20:381–98.

Board of Trustees of the University of Alabama v. Garrett. 2001. 531 U.S. 536.

Brown v. Board of Education of Topeka. 1954. 347 U.S. 483.

Cintron, Ralph. 2010. "Democracy and Its Limitations." In *The Public Work of Rhetoric: Citizen-Scholars and Civic Engagement,* edited by John M. Ackerman and David J. Coogan, 98–116. Columbia: University of South Carolina Press.

City of Boerne v. Flores. 1997. 521 U.S. 507.

Ely, John Hart. 1980. *Democracy and Distrust: A Theory of Judicial Review.* Cambridge: Harvard University Press.

Employment Division, Department of Human Resources of Oregon v. Smith. 1990. 494 U.S. 872.

Erickson v. Pardus. 2007. 551 U.S. 89.

Fisher v. University of Texas I. 2013. 570 U.S. 297.

Fisher v. University of Texas II. 2016. 579 U.S. 365.

Fiss, Owen. 1976. "Groups and the Equal Protection Clause." *Philosophy and Public Affairs* 5:107–77.

Gotanda, Neil. 1991. "A Critique of 'Our Constitution Is Color-Blind.'" *Stanford Law Review* 44:1–68.

Grutter v. Bollinger. 2003. 539 U.S. 306.

Hernandez v. New York. 1991. 500 U.S. 352.

Karst, Kenneth L. 1977. "Foreword: Equal Citizenship Under the Fourteenth Amendment." *Harvard Law Review* 91:1–68.

Katzenbach v. Morgan. 1966. 384 U.S. 641.

Kimel v. Florida Board of Regents. 2000. 528 U.S. 62.

Lawrence, Charles R., III. 1987. "The Id, the Ego, and Equal Protection: Reckoning with Unconscious Racism." *Stanford Law Review* 39:317–88.

Metro Broadcasting, Inc. v. F.C.C. 1990. 497 U.S. 547.

Obergefell v. Hodges. 2015. 576 U.S. 644.

Parents Involved in Community Schools v. Seattle School District No. 1. 2007. 551 U.S. 701.

Plessy v. Ferguson. 1896. 163 U.S. 537.

Regents of the University of California v. Bakke. 1978. 438 U.S. 265.

Reinert, Alexander A. 2015. "Measuring the Impact of Plausibility Pleading." *Virginia Law Review* 110:2117–83.

Ricci v. DeStefano. 2009. 557 U.S. 557.

Romer v. Evans. 1996. 517 U.S. 620.

Schmidt, Christopher. 2008. "*Brown* and the Colorblind Constitution." *Cornell Law Review* 94:203–38.

Shelby County v. Holder. 2013. 570 U.S. 529.

Siegel, Reva. 2003. "Equality Talk: Anti-Subordination and Anti-Classification Values in Constitutional Struggles over *Brown*." *Harvard Law Review* 117:1470–1547.

United States v. Carolene Products Co. 1938. 304 U.S. 144.

United States v. Morrison. 2000. 529 U.S. 598.

Washington v. Davis. 1976. 426 U.S. 229.

Zietlow, Rebecca E. 2006. *Enforcing Equality: Congress, the Constitution, and the Protection of Individual Rights.* New York: New York University Press.

———. 2008. "The Judicial Restraint of the Warren Court (and Why It Matters)." *Ohio State Law Journal* 69:25–301.

15

WHOSE FREEDOM? JUSTICE KENNEDY'S
SOVEREIGNTY, AUTONOMY, AND LIBERTY
DISCOURSES IN IMMIGRATION CASES

Leticia M. Saucedo

Justice Anthony Kennedy is widely recognized for his attempts to protect individual liberty, autonomy, and dignity against government intrusion (Knowles 2019, 4). In cases involving immigration, however, the federal government's autonomy interest often outweighed the due process or individual rights of immigrants. When the immigrant did prevail, Justice Kennedy constructed a narrative of the *deserving immigrant*, one who is worthy of and willing to participate in the US political community and who therefore should be accorded individual rights. In particular, immigrants who Justice Kennedy perceived had commonalities or assimilationist characteristics were deemed deserving of dignity protections. Justice Kennedy utilized rhetorical devices effectively to make the distinction between the deserving and undeserving immigrant, all the while protecting the authority of the federal government to exercise its discretion for the sake of protecting the nation from nonconforming outsiders.

The legal scholar Russell Robinson has observed that "the empathy and dignity that guided Justice Kennedy's pathbreaking sexual orientation decisions failed to trickle down to reach the minorities in the immigration and national security cases" (2019, 1071). Robinson argues that Justice Kennedy's opinions betrayed a view of the acceptable immigrant as one who fit within the mold of the white, heterosexual Christian. From Justice Kennedy's position as a white, heterosexual Christian, he could assume that the assimilable immigrant was one who accepted those values. Interestingly, Justice Kennedy's views were not so transparent in his opinions. Instead, his point of view as one in the majority white, heterosexual, Christian world that he occupied was implied in his discussions regarding who was deserving and who was not. His rhetoric assumes the centrality of his perspective and so appears unremarkable.

Justice Kennedy makes little reference to the positionality of the migrants who came before the Court. Instead, many of his opinions delve into the intricacies of the statute and statutory interpretation. There are clues, however, to Justice Kennedy's view that the statute's design favors those immigrants who will be easily assimilable. In this chapter, I explore Justice Kennedy's immigration opinions to reveal how he used sovereignty and liberty arguments to make room for deserving immigrants and exclude undeserving ones. As Robinson points out, Justice Kennedy's position as a white man "at the center of national identity" facilitated his reasoning surrounding assimilability (2019, 1031). If his views stemmed from the center of national identity in the immigration cases, it would be a logical next step for Justice Kennedy to invoke the will of the people to keep out nonassimilable immigrants. Robinson claims that these decisions were racialized. This may have been the case in the sense that deserving and assimilable immigrants share white, heterosexual Christian traits. This chapter explores the rhetoric Justice Kennedy utilized to speak from the center of national identity in distinguishing deserving from undeserving immigrants. His opinions created a particular immigration jurisprudence—one that protects those who are willing to assimilate into US civic culture against the overreaching of particular government branches but that protects the sovereignty of the federal government against those who are nonassimilable.

Justice Kennedy had ideas about the relative autonomy of each of the branches to represent the federal government in exercising its sovereign power, and he based his immigration opinions on those principles. He relied on both the institutional roles of government branches and the status of the immigrants in the cases to make decisions that ultimately affected the liberty interests of the immigrants. Whether he voted to protect the liberty interests of migrants or the authority of the federal government, Justice Kennedy spoke in terms of institutional competence, giving the benefit of the doubt to migrants only when their interests coincided with what he considered broader civic, political, and economic US values. Sovereignty and separation of powers, then, are twin pillars in Justice Kennedy's framing of the stories of the foreign individuals in the immigration cases.

Consider Justice Kennedy's dissent in *Zadvydas v. Davis* (2001), in which he argued that the Supreme Court overstepped its power when it decided that post-removal detention beyond six months might violate due process; or his concurrence in *Trump v. Hawaii* (2018), in which he argued that the president has the authority to issue a travel ban, assuming that the president acts in good faith; or his concurrence in *Kerry v. Din* (2015), in which he argues that the courts have no authority to go behind executive discretion in visa denial cases, even when the individual asserting a liberty interest is a US citizen; or his Ninth Circuit opinion in *Chadha v. Immigration and Naturalization Service* (1980), in which he held that Congress overstepped its delegation authority by instituting a one-house veto of cancellation of removal decisions. In all of these cases, Justice Kennedy's rhetorical construction of the immigrant as deserving or undeserving buttressed his views about the role of the different government branches. His empathy was conditioned on his rhetorical presentation of the assimilability of the immigrants in question.

Liberty, Autonomy, Sovereignty, and Civic Participation

In a post-9/11 speech to the American Bar Association, Justice Kennedy spoke of the work of maintaining freedom as linked with the work of growing a culture of civic discourse, in order to counter enemies threatening the country from the outside. He noted, "In this century democracy's enemies come from outside the countries they seek to destroy. They . . . see a free and open society as a threat. Once again we face an assault on freedom" (Kennedy 2003). In part of this speech, Justice Kennedy asserts that law needs to uphold dignity as a right and expresses his concern for assaults on freedom from the outside.

But from whose perspective should the legal system view freedom? Who is included in the community of freedom seekers? Justice Kennedy assumes that all who share the economic values of free enterprise should be assimilated into the project of building the country. He draws from Yick Wo's story in *Yick Wo v. Hopkins* (1886) to make his point:

> Our own legal tradition has been shaped by persons who know there is injustice but must resort to the law to establish the general principles for righting it. Over 115 years ago, in this city, a man called Yick Wo went to court when local officials denied him a permit for his laundry business. He came to the Supreme Court of the United States. His case generated one of the most important equal protection decisions ever written. It is a tribute to our law and to our profession that a case involving a foreign

national gave meaning and scope to the equal protection rights of all Americans. Our case law system is built on the idea that individuals in any era can strive to vindicate personal rights, and that by their effort our law emerges stronger than before. (Kennedy 2003)

This language is similar to the characterizations of the plaintiffs in *Obergefell v. Hodges* (2015) as individuals who simply sought to assimilate to the cultural and societal expectations of marriage but who faced unequal government opposition. In *Obergefell*, Justice Kennedy extols the importance of marriage to the fabric of society and then depicts James Obergefell and his partner, John Arthur, as striving to participate in that important expression. "Far from seeking to devalue marriage," he notes, "the petitioners seek it for themselves because of their respect—and need—for its privileges and responsibilities" (*Obergefell* 2015, 658).

The legal scholar Melissa Murray (2016) contends that *Obergefell* and its companion, *United States v. Windsor* (2013), were part of an assimilationist project. The assimilationist position of the parties in these cases appealed to Justice Kennedy's view that government should not create barriers for those who accept the values embedded in marriage as an institution. Just as with the same-sex marriage cases, Justice Kennedy approaches immigration cases by weighing the interests of the states and the federal government and the values they represent against the interests and the values of the immigrants. I next review some examples of Justice Kennedy's jurisprudence to demonstrate this thesis.

Arizona v. United States

In *Arizona v. United States* (2012), Justice Kennedy clearly stated that the principle of sovereignty gave the federal government authority, as against the states, over immigration. He concluded for the majority that the federal government had almost exclusive authority over immigration regulation, which preempted state enforcement efforts over immigration status. Importantly, he reached his conclusion, in part, by characterizing Arizona's law as an infringement on the federal government's authority to determine which immigrants deserve to assimilate into US society. He stressed the importance of upholding the flexibility of the executive branch to balance immigration enforcement with foreign-policy objectives (*Arizona* 2012, 397). He also emphasized the importance of allowing the executive branch to exercise discretion in immigration enforcement as a matter of agency expertise (397).

In reinforcing the federal government's exclusive power to regulate immigration, Justice Kennedy then invoked images of deserving immigrants. "Discretion in the enforcement of immigration law embraces immediate human concerns," the opinion noted. "Unauthorized workers trying to support their families, for example, likely pose less danger than alien smugglers or aliens who commit a serious crime. The equities of an individual case may turn on many factors, including whether the alien has children born in the United States, long ties to the community, or a record of distinguished military service" (*Arizona* 2012, 396).

Finally, Justice Kennedy invoked the assimilationist principle by describing a citizenship ceremony, the culmination of the ideal immigrant story: "Immigration policy shapes the destiny of the Nation. On May 24, 2012, at one of this Nation's most distinguished museums of history, a dozen immigrants stood before the tattered flag that inspired Francis Scott Key to write the National Anthem. There they took the oath to become American citizens. . . . These naturalization ceremonies bring together men and women of different origins who now share a common destiny. They swear a common oath to renounce fidelity to foreign princes, to defend the Constitution, and to bear arms on behalf of the country when required by law" (*Arizona* 2012, 415). Justice Kennedy's description of the naturalized citizens tracks the melting pot narrative: "The history of the United States is in part made of the stories, talents, and lasting contributions of those who crossed oceans and deserts to come here" (397).

The "nation of immigrants" narrative supports invoking sovereignty to uphold an assimilationist perspective of integration. The state has the responsibility to determine how to use its police powers to ensure that individuals are not harmed by the evolving immigrant nature of our nation. In exercising sovereignty, the federal government expresses the will of the people, which is not necessarily one that includes foreigners. As Justice Kennedy noted, "The National Government has significant power to regulate immigration. With power comes responsibility, and the sound exercise of national power over immigration depends on the Nation's meeting its responsibility to base its laws on a political will informed by searching, thoughtful, rational civic discourse" (*Arizona* 2012, 416).

This expression assumes the immigrant as outsider and, as such, one whose dignity interests may not factor into the balance of individual liberty against sovereignty interests. But the nation-of-immigrants narrative suggests that not all immigrants need remain outside the polity. Those who seek to integrate into the melting pot may have dignity interests worth protecting.

The distinction that Justice Kennedy made here establishes both that there are deserving immigrants and that the states cannot use sovereignty principles to decree all immigrants as undeserving.

Justice Kennedy's position responded to Justice Antonin Scalia's extreme position that states should be able to judge for themselves what the nature of their polity should be. Justice Scalia dissented from the opinion, which he excoriated for "depriv[ing] States of what most would consider the defining characteristic of sovereignty: the power to exclude from the sovereign's territory people who have no right to be there" (*Arizona* 2012, 417). Justice Scalia's version of the case presented Arizona and its citizens as victims. "Arizona bears the brunt of the country's illegal immigration problem," he noted. "Its citizens feel themselves under siege by large numbers of illegal immigrants who invade their property, strain their social services, and even place their lives in jeopardy" (436).

Justice Kennedy's rhetoric about immigrants seeking to naturalize, on the other hand, provided the counternarrative for how the Court should weigh the interests of immigrants. He did not seem to disagree that a decision should be made about who should be allowed to enter the United States. The disagreement was over institutional roles and whether the decision should be made at a federal level.

Chadha v. Immigration and Naturalization Service

In line with Justice Kennedy's portrayal of Yick Wo as the deserving immigrant, when he was a circuit court judge, he portrayed Jagdish Chadha—the protagonist in the drama over the executive line-item veto—in positive terms. In this case, Chadha's assimilability lay in his educational background. Judge Kennedy's portrayal of Chadha is important to his conclusion in this case. Chadha was a well-educated individual who came to the United States on a student visa. He received bachelor's and master's degrees from US schools before his visa expired and he was found deportable (*Chadha* 1980, 411).

Chadha faced deportation after his student visa expired. The immigration court suspended his deportation, pursuant to a statute that allowed for relief from deportation. The same statute allowed the House of Representatives to reverse the court's suspension of deportation, and it did (Immigration and Nationality Act, §244(c)(2)). Chadha challenged the one-house veto as unconstitutional. At the Ninth Circuit, Judge Kennedy agreed with Chadha that the one-house veto interfered with the executive authority and with the right of noncitizens to rely on court interpretations of the Immigration and

Nationality Act. Judge Kennedy concluded that allowing unicameral legislative disapproval in this case would give Congress "flexibility [that] is but the structural twin of lawless rule" and reinstated the attorney general's decision to stay deportation (*Chadha* 1980, 436).

Justice Kennedy's depiction of Chadha in public venues after the case was decided is telling. I was present at McGeorge School of Law when Justice Kennedy gave a talk to constitutional law students in 2013. Justice Kennedy mentioned Chadha as he urged students to remember that cases involving highly technical and abstract legal principles are many times cases involving life-changing issues for everyday human beings. He told the story of how he was reminded of this observation. He recounted being at a Tower Records store in the San Francisco area buying music for his family some time after *Chadha* was decided. He went to the counter, where a hard-working clerk rung up his purchases and took his credit card. When the man saw the name on the credit card, he asked Justice Kennedy whether he was *the* Judge Kennedy from the Ninth Circuit. Justice Kennedy answered in the affirmative, at which point Jagdish Chadha said to him excitedly, "I am Chadha!" Just as in his retelling of the Yick Wo story as a tale of an immigrant seeking to contribute, his recounting of his experience with Chadha portrays him as a deserving immigrant facing unnecessary structural governmental obstacles to integration.

The Nonassimilationist Cases

The same structural arguments that Justice Kennedy utilized to uphold the liberty interests of good immigrants operated to protect the sovereign from undesirable immigrants. The following cases involve examples of this rhetorical move.

Immigration and Naturalization Service v. Aguirre-Aguirre

In *Immigration and Naturalization Service v. Aguirre-Aguirre* (1999), Justice Kennedy constructed an image of an immigrant who does not fit with US political decorum: one can only go so far in voicing political views, and violence goes too far. The determination over how far is too far, moreover, belongs in the executive branch, which has the flexibility and expertise to make determinations about the political nature of a crime. Juan Anibal Aguirre-Aguirre had been convicted of burning and looting buses to protest increases in public transportation fares and the disappearance or murder of students. Although he was not eligible for asylum, he sought withholding of removal because he would be persecuted if he returned to his home country of Guatemala. The immigration statute required that the Immigration and Naturalization Service (INS) make a determination balancing the political nature of his crime against its common law character (*Aguirre-Aguirre* 1999, 422). The immigration court held that the crime was out of proportion with the political aspect of the action (421). The Board of Immigration Appeals decided that Aguirre-Aguirre's political messages of dissatisfaction with the Guatemalan government were "outweighed by their criminal strategy" (422–23).

The Ninth Circuit held that the INS should instead have balanced the nature of the crime against the threat of persecution. Justice Kennedy disagreed with the Ninth Circuit and gave great deference to the agency to weigh the political crime against its common law character.

In Justice Kennedy's view, Aguirre-Aguirre was undeserving because his underlying act of violence, even if done for political reasons, marked him as unassimilable. Justice Kennedy emphasized, however, that the ultimate determination belongs to the administrative agency (*Aguirre-Aguirre* 1999, 431). This position makes it easier for front-line employees to severely limit the claims of asylum applicants who engaged in political activity—often in the midst of a violent government response—that ultimately drove them to the United States. Without mentioning race, Justice Kennedy endorsed a standard that closes the avenues to remain in the United States to Latino/a political dissidents. He did this in the name of foreign affairs. If the judiciary were to determine that the political nature of a crime outweighed its political character, there might be consequences that implicate foreign relations. This rationale reveals an understanding of political crimes from the position of governments facing them rather than from the perspective of the individual seeking protection from persecution. It has a damning effect on immigrants from Latin America, especially, where geopolitical considerations are made alongside determinations of political persecution.

Zadvydas v. Davis

In weighing the limits of sovereignty, Justice Kennedy dissented from a case in which the respondent, Kestutis Zadvydas, faced indefinite detention—a denial of liberty interest if ever there was one—after his removal proceeding (*Zadvydas* 2001, 682). At issue was a provision of the Immigration and Nationality Act that allows for post-removal detention while the government makes preparations for physical removal. The statute allows for a ninety-day removal period, but the government can continue to detain the noncitizen under certain conditions, subject to periodic review of the reasons for detention (683). In this case, Zadvydas had a long criminal record, which was the basis for his removal. The agency had been unable to get Zadvydas's country of origin to accept him, and he was held in post-deportation detention for over two years (683).

The majority opinion in this case noted that the statute seemingly authorized indefinite detention of these individuals inside the United States and that this interpretation of the statute would raise due process considerations (*Zadvydas* 2001, 683). Applying the canon of constitutional avoidance, the majority held that the post-removal detention statute should be read to authorize detention to a period reasonably necessary to effect the deportation and that it does not permit indefinite detention (699).

Justice Kennedy dissented, pointing to the role of the executive branch in protecting the country's sovereignty. Highly critical of the majority, he opined that the majority was wrong to insert itself into foreign affairs, to rewrite the statute in contravention of congressional intent, and to undermine Congress's safety concerns (*Zadvydas* 2001, 705–8). He invoked several examples of unassimilable immigrants, all convicted of crimes, including Zadvydas. His examples included Cambodians, Laotians, Vietnamese, and Zadvydas, who was of Lithuanian descent but was born in Germany and an outsider in both countries. His outsider, noncitizen status in both Lithuania and Germany bolstered Justice Kennedy's view that some immigrants who are unassimilable should not be free to roam in the United States (721)—this despite the fact that in each example, the individuals had served their time in prison and were then held indefinitely in immigration detention.

But Justice Kennedy did not stop there. He also worried about the ability of immigrants who entered the country without authorization to remain free if they could not return to their home countries. Here he invoked the example of Mariel Cubans who were convicted of small crimes but who could not be returned to Cuba. In describing their nonassimilability, Justice Kennedy explained that the due process right to freedom from indefinite detention hinged on the status of the individual. "It must be made clear these aliens are in a position far different from aliens with a lawful right to remain here," he wrote. "They are removable, and their rights must be defined in accordance with that status. The due process analysis must begin with a 'careful description of the asserted right'" (*Zadvydas* 2001, 720; citations omitted).

Here the immigrants' criminal records defined their status as undeserving. That undeservedness gives an immigrant's interest little weight. Justice

Kennedy characterized the majority opinion as an impingement on federal sovereignty because it requires the executive branch to submit the status of repatriation efforts to the judiciary. He considered this an imposition on the executive branch's operation of sovereignty (*Zadvydas* 2001, 722). Rather than placing weight on the liberty interest of the detainee, Justice Kennedy sided with the federal government's autonomy/sovereignty interest. As long as the initial detention was protected by procedural safeguards, Justice Kennedy remained satisfied that the process due the undeserving immigrant was less weighty than the government's autonomy interest (721–22).

Kerry v. Din

Just as in *Zadvydas*, Justice Kennedy's approach to the balance between individual dignity interests and federal sovereignty interests in *Kerry v. Din* weighed heavily in favor of the federal government. Congressional determination of what constitutes due process—in this case, notice of a visa denial—sufficed to ensure a liberty interest, even when the liberty interest at stake was the ability of a citizen to reunite with her noncitizen spouse. Fauzia Din, a US citizen, sued the government when her husband, an Afghan citizen, was denied a visa (*Kerry* 2015, 88). Din's husband was denied a visa because he was inadmissible under 8 USC §1182(a)(3)(B)'s terrorism bar, based on his having worked for the Taliban government at some point in his past. Din alleged a due process violation when the government refused to give her an adequate explanation for the visa denial. Justice Scalia, for the Court, wrote that there was no such constitutional right because Din did not suffer a deprivation of liberty (89–92).

Justice Kennedy concurred, arguing that even if Din had a protected liberty interest, "the notice she received regarding her husband's visa denial satisfied due process" and emphasizing that Din "received all the process to which she was entitled" (*Kerry* 2015, 102). He argued that courts had no authority to "look behind the exercise of [executive] discretion . . . or test it by balancing its justification against" a citizen spouse's constitutional right (104).

As Russell Robinson notes in his critique of the opinion, "In short, Justice Kennedy gave no weight to Din's interest in living together with her husband in America. He concluded that 'respect for the political branches' broad power over the creation and administration of the immigration system' counsels against requiring the government to disclose the underlying facts and allowing Din to challenge them. Justice Kennedy's concurrence declined even to discuss Din's personal stake in the visa decision—that is, how enforced separation from her husband would impact the integrity of their union" (2019, 1053). The weight of the individual interest here again depends on Din's status. She is the wife of a suspected Taliban member. Importantly, Justice Kennedy's opinion portrays the relative weight of interests between the individual and the federal government as lopsided. The interest of the wife of a suspected terrorist—even if she is a US citizen—is less weighty than the interest of the government in securing the safety of the country against outside forces. In making this rhetorical turn, Justice Kennedy prioritized sovereignty principles over the interests of both the foreign national and his citizen spouse. In determining the people whose will must be protected through institutional roles, Justice Kennedy tied Din to her husband, leaving them outside the polity, even when her husband's liberty interests might otherwise be more fully protected because of the marriage. In so doing, Justice Kennedy framed the question as one of the role of a government branch in exercising its sovereignty/autonomy principles, rather than an issue of government action potentially endangering liberty. Ironically, this means that the wife seeking the entry of her Afghan husband will not, in the words of Justice Kennedy's *Obergefell* decision, be able to experience how "marriage responds to the lonely person who might call out only to find no one there" (2015, 667).

Trump v. Hawaii

Trump v. Hawaii, the challenge to the Trump administration's Muslim ban, questioned the rationales behind the administration's decision to ban from entry groups of people from mostly Muslim countries. Instead of interrogating either the rationales for these decisions or the anti-Muslim statements made by President Trump in his Twitter feeds, the Court, and Justice Kennedy, assumed both the rational basis and the good faith of the administration in making its decision.

The state of Hawaii and three individuals with foreign relatives challenged a presidential proclamation that limited immigration from specified countries for ninety days (*Trump* 2018, 2403). The president justified the proclamation by stating that these countries failed to meet information-sharing standards and/or posed a national security risk (2403). The state of Hawaii argued that the proclamation exceeded executive authority under the Immigration and Nationality Act and violated the Establishment Clause of the First Amendment (2403). The federal government argued for its sovereignty interest in the exclusion of noncitizens and that noncitizens had no individual right to enter the United States (2407).

The majority held that the president did not exceed his authority under the INA because the text of the INA allows for deference to the judgment of the executive branch (*Trump* 2018, 2408). The Court further supported its holding by noting that if Congress wished to limit presidential power in the INA to emergencies, it would have done so in the text of the INA (2414).

Writing separately in concurrence, Justice Kennedy elevated sovereignty interests and executive authority on matters of foreign affairs (*Trump* 2018, 2424)—but not without a reprimand to the executive branch that judicial deference comes with a heightened responsibility to adhere to constitutional standards. Here Justice Kennedy did not question the good faith or the integrity of the Trump administration directly. Instead, he resorted to institutional roles and the interest of the federal government in exercising its sovereignty to keep out undeserving immigrants. The undeserving immigrants in this case were nonwhite, Muslim immigrants. But, by operating on a level of abstraction, Justice Kennedy could condone a Muslim ban in the name of institutional autonomy without having to reach the question of individual dignity interests. At this level of abstraction, assuming the good faith of the government actors, the three branches could achieve a free and open society.

Conclusion

The day before Justice Kennedy announced his retirement, he issued his concurrence in *Trump v. Hawaii*. The case exemplified Justice Kennedy's approach to the immigration cases, which limited empathy and dignity considerations to those immigrants he deemed deserving. Deserving immigrants, in turn, were ones to which Justice Kennedy assigned assimilability traits. Underserving immigrants, by contrast, were accorded due process rights only according to their status as nonassimilable. The interests of those immigrants proved less weighty than the autonomy and sovereignty of the federal government. As Robinson notes, those immigrants also tended to be nonwhite. Importantly, Justice Kennedy's opinions reflected a consistent faith in the role of government in protecting freedoms of people seeking to assimilate—that is, deserving immigrants—but also in the autonomy and authority of the federal government, expressed through its different branches, to distinguish deserving from undeserving immigrants in order to remain faithful to the people's will. Ironically, this also means that immigrants and their families will need to establish deservedness to seek liberty protections.

References

Arizona v. United States. 2012. 567 U.S. 387.

Chadha v. Immigration and Naturalization Service. 1980. 634 F.2d 408.

Immigration and Naturalization Service v. Aguirre-Aguirre. 1999. 526 U.S. 415.

Kennedy, Anthony. 2003. Speech at the annual meeting of the American Bar Association, August 9, 2003. Available at https://www.supremecourt.gov/publicinfo/speeches/viewspeech/sp_08-09-03.

Kerry v. Din. 2015. 576 U.S. 86.

Knowles, Helen J. 2019. *The Tie Goes to Freedom: Justice Kennedy on Liberty*. Updated ed. Lanham, MD: Rowman and Littlefield.

Murray, Melissa. 2016. "*Obergefell v. Hodges* and Nonmarriage Inequality." *California Law Review* 104:1207–58.

Obergefell v. Hodges. 2015. 576 U.S. 644.

Robinson, Russell. 2019. "Justice Kennedy's White Nationalism." *UC Davis Law Review* 53:1027–72.

Trump v. Hawaii. 2018. 585 U.S. ___, 138 S. Ct. 2392.

United States v. Windsor. 2013. 570 U.S. 744.

Yick Wo v. Hopkins. 1886. 118 U.S. 356.

Zadvydas v. Davis. 2001. 533 U.S. 678.

PART 6

ASSESSMENT

16

RHETORICAL VISION AND JUDGMENT:
DID JUSTICE ANTHONY M. KENNEDY JUDGE WELL?

David A. Frank

Let rhetoric be [defined as] an ability, in each [particular] case, *to see* the available means of persuasion.

—Aristotle

On March 12, 2021, Justice Anthony M. Kennedy addressed a virtual working papers conference designed to engage the editors and contributors of this volume in dialogue and argument about his Supreme Court decisions. Justice Kennedy delivered his recorded address from his Supreme Court chambers. He dedicated his address to the theme of civility. The editors and contributors were struck by Justice Kennedy's thoughtful, meditative style, confirming the observation of Ashutosh Bhagwat, who clerked for Justice Kennedy and is the author of chapter 9, that "one of Justice Kennedy's notable personal characteristics is that he seems incapable of vitriol or unkindness, in any setting": "I have never truly heard him speak an unkind word about another human being, even when such words might have been deserved" (2016, 388). These impressions of Justice Kennedy's ethos, most notably his apparent goodwill, earned the respect of the editors and contributors, but no one in his audience was deterred by this consensus from answering this book's guiding question mainly in the negative: Did Justice Kennedy judge well?

In judging Justice Kennedy's decisions, the editors and authors, representing the fields of law and rhetoric, explore the methods and criteria used to make judgments. Their insights and contributions, developed by leading scholars in both fields, advance our understanding of the relationship between rhetoric and judgment and the quality of Justice Kennedy's decisions. I devote this chapter to three most noteworthy insights offered by the studies in this volume. They are (1) the unappreciated power of classical and contemporary rhetorical theories and methods to inform legal decision-making and judgment, (2) the rhetorical standards needed to identify the humane vision and blind spots in Justice Kennedy's decisions, and (3) the further development of a rhetorical theory of judging well. Because these three topics are grounded in the concept of rhetorical knowledge, I begin by exploring that concept.

Rhetorical Knowledge in Justice Kennedy's Opinions

Scholars have noted that the values of equality, liberty, dignity, and freedom anchored Justice Kennedy's decisions in his role as an associate justice. The editors and contributors agree that Justice Kennedy did make use of these values to judge well in the gay-marriage case. His deep empathy for gay people is evident in his rich depiction of their individuality and character in *Obergefell v. Hodges* (2015), the case in which Justice Kennedy established the right to gay marriage under the federal Constitution. However, even here, as Elizabeth C. Britt persuasively argues in chapter 12, Justice Kennedy's view of marriage as the best familial form is deeply problematic.

Blind spots affected Justice Kennedy's vision and application of these values. They revealed themselves in misjudgments in several important cases. Justice Kennedy displayed profoundly flawed images of women, people of color, and immigrants in his decisions. As Kathryn Stanchi concludes in chapter 13, Justice Kennedy did not judge well in women's rights cases. His image of women in these cases, Stanchi explains, is flat, "with little agency or complexity," a judgment corroborated by Britt in chapter 12. Rebecca E. Zietlow (chap. 14) and Leticia M. Saucedo (chap. 15) identify similar blind spots in Justice Kennedy's depictions of race and immigrants, leading to defective judgments.

Justice Kennedy's decisions are products of rhetoric. As the studies in this volume suggest, the process of judging and the product of legal judgments are not simple functions of mathematical calculations; they require a rhetorical method. As James A. Gardner explains in chapter 10, "The very idea that 'judgment' needs to be exercised in certain circumstances implies some degree of both complexity and discretion; we do not speak of 'judgment' in cases where tasks call merely for mechanical, discretionless administration." Judgment, rather than calculation, is called for when a judge, in Gardner's words, must "sift and evaluate conflicting evidence" and when "the meaning of controlling texts or precedents" is "obscure and indeterminate." There are, as Gardner rightly points out, easy cases in which the precedents are clear and the evidence is compelling. In such cases, judgments may resemble calculations. In stark contrast, hard cases, Gardner argues, require struggle with conflicting evidence and precedents that do not offer good mooring for judgment.

Hard cases require rhetoric as a method of interpretation, criticism, and as Aristotle observed in his *Rhetoric*, judgment. Argument and argumentation are the vehicles for rhetorical judgments (Zarefsky 2019; Perelman and Olbrechts-Tyteca 1969; Mercier and Sperber 2017). Sean O'Rourke, in chapter 5, nests the process of argument and argumentation in the ancient method of *controversia*. He writes, "Controversial thinking is a way of approaching the world, a rhetorical stance, predicated on the assumption that doubt begets possibilities for argument. It serves as an inventional activity by cultivating fitting responses to the factual, legal, and equitable demands of a case and is evident in the text that the rhetor produces. At its heart is the *quaestio*, the question." Here O'Rourke identifies the essential characteristics of the rhetorical method: it begins with questions rather than answers or a predetermined methodology; it assumes uncertainty in precedent and evidence; it seeks to discover and invent good but not perfect judgments; it strives for solutions that fit the problem in its temporal situation; and it draws from and creates rhetorical knowledge in the service of justice.

In chapter 7, Francis J. Mootz III defines and describes rhetorical knowledge as a social construction, one that "is no less a form of knowledge than logical or empirical knowledge." Rhetorical knowledge emerges from "practical encounters that have critical dimensions," taking the form of argument and argumentation (Mootz 2006, xvi). Rhetorical knowledge is only as strong as the arguments supporting it. Rhetorical method neither "achieves . . . apodictic certitude nor collapses into a relativistic irrationalism," as Mootz argues in his article "Judging Well" (Mootz 2018, 16).

One can judge well or poorly with rhetoric—the judgments themselves constitute rhetorical knowledge, as they do establish values and precedents that have survived the tests of *controversia*. Neither the rhetorical method nor subsequent judgments that are the result are immaculate or beyond the pale of error, prejudice, and mistake. Rhetorical knowledge can serve as precedent, as an anchor for preferred values and action. And rhetorical knowledge remains open to challenge, change, and reformation. When, for example, Justice

Kennedy argues in *Lawrence v. Texas* (2003) that the Supreme Court was "wrong" in *Bowers v Hardwick* (1986), the case that upheld laws against homosexuality, he was rejecting what had been justified by the court and a legitimate expression of rhetorical knowledge and then setting forth a better version.

Mootz calls our attention to Justice Kennedy's natural law argumentation and to the consensus of the world community in *Roper v. Simmons* (2005) that minors should not be treated as adults in capital cases as illustrations of rhetorical knowledge. Justice Kennedy's natural law argument is one of several arguments in his decision in *Roper*; it does not, as Mootz insists, reign supreme. There are several arguments in *Roper* that have different starting points but converge on the same conclusion: minors should not be treated as adults. "We should not confuse recourse to natural law argumentation," Mootz writes, "with following a method that generates the correct method" (chap. 7 in this volume). No one methodology or strategy produces rhetorical knowledge. A natural law methodology or natural law used as a primary strategy would constrain judgment to a deduction, with natural law serving as the major premise, or confine it to a calculation.

Rhetorical knowledge is contingent on the good reasons that are seen and understood by the judge. Indeed, as Mootz concludes, "Natural law argumentation is not always persuasive" (chap. 7 in this volume). Natural law is sometimes persuasive, depending on the question it answers. More broadly, the roles of persuasion and rhetoric in judging rhetorical knowledge were clearly understood by ancient Greek and Roman rhetoricians as well as modern scholars, leading to the first of three insights (among many) developed in this volume.

Three Insights into Justice Kennedy's Rhetoric

With the preceding understanding of the nature of rhetorical knowledge, we are in a position to elaborate on the three key insights to be gained from this volume.

Classical and Contemporary Rhetorical Theories: Equipment for Judging Well

During the two virtual working paper conferences devoted to this volume, hosted by the McGeorge School of Law and the Anthony M. Kennedy Chair at McGeorge School of Law—currently held by Leslie Jacobs, the author of chapter 11—participants sounded a recurring qualification: "I'm not a legal scholar, but . . ." and "I'm not a scholar of rhetoric, but . . ." As the chapters reveal, the contributors were more than willing to trespass disciplinary boundaries in their chapters. Fortunately, the two working paper conferences and subsequent revisions of the book chapters by their authors yielded an interdisciplinary approach blending legal studies with rhetoric to explain and assess Justice Kennedy's opinions.

We were privileged to have some of the leading scholars of ancient and modern rhetorical theory and criticism provide histories of rhetoric and its relationship to judgment and to legal reasoning. Two of the most prominent scholars of ancient rhetoric and of Aristotle's *Rhetoric*, Michael Gagarin and Eugene Garver, draw from classical theories of rhetoric to explain and evaluate Justice Kennedy's decisions. As they observe, the rhetorical tradition, which spans two thousand years in Western culture, sets forth methods that are not an all-inclusive methodology or a preexisting strategy, but it does set up approaches and standards for discovering, inventing, and judging the decisions offered by advocates and judges. Rhetorical methods do have several essential characteristics that have evolved over time.

George Kennedy translates Aristotle's definition of "rhetoric" as "an ability, in each [particular] case, *to see* the available means of persuasion" (Aristotle 1991, 37; emphasis added). A robust rhetorical vision is capable of seeing and understanding humans and their affections, desires, traumas, and modes of reasoning (Hawhee 2011). A rhetorical vision must include all the proofs that are important in judgment, including ethos (character), pathos (emotions), and the role of reason in human affairs (Garver 2011). This vision must include all the audiences affected by a judge's judgment. Chaïm Perelman and Lucie Olbrechts-Tyteca, in their contemporary revision of Aristotelian rhetoric, observe that the audience is a "visualized . . . construction" made by the speaker; this visualization, they conclude, "should be adequate to the occasion" (1969, 19). If the occasion calls for judgment, then the judge must have properly and humanely constructed the audience of the judge's decision. Sight and vision are at the core of rhetoric, its method, and its judgments. Several authors in this book target Justice Kennedy's moral vision for praise and blame.

Socrates, as Garver astutely illustrates, understood the forces of piety and pollution in clouding rhetorical visions. The question that Socrates poses to Euthyphro, Garver rightly reminds us, remains a constant: Is something true and right because it has earned the consensus of the community or because that something is true and right in principle? A community's consensus about piety has a counterpart in the fear of communal pollution. This fear is based on a consensus that "there is something critically wrong with our community, and it has to be purged and cleansed" (chap. 2 in this volume). Piety and pollution are powerful drivers in the formation of Justice Kennedy's rhetorical vision.

Justice Kennedy's rhetorical vision was infused with empathy for gay people and a fear of pollution when faced with cases dealing with abortion, race, and nonassimilated immigrants. Stanchi writes that Justice Kennedy's "opinions in gay civil rights cases are widely lauded as showing deep empathy for the liberty, dignity, and autonomy of gay people"; however, "Justice Kennedy's empathy is limited," because "his empathy for some people stands in contrast to his blind spots to the suffering of other marginalized groups" (chap. 13 in this volume). A judge's rhetorical vision can be judged. These judgments, as the studies in this volume illustrate, have rhetorical methods.

Rhetorical methods, Michael Gagarin writes in chapter 1, link ancient and modern methods of legal interpretation and the search for justice. Stanchi's chapter corroborates Gagarin's insight that classical Athens offers an example of a relatively stable judicial system that yielded useful rhetorical knowledge. Rhetorical methods cannot be reduced to a methodology, as Mootz (2018) observes, and do not dictate in advance of a case what interpretative strategy should be used. Rather, the methods of rhetoric capture questions that recur when evidence conflicts, precedents fail to give guidance, and a judge must judge.

Martin Camper, Susan Provenzano, and Sean O'Rourke demonstrate in their chapters (3, 4, and 5, respectively) the value of the ancient Greek and Roman rhetorical methods of interpretative stases. Camper, Provenzano, and O'Rourke invite readers to appreciate the power of the interpretative stases developed in Cicero's *De inventione*, the *Rhetorica ad Herennium*, and Quintilian's *The Orator's Education*. These works set forth questions designed to help interpret how law might be applied and what arguments might be used to judge human action. In addition to interpretative stases, O'Rourke includes *controversia* and topical argument as vehicles for generating insight.

Modern rhetorical theories, which are often anchored in the texts of Aristotle, Cicero, and Quintilian, offer contemporary embellishments of ancient rhetorical methods and procedures of judgments. Rountree and Mootz, in their chapters, appropriate the two most important modern contributions to rhetorical theory and method, the new rhetorics of Kenneth Burke and Chaïm Perelman and Lucie Olbrechts-Tyteca, to broaden the aperture of ancient rhetorical theory. Burke, Rountree rightly observes, offers a sophisticated grammar of rhetoric and motives, one that draws from a dramatist paradigm. Building from the rhetorics of Cicero and Aristotle, Burke identifies "terministic screens," which shape how we see and then represent the world through symbols (Burke 1966). Burke's rhetorical theory, Rountree observes, explains how terministic relationships between the various components of action are constructed rhetorically. Applying Burkean analysis to Justice Kennedy's judgment in *Lawrence*, Rountree finds that it developed "systematically and persuasively," serving as a good example of judging well, based as it was on a more enlightened view of human nature and homosexual actions (chap. 6 in this volume). The Burkean screen broadens the vision of judgment, which might help judges identify their blind spots. Rountree's chapter provides a splendid illustration of a critic using Burkean rhetorical theory to explain how a judge judges well.

Mootz calls on Perelman and Olbrechts-Tyteca's notion of the universal audience to judge Justice Kennedy's opinion in *Roper v. Simmons*. Perelman and Olbrechts-Tyteca's new rhetoric features three audiences: particular, composite, and universal. All are visualized constructions of the one who seeks to persuade. The universal audience is the speaker's visualization of the audience that is most capable of using effective and humane reason (Crosswhite 2013). Justice Kennedy, Mootz argues, invites the domestic audience in the United States to consider the judgment of the world community: minors should not be treated as adults. This is an argument based on the natural law tradition. As an argument, Mootz continues, it is not meant to be a methodology; indeed, "it is no method at all; it is a type of argument" (chap. 7 in this volume). As a type of argument, one affirmed by Justice Kennedy's construction of a universal audience, natural law argumentation helps locate blind spots that may be the result of more local and provincial views of audiences.

Modern rhetorical theory, Rountree and Mootz explain, complements ancient expressions of rhetorical reasoning, which are based in questions designed to enhance the vision of the advocate, judge, and critic—interpretative stases, *controversia*, and topical arguments. Burke's framework and Perelman and Olbrechts-Tyteca's focus on the audience offer advocates, judges, and critics the equipment necessary to identify flaws in their reasoning. This rhetorical equipment allows a second contribution made by the contributors to this volume to be set forth.

Rhetorical Standards Identifying the Humane Vision and Blind Spots in Justice Kennedy's Decisions

Elizabeth Britt, Kathryn Stanchi, Rebecca E. Zietlow, and Leticia M. Saucedo feature Justice Kennedy's judicial failures, which they trace to an ocular deficiency. Justice Kennedy could not or did not see the women or persons of color or immigrants in their full humanity, unlike his capacity to understand, in Stanchi's word, gays as "fully human, rounded characters with feelings, agency, and life" (chap. 13 in this volume). Justice Kennedy's blind spots, as Britt, Stanchi, Zietlow, and Saucedo explain, can be traced to the ideological "template" (Britt, chap. 12 in this volume), "picture" (Stanchi, chap. 13 in this volume), extension of "empathy" (Zietlow, chap. 14 in this volume), and "positionality" (Saucedo, chap. 15 in this volume). While they identify Justice Kennedy's blind spots, which emerge out of his rhetorical vision, they are puzzled and challenged by the empathy and dignity demonstrated in his sexual orientation decisions. As Saucedo exclaimed during one of the virtual sessions, Justice Kennedy could judge both well and poorly.

I struggle with this contradiction in Justice Kennedy's body of work and ask this question: Shouldn't we expect a judge to possess a rhetorical vision that is expressed consistently across cases? Gardner's chapter offers a novel and insightful answer. In hard cases, members of the Supreme Court must provide evidence that they struggled with opaque precedents and evidence that conflicts. These struggles should enhance the credibility—the ethos—of the judge if these struggles are effectively revealed to the judge's audience. "Justice Kennedy's struggles often seemed unconvincing and idiosyncratic," concludes Gardner (chap. 10 in this volume).

Gardner's case study of struggle is Justice Kennedy's swing opinion in *Vieth v. Jubelirer* (2004). In this case, Gardner argues, Justice Kennedy "had refused to do the one thing every judge must do: decide." Justice Kennedy, Gardner continues, "had struggled" with the case but "had in the end lacked the internal fortitude to resolve his struggle one way or the other; instead of mastering the judicial task, it had mastered him" (chap. 10 in this volume). Yet Justice Kennedy did command the internal fortitude to decide sexual orientation cases and cases involving women, persons of color, and immigrants.

Gardner and other contributors to this volume identify three patterns in Justice Kennedy's judicial rulings: those that are indecisive (e.g., *Vieth*), humane (e.g., *Lawrence v. Texas*), and inhumane (e.g., *Gonzales v. Carhart* [2007]). What, then, did Justice Kennedy do or not do to create these patterns? As Gardner explains, the Supreme Court exists to decide hard cases; Justice Kennedy failed in *Vieth* to render a clear judgment and did not meet this responsibility. The decision, as Gardner notes, "struck most readers as a catastrophic failure" (chap. 10 in this volume).

What kind of failure, then, was the *Vieth* opinion? Scholars of rhetoric would describe it as failure of argument invention and, with Mootz, point to Giambattista Vico's *New Science* (1968) for insight on the rhetorical understanding of *inventio*, the first canon of rhetoric. Vico's take on invention held that it is a capacity, an ability, to bring "things together that are disparate and widely separated" (Mooney 1976, 581, 586). Vico's sense of *inventio*, Edward Said writes, "means finding things that otherwise lie hidden beneath piety, heedlessness, or routine" (1983, 53). Justice Kennedy's inventional failure can be explained by flaws in his and the Supreme Court's decision-making procedures—that *interpretative stases* and *controversia* were not in play or were inadequately deployed.

Gardner displays many of the inventional opportunities available to Justice Kennedy, which he did not see or use. Justice Kennedy had the option of joining the plurality in *Vieth*. He could have endorsed one of the many standards offered by the litigants or his colleagues on the Court. He had available to him a huge literature in legal studies and political science that offered appealing standards. He had the option of inventing his own standard. Instead, as Gardner concludes, Justice Kennedy absolved himself of responsibility for making a decision because he did not struggle to discover or invent the needed rules or standards to issue a definitive decision.

What, then, explains Justice Kennedy's capacity to judge well in the sexual orientation cases? The simple answer: he saw gays as fully human. His rhetorical vision included his friend Gordon Schaber, who had served as dean of the McGeorge Law School. Schaber had "enlisted a young Mr. Kennedy to teach night classes and nurtured his career." Harvard's Lawrence Tribe reported that Schaber "said Tony Kennedy was entirely comfortable with gay friends. . . . He said he never regarded them as inferior in any way or as people who should be ostracized." His views on gays were the result "of his custom—in the words of one good friend, Judge Alex Kozinski of the United States Court of Appeals for the Ninth Circuit—of stepping into the skin of those his decisions affect" (Stolberg 2015). Kozinski, unfortunately, is not quite right. Justice Kennedy was not fully capable of "stepping into the skin" of women (see Britt's and Stanchi's chapters in this volume), communities of color (see Zietlow's chapter), and nonassimilated immigrants (see Saucedo's chapter). Justice Kennedy's rhetorical vision was afflicted with blind spots.

Developing the Principles of Judging Well by Noting the Blind Spots in Justice Kennedy's Rhetorical Vision

Russell K. Robinson, whom Saucedo cites, uses "doctrinal intersectionality" to challenge the "single axis of gay and lesbian rights" (2019, 1071) used by those who rightly applaud Justice Kennedy's decisions in *Romer v. Evans*

(1996) and *Obergefell*. When the full spectrum of cases that Justice Kennedy decided is considered, which requires the addition of axes of race, nationality, and class, Robinson argues that Justice Kennedy's rhetorical vision is tethered to white nationalism; he defines the ideology of white nationalism as "the belief that white people, especially white men, should remain at the center of national identity and hold a disproportionate amount of political and economic power" (2019, 1031). Yet Justice Kennedy's rhetorical vision should not be reduced to white nationalism, as his rulings on sexual orientation cases and other cases are not ruled by white nationalism. This ideology helps to explain Justice Kennedy's defective rhetorical vision, offering a through line connecting his formulaic reasoning concerning the suffering of women, people of color, and nonassimilated immigrants.

The Image of Women in Kennedy's Decisions

"The contrast between the portrayal of women in Justice Kennedy's abortion jurisprudence," writes Stanchi, "and his portrayal of people in the gay civil rights cases is stark." In cases affecting women, they "are often missing from the narrative or, if mentioned, are reduced to one-dimensional stock characters." Justice Kennedy's decisions in gay civil rights cases, Stanchi rightly observes, present people who are "rounded characters with feelings, agency, and life" (chap. 13 in this volume). There is no individual woman in Justice Kennedy's abortion jurisprudence who serves the same function as Gordon Schaber in his gay civil rights line of cases.

For those who are not quite persuaded that Justice Kennedy's treatment of gay civil rights is "starkly" different from his approach to cases affecting women, I point to Stanchi's arresting chart (table 13.1). Stanchi's word counts reflect Justice Kennedy's rhetorical vision, one that is humane and robust in the gay rights cases of *Obergefell* and *Lawrence* and inhumane and flat in the women's rights cases of *Gonzales* and *Ohio v. Akron Center for Reproductive Health* (1990). Stanchi properly scores Justice Kennedy for "his blind spots to the suffering" of marginalized groups other than gays.

If Justice Kennedy needed to understand the suffering of individual women as they faced the choice of abortion, he had the opportunity. An amicus brief filed on behalf of the Institute for Reproductive Health Access and Fifty-Two Clinics and Organizations offered testimonials from more than 150 women who sought second-trimester abortions. That Justice Kennedy did not take this opportunity suggests a failure of rhetorical vision and invention; his resulting portrayal of women, as Stanchi notes, lacked depth and nuance.

To be sure, there were other briefs filed detailing "adverse emotional affects" that women have suffered as a result of abortions. Because abortion is a hard case, it is incumbent, as Gardner writes, for judges to struggle, which Justice Kennedy does not do when he depicts women without agency or will or facing truly tragic decisions.

The Image of Race in Justice Kennedy's Decisions

One anchor in Justice Kennedy's rhetorical vision of white nationalism, identified by Zietlow, is his anticlassification doctrine. Race, Justice Kennedy held, should not be used as a category even if a racial category is needed to identify systemic racism. "In race-equality cases," Zietlow writes, "Justice Kennedy applied a rigidly formalistic anti-classification approach that left little room for empathy and imposed barriers to achieving substantive equality." As a rhetorical device, the anticlassification frame is effective "because it is a common topos, an idea present in the common culture" (chap. 14 in this volume).

In adopting anticlassification as a formal methodology, Justice Kennedy violated the principle of rhetorical reasoning that Mootz suggests is essential to judging well: "One does not judge well by following a methodology" (2018, 35). By using a doctrine of anticlassification and requiring the demonstration of discriminatory intent in racial cases, Justice Kennedy "makes it virtually impossible to use litigation to address the systemic racism that permeates our society" (Zietlow, chap. 14 in this volume). The empathy that Justice Kennedy demonstrates in gay rights cases is absent in cases affecting women and in racial cases, concludes Zietlow: "Justice Kennedy imposed significant barriers to minorities alleging race discrimination and limited government actors from adopting affirmative measures to remedy that discrimination. In the field of racial equality, Justice Kennedy showed no empathy. . . . This is not judging well." This lack of empathy, informed by white nationalism, extended to his treatment of nonassimilated immigrants.

The Image of Nonassimilated Immigrants in Justice Kennedy's Decisions

The specter of white nationalism is explicit in Justice Kennedy's immigration cases. As Saucedo observes, Justice Kennedy created a binary classification system in his immigration cases, the assimilated and nonassimilated immigrant. Only the assimilated immigrant, Justice Kennedy held, was deserving of protection and citizenship. His rhetorical vision, "his point of view," writes Saucedo, "as one in the majority white, heterosexual, Christian world that he occupied was implied in his discussions regarding who was deserving and who was not" (chap. 15 in this volume). This binary system is cruel in its application.

A formal methodology is at work in these cases, informed by an "assimilationist project." Deserving immigrants, those who wish to assimilate and seek to "integrate into the melting pot" that is the United States, "have dignity interests worth protecting." In a series of cases, Justice Kennedy extended protections to immigrants who committed to assimilation; immigrants who did not make this commitment were left to suffer, justifying Saucedo's claim that "Justice Kennedy's approach to the immigration cases . . . limited empathy and dignity considerations to those immigrants he deemed deserving" (Saucedo, chap. 15 in this volume). The assimilationist project meant that "the empathy and dignity that guided Justice Kennedy's pathbreaking sexual orientation decisions failed to trickle down to reach the minorities in immigration and national security cases" (Robinson 2019, 1071). The same problem, a commitment to a formal methodology, presents itself in Justice Kennedy's free speech cases.

The Image of the Ideal Citizen in Justice Kennedy's Free Speech Cases

Ashutosh Bhagwat, who witnessed when he served as Justice Kennedy's clerk how he thought through hard cases, devotes his chapter to Justice Kennedy's free speech optimism. Justice Kennedy, Bhagwat observes, presented an aspirational view of US democracy, and he idealized the US citizen. The "people," Justice Kennedy maintained, were well equipped and capable of judging the messages put before them. The government and public officials, in contrast, were not to be trusted. The US citizen would hold the government and its representatives accountable through free speech and debate.

Justice Kennedy's "relentlessly optimistic vision of the role of citizens in our democracy and the ability of citizens to parse and engage in public dialogue" became a methodology that he applied to all the free speech cases that came before him. Bhagwat puts a positive gloss on Justice Kennedy's motive; he saw himself as an educator and believed that free speech and debate would serve a pedagogical function. However, *Citizens United v. Federal Election Commission* (2010) and other cases demonstrated the need for the regulation of speech, suggesting that the "gap between his rhetoric and the real world seems unbridgeable." Regrettably, Justice Kennedy's idealization of the US citizen and the role he assumed as an educator constricted his vision, preventing him from "adopting a more limited and balanced approach to First Amendment rights," one better suited for a political reality dominated by corporate money and internet platforms that use algorithms to distort the public space (Bhagwat, chap. 9 in this volume).

Susan Provenzano draws on classical stasis theory to offer a limited defense of Justice Kennedy's free speech doctrine. She is careful to note that "Justice Kennedy judged *relatively* well" in the *Legal Services Corporation v. Velazquez* (2001) case "by developing rhetorical knowledge with an argumentative expansiveness that advanced natural liberty and speech rights." In this case, Justice Kennedy did not use a distinct methodology, a formal strategy, or deductive reasoning. Rather, his reasoning curved "along two paths" that depend on rhetorical knowledge. Justice Kennedy invented a "new line of argumentation" using "conventional topos of inductive reasoning from precedent to neutralize" the opposing arguments. Although these lines of argument were deemed problematic, they were stronger than those of Justice Kennedy's colleagues. Provenzano concludes that Justice Kennedy "engaged in a reasoned elaboration" with an "interpretive vibrance and dynamic argumentation, important hallmarks of judging well" (chap. 4 in this volume).

We are then left with two perspectives on Justice Kennedy's free speech doctrine, one offered by Bhagwat and the other by Provenzano, that are both reasonable and supported by evidence. In the realm of rhetoric, one explored by Perelman (1982) and a host of others, both can be true at the same time. Bhagwat's more general claim is that Justice Kennedy approached free speech issues with a predetermined methodology.

The authors in this volume have identified patterns in Justice Kennedy's judgment using the prism of rhetoric. What does it mean to see his judgments as expressions of rhetoric? What, then, is the payoff of a volume dedicated to an assessment of Justice Kennedy's decisions? What contributions might these studies offer to a theory of judging well?

Did Justice Kennedy Judge Well? The Rhetoric of Judgment

Justice Kennedy's rhetorical vision, as the contributors to this volume explain, was humane, if limited, in gay rights cases; led to indecision in gerrymandering cases; and was afflicted with blind spots when he judged cases affecting women, people of color, and nonassimilated immigrants. In free speech cases, he used a methodology turning on an idealization of the US citizen's capacity to make good judgments, rather than the distressing reality of a US political system that distorts the structures of discourse necessary for healthy deliberation. Yet, even in free speech cases, as Provenzano demonstrates, he "judged *relatively* well" when he made use of a rhetorically inflected process of reasoning (chap. 4 in this volume).

Justice Kennedy could judge well and poorly—evidence that he, like all humans, is made of "crooked timber," that his rhetorical vision included apertures unfolding humane and inhumane judgments. He judged well in the gay rights cases, I would argue, because his rhetorical vision included embodied homosexuals—his relationship with Gordon Schaber was a concrete, empirical referent that contributed to his laudable empathy in these cases. Justice Kennedy's rhetorical vision of the lived experience of women, people of color, and nonassimilated immigrants was constricted, flawed, and untethered to the realities of abortion, race, and immigration. Britt, in her chapter, explains these limitations by excavating Justice Kennedy's impulse to view the issue of abortion from "nowhere"—from a purported site of objectivity and impartiality. Justice Kennedy's understanding of objectivity, Britt writes, is a script "that obscures law's patriarchal bias—its roots in and commitments to masculine privilege in favor of" an imaginary judge who takes a view from nowhere (chap. 12 in this volume). Feminist jurisprudential methods, Britt argues, offer an alternative rhetorical vision, one that embraces practical reasoning and expands the range of proofs beyond those authorized by the ideology of white nationalism.

Britt cites Kathryn Stanchi, Linda Berger, and Bridget Crawford's 2016 book *Feminist Judgments: Rewritten Opinions of the United States Supreme Court* as an illustration of feminist methods. The book, which is published in the Cambridge University Press Feminist Judgment Series, corroborates the argument that Britt makes in her chapter, that justice is better served with practical reasoning and with the recognition "that all forms of reasoning are necessarily biased" (chap. 12 in this volume). In my judgment, the rewritten opinions in the *Feminist Judgments* volume are better than the originals because the authors command a much stronger rhetorical vision.

In the same spirit, Jack Balkin's edited volume *What* Obergefell v. Hodges *Should Have Said* offers eleven opinions written by legal scholars, using the evidence available to Justice Kennedy in 2015, that are quite different from Justice Kennedy's lines of reasoning. Indeed, the limitations built into *Obergefell* that are identified in this volume are remedied in some of the rewritten opinions. The opinions put on display rhetorical methods and rhetorical knowledge, although the authors do not recognize or make use of rhetorical terminology.

Feminist Judgments, What Obergefell v. Hodges *Should Have Said,* and the chapters in this book help embellish Mootz's theory of judging well. They offer evidence for Mootz's claim that "judging well is not a deductive exercise that can be assessed in terms of logic, nor it is an empirical inquiry that can be assessed in terms of method" (2018, 36). Judging well in hard cases is a distinctly rhetorical exercise in which deduction and empirical inquiry can play roles alongside other modes of reasoning, including analogy; indeed, they may play starring roles in certain cases. Rhetorical reasoning does not presume a methodology, and it welcomes multiple methodologies, strategies, and new lines of argumentation.

The chapters in this book backfill Mootz's theory with their development of the rhetorical methods—the interpretative stases, controversial thinking, the *quaestio,* and so on—that offer the tools that advocates, judges, and critics need to develop a moral rhetorical vision. They help all those who are tasked with the responsibility of judgment to see all the available means of persuasion in a given case. These methods should help those who make judgments to seek out a full understanding of the audiences affected by their judgments. Rhetorical methods yield rhetorical knowledge, a form of understanding that can serve as a dependable touchstone until it is successfully challenged.

The chapters in this book also help to identify the normative standards needed to judge rhetorical knowledge with their analysis of Justice Kennedy's hard cases, standards that, in the rhetorical traditions, are posed in the form of questions. The temptations offered by deduction and bounded methodologies, with their precision and clarity, do not fit the complex and variegated facets of hard cases involving human beings. What the studies of the rhetoric of Justice Kennedy's judgment in this book reveal is the importance of rhetorical visions—their depth, breadth, and capacities of wisdom and empathy—in judgment.

Judging well, as this volume illustrates, requires judges to command a humane rhetorical vision, one developed by rhetorical methods, including struggle, the question, interpretative stasis, a proper construction of audiences, and argumentation drawing on plural truths. This vision, the rhetorical traditions teach us, is a function of struggle with precedents and conflicting evidence, the theme of Gardner's chapter in this volume. Rhetoric, Walter Ong writes in his *Fighting for Life,* is the vehicle to be used in these struggles: "rhetoric, out of which formal logic grew, proceeds also by opposition, but by contrast with formal logic, rhetoric deals typically with soft oppositions. Rhetorical oppositions are negotiable" (1980, 19). Rhetorical reasoning and knowledge resist binary thinking.

The question becomes the driving force in facing hard cases, not a formula or methodology to be applied. Michel Meyer (2017) has developed an extensive rhetorical theory based on the question. To answer the questions posed by hard cases, rhetoric offers the *quaestio*, interpretative stases, reasoned elaboration, *controversia*, and legal topoi. These methods produce knowledge that must be rhetorical; it should persuade audiences.

Legal decisions are directed to composite audiences (Perelman and Olbrechts-Tyteca 1969, 21–22), members of which may hold conflicting values and worldviews. Persuading the composite audience may be difficult because members of this audience may disagree about the interpretation of precedent and evidence. These disagreements may be reasonable. As a result, rhetorical knowledge might be persuasive to one audience and less so to another. The truly creative judge can build systems of justice that members of the composite audience find reasonable.

This case study of Justice Kennedy's rhetoric of judgments helps contribute to and develop Mootz's theory of judging well. This theory, which Mootz roots in the rhetorical tradition of Vico, Perelman, and Gadamer, honors but transcends logically rigorous but abstract conceptualizations of judging and judgment. It does so by rooting judgment in the rhetorical vision of advocates, judges, and critics.

Rhetorical visions can be assessed for their capaciousness and empathy and the degree to which they contribute to justice. The great wonder of rhetoric resides in its capacity of invention, that it can inspire, through its methods, the discovery and creation of rhetorical knowledge that can persuade the composite audience. This is the capacity that Vico celebrates in his *New Science*. This is an expression of "deep rhetoric" that James Crosswhite illuminates (2013). This facility is in evidence when advocates, judges, and critics "develop a public discussion along new lines of argumentation that motivate justified action" (Mootz, chap. 7 in this volume).

References

Aristotle. 1991. *Aristotle on Rhetoric: A Theory of Civic Discourse*. Translated by George Kennedy. New York: Oxford University Press.

Balkin, Jack M., ed. 2020. *What Obergefell v. Hodges Should Have Said: The Nation's Top Legal Experts Rewrite America's Same-Sex Marriage Decision*. New Haven: Yale University Press.

Bhagwat, Ashutosh. 2016. "Liberty or Equality." *Lewis & Clark Law Review* 20:381–98.

Bowers v. Hardwick. 1986. 478 U.S. 186.

Burke, Kenneth. 1966. *Language as Symbolic Action: Essays on Life, Literature, and Method.* Los Angeles: University of California Press.

Citizens United v. Federal Election Commission. 2010. 558 U.S. 310.

Crosswhite, James. 2013. *Deep Rhetoric: Philosophy, Reason, Violence, Justice, Wisdom.* Chicago: University of Chicago Press.

Garver, Eugene. 2011. *Aristotle's Politics: Living Well and Living Together.* Chicago: University of Chicago Press.

Gonzales v. Carhart. 2007. 550 U.S. 124.

Hawhee, Debra. 2011. "Looking into Aristotle's Eyes: Toward a Theory of Rhetorical Vision." *Advances in the History of Rhetoric* 14:139–65.

Lawrence v. Texas. 2003. 539 U.S. 558.

Legal Services Corporation v. Velazquez. 2001. 531 U.S. 533.

Mercier, Hugo, and Dan Sperber. 2017. *The Enigma of Reason.* Cambridge: Harvard University Press.

Meyer, Michel. 2017. *What Is Rhetoric?* Oxford: Oxford University Press.

Mooney, Michael. 1976. "The Primacy of Language in Vico." *Social Research* 43:581–600.

Mootz, Francis J., III. 2006. *Rhetorical Knowledge in Legal Practice and Critical Legal Theory.* Tuscaloosa: University of Alabama Press.

———. 2018. "Judging Well." *Washington University Jurisprudence Review* 11:1–37.

Obergefell v. Hodges. 2015. 576 U.S. 644.

Ohio v. Akron Center for Reproductive Health. 1990. 497 U.S. 502.

Ong, Walter J. 1980. *Fighting for Life: Contest, Sexuality, and Consciousness.* Ithaca: Cornell University Press.

Perelman, Chaïm. 1982. *The Realm of Rhetoric.* Notre Dame: University Press of Notre Dame.

Perelman, Chaïm, and Lucie Olbrechts-Tyteca. 1969. *The New Rhetoric: A Treatise on Argumentation.* Translated by John Wilkinson and Purcel Weaver. Notre Dame: University of Notre Dame Press.

Robinson, Russell K. 2019. "Justice Kennedy's White Nationalism." *UC Davis Law Review* 53:1027–72.

Romer v. Evans. 1996. 517 U.S. 620.

Roper v. Simmons. 2005. 543 U.S. 551.

Said, Edward W. 1983. *The World, the Text, and the Critic.* Cambridge: Harvard University Press.

Stanchi, Kathryn M., Linda L. Berger, and Bridget J. Crawford. 2016. *Feminist Judgments: Rewritten Opinions of the United States Supreme Court.* Feminist Judgments Series. New York: Cambridge University Press.

Stolberg, Sheryl Gay. 2015. "Justice Anthony Kennedy's Tolerance Is Seen in His Sacramento Roots." *New York Times,* June 21, 2015. https://www.nytimes.com/2015/06/22/us/kennedys-gay-rights-rulings-seen-in-his-sacramento-roots.html.

Vico, Giambattista. 1968. *The New Science of Giambattista Vico.* Rev. trans. of the 3rd ed. Ithaca: Cornell University Press.

Vieth v. Jubelirer. 2004. 541 U.S. 267.

Zarefsky, David. 2019. "Underlying Assumptions of Examining Argumentation Rhetorically." *Argumentation* 34:1–13.

CONTRIBUTORS

Ashutosh Bhagwat is a Distinguished Professor of Law and the Boochever and Bird Endowed Chair for the Study and Teaching of Freedom and Equality at the University of California, Davis School of Law. He is the author of *Our Democratic First Amendment*, *The Myth of Rights*, and numerous articles and book chapters on constitutional and administrative law. His scholarship focuses particularly on the First Amendment and democratic theory.

Elizabeth C. Britt is Professor of English at Northeastern University. A feminist rhetorical theorist and critic whose research focuses on legal rhetoric, she is the author of *Reimagining Advocacy: Rhetorical Education in the Legal Clinic*, *Conceiving Normalcy: Rhetoric, Law, and the Double Binds of Infertility*, and articles in such journals as *Rhetoric Society Quarterly* and *Law, Culture and the Humanities*.

Martin Camper is Associate Professor of Writing and Director of the Center for the Humanities at Loyola University Maryland. He is the author of *Arguing over Texts: The Rhetoric of Interpretation* and a number of articles that have appeared in journals such as *Philosophy and Rhetoric*, the *Journal of Communication and Religion*, and *Argumentation and Advocacy*. His research concerns textual interpretation, religious rhetoric, disagreement, and argumentation.

David A. Frank is Professor of Rhetoric (Emeritus) at the Robert D. Clark Honors College, University of Oregon. He is author, most recently, of a digital exhibition of James Blue's documentary *The March*, the result of an Andrew R. Mellon grant. In numerous articles and book chapters, he has offered studies of rhetorical history and theory, with a focus on the new rhetoric project of Chaïm Perelman and Lucie Olbrechts-Tyteca. He has also written on the rhetoric of the Israeli-Palestinian conflict and the rhetoric of Barack Obama.

Michael Gagarin is James R. Dougherty, Jr. Centennial Professor of Classics (Emeritus) at the University of Texas at Austin. His current interests are ancient Greek law and rhetoric. His most recent books are *Writing Greek Law*, *The Laws of Ancient Crete, c. 650–400 BCE* (with Paula Perlman), and *Democratic Law in Classical Athens*. He is also the series editor of the fifteen-volume Oratory of Classical Greece (translations of the Greek orators) and the editor in chief of the seven-volume *Oxford Encyclopedia of Ancient Greece and Rome*.

James A. Gardner is Bridget and Thomas Black SUNY Distinguished Professor at the University at Buffalo School of Law, State University of New York, where he specializes in constitutional law and democracy. He is the author of *What Are Campaigns For? The Role of Persuasion in Electoral Law and Politics* and coauthor of *Legal Argument: The Structure and Language of Effective Advocacy*.

Eugene Garver is Professor Emeritus at Saint John's University, Minnesota. His latest book is *Spinoza and the Cunning of Imagination*. Earlier books include a trilogy on Aristotle's *Rhetoric, Ethics,* and *Politics*. He also traveled by bicycle from Cairo to Cape Town.

Leslie Gielow Jacobs is the Anthony Kennedy Professor and Executive Director, Capital Center for Law & Policy, at McGeorge School of Law, University of the Pacific. She is the coauthor of *Global Issues in Constitutional Law* and *Global Issues in Freedom of Speech and Religion* and has recently served as Special Rapporteur for the United States to the 2022 International Academy of Comparative Law on Freedom of Speech and Regulation of Fake News. She has written and comments extensively on constitutional law, government structures, and individual rights.

Francis J. Mootz III is Professor of Law at the McGeorge School of Law, University of the Pacific. He is the author of *Rhetorical Knowledge in Legal Practice and Critical Legal Theory* and *Law, Hermeneutics and Rhetoric* and coeditor of *Justice Scalia: Rhetoric and the Rule of Law*. In numerous articles and book chapters, he has explored the rhetorical and hermeneutical dimensions of law.

Sean Patrick O'Rourke is Professor and Chair of the Rhetoric Program and Professor and Chair of the American Studies Department at Sewanee: The University of the South, where he also serves as director of the Center for Speaking and Listening. He is coeditor of *Rhetoric, Race, Religion, and the Charleston Shootings: Was Blind but Now I See, Like Wildfire: The Rhetoric of the Civil Rights Sit-Ins,* and *On Fire: Five Civil Rights Sit-Ins and the Rhetoric of Protest*. He teaches and writes about rhetoric, protest, and legal rights.

Susan E. Provenzano is Assistant Professor of Law at the Georgia State University College of Law. Her work applying philosophical and rhetorical theories of meaning to the law has appeared in the *Indiana Law Journal*, the *Tennessee Law Review*, and the *Nevada Law Journal*. She has written a book on appellate advocacy, along with several book chapters. Her most recent publications are "Can Speech Act Theory Save Notice Pleading?" and "How Rhetoric Reveals Judicial Motives."

Clarke Rountree is Professor Emeritus of Communication Arts at the University of Alabama in Huntsville. He is the author of *Judging the Supreme Court: Constructions of Motives in Bush v. Gore* and coeditor of *National Rhetorics in the Syrian Immigration Crisis: Victims, Frauds, and Floods,* and he has published four other books and numerous essays. He studies US Supreme Court rhetoric, political rhetoric, and the rhetorical concepts of Kenneth Burke.

Leticia M. Saucedo is Martin Luther King, Jr. Professor of Law at the University of California, Davis School of Law. Her research interests lie at the intersections of employment, labor, and immigration law. Her review articles have appeared in the *Washington University Law Review, Notre Dame Law Review, North Carolina Law Review, UC Davis Law Review*, and *Ohio State Law Journal*, among others.

Darien Shanske is Professor of Law at University of California, Davis School of Law. He is the author of *Thucydides and the Philosophical Origins of History*, "Thucydides and Law: A Response to Leiter," and "Revitalizing Aristotle's Doctrine of Equity." He is a prolific scholar of tax law, as well as an expert in ancient Athenian law.

Kathryn Stanchi is the E. L. Cord Professor of Law at the William S. Boyd School of Law, University of Nevada, Las Vegas. She is a principal organizer of the United States Feminist Judgments Project, coeditor of *Feminist Judgments: Rewritten Opinions of the United States Supreme Court*, and executive editor of multiple *Feminist Judgments* volumes. She is the coauthor of the book *Legal Persuasion: A Rhetorical Approach to the Science* and the recent article "The Rhetoric of Racism in the United States Supreme Court." Her scholarship focuses on the intersection between rhetoric and language and the law's potential for social justice.

Rebecca E. Zietlow is Distinguished University Professor and Charles W. Fornoff Professor of Law and Values at the University of Toledo College of Law. She is the author of *The Forgotten Emancipator: James Mitchell Ashley and the Ideological Origins of Reconstruction* and *Enforcing Equality: Congress, the Constitution, and the Protection of Individual Rights*. In numerous articles and book chapters, she has explored the history and meaning of the Reconstruction Amendments, constitutional equality and workers' rights, and constitutional interpretation outside the courts.

INDEX OF CASES

RHETORIC AND **DEMOCRATIC** DELIBERATION